CHILD POVERTY AND INEQUALITY

NEW PERSPECTIVES

Isabel Ortiz

Louise Moreira Daniels

Sólrún Engilbertsdóttir

Editors

Division of Policy and Practice

Cover design: Upasana Young
Cover and back photos:
© UNICEF/NYHQ1996-0909/LeMoyne
© UNICEF/INDIA-00073/Shankar
© UNICEF/PHIA2009-0011/Lovell
© UNICEF/NYHQ2007-2671/Giacomo Pirozzi

Child Poverty and Inequality: New Perspectives
Isabel Ortiz, Louise Moreira Daniels, Sólrún Engilbertsdóttir (Eds)

© United Nations Children's Fund (UNICEF), Division of Policy and Practice, New York 2012
ISBN: 978-1-105-53175-0

Contents

Contributors

Hanna Alder is Programme/Research Officer at the Overseas Development Institute (ODI).

Sabina Alkire is Director at the Oxford Poverty and Human Development Initiative (OPHI), Oxford University.

Armando Barrientos is Research Director of the Brooks World Poverty Institute, University of Manchester.

Sheridan Bartlett is Senior Research Associate in the Human Settlements Program at the International Institute for Environment and Development (IIED) and Managing Editor of IIED's journal, *Environments and Urbanization.*

Laurence Chandy is a Fellow at the Brookings Institution.

Alex Cobham is Chief Policy Advisor for Christian Aid.

Paul Collier is Professor of Economics, Director for the Centre for the Study of African Economies at the University of Oxford and fellow of St. Antony's College.

Sarah Cook is Director of the United Nations Research Institute for Social Development (UNRISD).

Giovanni Andrea Cornia is Professor of Development Economics, University of Florence, and former Chief Economist at UNICEF.

Matthew Cummins is Social and Economic Policy Specialist, Division of Policy and Practice, UNICEF.

Sólrún Engilbertsdóttir is Policy Analyst at the Social Policy and Economic Analysis Unit, Division of Policy and Practice, UNICEF.

Gaspar Fajth is Regional Social Policy Advisor at UNICEF's Eastern and Southern Africa Regional Office.

Geoffrey Gertz is Research Analyst at the Brookings Institution.

Caroline Harper is Associate Director of the Chronic Poverty Research Centre and a Research Fellow at Overseas Development Institute.

Sir Richard Jolly is Research Associate at the Institute of Development Studies (IDS) and former Assistant Secretary General, UNICEF.

Jomo Kwame Sundaram is United Nations Assistant Secretary-General for Economic Development in the United Nations Department of Economic and Social Affairs (UN DESA).

Nicola Jones is Research Fellow at the Overseas Development Institute (ODI).

Naila Kabeer is Professor of Gender and Development at the School of Oriental and African Studies (SOAS), University of London.

Bill Kerry is Co-founder and Director of The Equality Trust.

Sharmila Kurukulasuriya is a Poverty Specialist formerly at the Social Policy and Economic Analysis Unit, Division of Policy and Practice, UNICEF.

Nora Lustig is Samuel Z. Stone Professor of Latin American Economics at Tulane University and non-resident fellow at the Center for Global Development (CGD).

Bruno Martorano is Staff Consultant at UNICEF's Innocenti Research Center.

Alberto Minujin is Professor at The New School and at Columbia University.

Louise Moreira Daniels is Policy Analyst, Division of Policy and Practice, UNICEF.

Deepa Narayan is former Senior Advisor in the Poverty Reduction and Economic Management Network of the World Bank.

Isabel Ortiz is Associate Director, Policy and Practice, UNICEF.

Paola Pereznieto is Research Fellow in the Social Development Programme at Overseas Development Institute (ODI).

Kate Pickett is Professor of Epidemiology at the University of York and a National Institute for Health Research Career Scientist.

Amjad Rabi is Social Policy Specialist, UNICEF Zimbabwe.

José Manuel Roche is Research Officer at Oxford Poverty and Human Development Initiative (OPHI).

Andy Sumner is Research Fellow at the Institute of Development Studies (IDS) and Visiting Fellow at the Centre for Global Development (CGD).

Timo Voipio is Chair of the Poverty Reduction Network (POVNET), OECD-DAC Paris, and Senior Adviser for Global Social Policy, Ministry of Foreign Affairs for Finland.

Richard Wilkinson is Professor Emeritus of Social Epidemiology at the University of Nottingham.

Jennifer Yablonski is Social Protection Specialist at the Social Policy and Economic Analysis Unit, Division of Policy and Practice, UNICEF.

Acknowledgements

This volume is the result of over two years of UNICEF's work on multidimensional child poverty and inequality. The editors of this book would like to thank all the contributors, not only for their papers but also for the support provided to other efforts crucial to child wellbeing. Special thanks to Gaspar Fajth, Sharmila Kurukulasuriya, Alberto Minujin and Giovanni Andrea Cornia for their pioneering work in UNICEF in this area, as well as to Richard Morgan, Director of Policy and Practice, UNICEF, for his guidance and comments during these past years.

Introduction

While poverty reduction has become a central feature of the international development agenda, the 21st century starts with vast asymmetries in terms of income, access to food, water, health, education, housing, or employment for families. Half of the world's children are below the international poverty line of $2 a day and suffer from multiple deprivations and violations to basic human rights. More than eight million children die each year (some 22,000 per day), and most of their deaths are preventable. Hunger, malnutrition and lack of safe drinking water contribute to at least half of child mortality. The urgency to address these inequalities cannot be more stressed.

The consequences of poverty and inequality are very significant for children. Children experience poverty differently from adults; they have specific and different needs. While an adult may fall into poverty temporarily, falling into poverty in childhood can last a lifetime – rarely does a child get a second chance at an education or a healthy start in life. Even short periods of food deprivation can impact children's long-term development. If children do not receive adequate nutrition, they grow smaller in size and intellectual capacity, are more vulnerable to life-threatening diseases, perform worse in school, and ultimately, are less likely to be productive adults. Child poverty threatens not only the individual child, but is likely to be passed on to future generations, entrenching and even exacerbating inequality in society.

This volume is a compilation of recent thinking on the issue of child poverty and inequalities. It draws on over two years of UNICEF's collaboration with innovative and leading thinkers on these matters. Papers in this volume discuss child poverty measurement, trends in global poverty and inequality, outcomes for children, and policies to address them.

We start by revising how poverty is measured, calling for new multidimensional poverty measurements to better appreciate the reality of children in the world. According to orthodox estimations of an international extreme poverty line of $1 a day, the total number of poor people around the world has declined drastically; approximately one billion people have escaped extreme poverty since 1981. This approach celebrates that poverty reduction of this magnitude is unparalleled in history; never before have so many people been lifted out of poverty over such a brief period of time.

However, many have noted shortcomings in these estimates. To start, while the number of people living in extreme poverty on less than $1 a day (adjusted to $1.25 a day measured at 2005 international prices), declined globally from 1.9 billion in 1981 to 1.4 billion in 2005, this decline was largely due to progress in China and East Asia; however, the absolute number of people living in poverty actually went up during this period in Sub-Saharan Africa, as in many developing countries in other regions. Additionally, there are concerns about an international income-based poverty line as a meaningful measure of poverty. Evidence suggests that such poverty lines misrepresent the actual extent of poverty. Many criticisms have emerged on how they are adjusted with time; for instance, the World Bank's adjustment of poverty lines is not based on the United States rate of inflation; had it been taken into account, the original $1 a day would have become $1.45 a day for 2005, with obvious implications for the corresponding estimates of people in poverty, and hence, for the achievement of the Millennium Development Goals poverty target by 2015. Further, the companion $2 a day poverty line was never adjusted. Even if extreme poverty has reduced significantly in some countries like

China, inequalities in income, wealth and others has increased. Thus, the pace of progress is unequal.

New approaches show an understanding of poverty as multidimensional. As long as policy debates focus solely on income poverty, children and their priorities will be missed out, and the battle to end the cycle of poverty will be undermined. UNICEF is working to mainstream a multidimensional approach of poverty, to reflect how and where children are experiencing poverty, and to allow a different set of policy responses that would structurally address children being lifted out of poverty in the long-term by addressing their different deprivations.

In *"Making the Case for Child Poverty,"* Alberto Minujin discusses the idea that child poverty differs from adult poverty and explains why it should be measured differently, providing examples of some initiatives that use multidimensional approaches. Furthermore, he discusses how child poverty can be inserted in the policy discourse.

In *"Beyond Headcount: The Alkire-Foster Approach to Multidimensional Child Poverty Measurement,"* Sabina Alkire and José Manuel Roche discuss their methodology for multidimensional poverty measurement, and how it can be used to inform policy. This methodology formed the basis for the now well-known Multidimensional Poverty Index (MPI).

Using the progressive University of Bristol methodology, Sharmila Kurukulasuriya and Sólrún Engilbertsdóttir demonstrate in *"A Multidimensional Approach to Measuring Child Poverty"* how a multidimensional approach is an essential supplement to the traditional income approach to poverty. In addition they discuss how such multidimensional child poverty measures can inform child friendly policies.

Deepa Narayan, in *"The Dynamics of Poverty,"* reminds us that poverty is not only a multidimensional, but a dynamic phenomenon. She discusses how people fall into it, and move out of poverty. The study she highlights shows that, across 500 communities studied, close to half the population is moving up or down, often with the same people falling and rising at different times, and that the reasons for moving out of poverty and for falling into it are different. She also discusses several policy implications to her findings.

In *"The Changing State of Global Poverty,"* Laurence Chandy and Geoffrey Gertz discuss new trends on global poverty. They provide estimates of global poverty, and compare rates of progress over time. Most importantly, they point out that the global poverty landscape is quickly being redrawn. Between 2005 and 2015, Asia's share of global poverty is expected to fall from two-thirds to one-third, while Africa's share more than doubles from 28% to 60%. With the graduation of some of the world's biggest developing countries into middle income-country (MICs) status, poverty is no longer concentrated in low-income countries (LICs), the largest number of poor people are in in the wealthier MICs. In LICs, they discuss the fact that poverty is becoming increasingly concentrated in fragile and conflict-afflicted states. Finally, they discuss how these trends affect organizations committed to improving the wellbeing of children across the developing world.

Caroline Harper, Hanna Alder and Paola Pereznieto, in *"Escaping Poverty Traps – Children and Chronic Poverty,"* discuss the importance of chronic poverty to development, what the drivers of chronic poverty are, how children are disproportionately affected, and how chronic poverty, in particular children's chronic poverty, can be addressed. They provide key policy recommendations to tackling the issue.

Going deeper on what is needed for children's equity, Naila Kabeer's *"Can the MDGs Provide a Pathway to Social Justice? The Challenge of Intersecting Inequalities"* stresses that the focus on the Millennium Development Goals (MDGs) on 'average' measures of progress fails to capture the unequal pace of this progress and the systematic exclusion of certain groups in society, and demonstrates how the effects of social exclusion are detrimental to child well-being. The wealth of Kabeer's analyses relies on highlighting how cultural, special, economic and political inequalities make people deprived of voice and influence in the decisions that affect their lives and their communities, calling for attention to issues of caste, race, ethnicity, language and religion given they are among the most common markers of exclusion.

Jomo Kwame Sundaram, in *"Rethinking Poverty,"* discusses the most striking findings presented in UNDESA's recent publication of the same title. He describes global poverty trends and distribution patterns over the last 20 years, and asserts the need for rethinking policy approaches, starting by the need for multidimensional poverty measurements. He emphasizes that the global financial, food, and fuel crises, as well as the ongoing effects of climate change threaten efforts to greatly reduce extreme poverty, undermining some gains achieved since the 2000 Millennium Summit. The mixed record of poverty reduction calls into question the efficacy of conventional approaches involving economic liberalization accompanied by targeted safety nets and services. Key policies for poverty reduction include macroeconomic policies focused on the stability of real output, incomes and employment; universal social policies focused on the determinants of asset and income inequality as well as poverty, such a social protection floor; and the promotion of participation, inclusion and voice of poor people.

Sarah Cook, in *"Combating Poverty and Inequality: Structural Change, Social Policy and Politics,"* highlights some of the main messages from the UNRISD Report of the same title. Cook points that poverty reduction requires growth and structural change that generate productive employment, as well as comprehensive social policies. Social policy, as a transformative instrument against poverty and inequality, must transcend its residual role of safety nets and engage with broad public policy issues of distribution, protection, production and reproduction. Most countries that have successfully reduced poverty adopted heterodox policies that reflected their national conditions, rather than fully embracing market-conforming prescriptions. Countries and peoples must be allowed the policy space to adopt different models of development where aspects of livelihood and food security, land reform, cultural rights, gender equity, social policy and associative democracy figure prominently. She explains why it is essential to take politics and power relations into account in order to reduce poverty and inequality.

Sir Richard Jolly, in *"UNICEF, Economists and Economic Policy: Bringing children into development strategies,"* explains the transformation occurred in UNICEF since earlier times. From as early as 1947, UNICEF recognized the importance of economic policy for children and has sought the help of development economists in mapping out what this might involve. UNICEF was about to be transformed from a UN emergency agency for children to one dealing with children's long-term needs, questioning how the needs of children and youth can be integrated into the general objectives of development. In his account of UNICEF's intellectual history, he explains how addressing economic development for children became even more acute in the adjustment period of the 1980s. The legacy of "Adjustment with a Human Face" turned into "Development with a Human Face" in later years. UNICEF developed the concept of First Call for Children, which means essentially that in bad times as in good, countries should ensure that children's priority needs should have a first call on resources – a principle accepted by most families for their own children but still only rarely recognized in national economic policy. Dedicated UNICEF officials have been working hard on this commitment to economic policy work in the context of children's rights.

Nicola Jones and Andy Sumner further support Jolly's arguments in "*Child Poverty, Policy and Evidence: Mainstreaming Children in International Development.*" They describe the types of knowledge being generated about the nature, extent and trends in child poverty and well-being in developing country contexts, and discuss another way of conceptualising child poverty and well-being: 3D child wellbeing. Finally, they identify and discuss three clusters of factors that support policy change: policy ideas and narratives; policy actors and networks; and policy contexts.

A set of contributions in this volume focuses on the importance of social protection for children. Armando Barrientos' provocative piece, "*Just Give Money to the Poor - And Children Will Benefit,*" presents some of the most interesting points coming out of his research on cash transfers to the poor. He addresses the positive impact for children, especially girls, and states that direct transfers to households in poverty are an essential component of poverty reduction and development strategies in the South, as they enable poor households to access services and link up to growth. Barrientos also addresses questions related to the efficacy of child-focused transfer programs, of the impact of cash transfers on child labor, and the feasibility of such programs in low income countries, among other issues.

The UN Secretary General called to achieve the Millennium Development Goals, which "will need accelerated interventions in key areas. These interventions should be framed within the broader development framework of national development strategies. The immediate priority would be to ensure the sustainability of economic recovery....Progress must be protected in an era of increased economic insecurity arising from global economic instability, volatile food prices, natural disasters and health epidemics. This requires universal social protection and measures to support the most vulnerable communities." Responding to this call, Isabel Ortiz, Gaspar Fajth, Jennifer Yablonski and Amjad Rabi, in "*Social Protection: Accelerating the MDGs with Equity,*" point out how MDG progress is measured in terms of national averages but these statistical averages often disguise that progress has not accrued to those at the bottom - arguably those who need it most. They show how social protection is essential to accelerate MDGs with equity by facilitating access to essential services and decent living standards. Specifically, they present evidence that social protection contributes to MDGs 1, 2, 3, 4, 5 and 6[1] - with stronger impacts for disadvantaged children.

Crises often oblige policy-makers to rethink development models. Ortiz et al. point out that the 1929 financial crash led to a New Deal in which social protection systems were used as a powerful tool to raise living standards and domestic demand in many countries. Likewise, the current crisis is an opportunity to rethink development. Social protection has been a major component of fiscal stimulus plans in the first phase of the crisis (2008-09); on average, an estimated 25% of fiscal stimuli were invested in social protection measures in both developing and higher income countries—though progress is currently threatened by fiscal consolidation processes. The UN has called for a social protection floor, below which nobody should fall, to provide a minimum set of social services and transfers for all. In the aftermath of the global

---

[1]MDG 1: Eradicate Extreme Poverty and Hunger; MDG 2: Achieve Universal Primary Education; MDG 3: Promote Gender Equality and Empower Women; MDG 4: Reduce Child Mortality; MDG 5: Improve Maternal Health; MDG 6: Combat HIV/Aids, Malaria and Other Diseases.

crisis, there is a historical opportunity to expand social protection in developing countries.

Timo Voipio, in *"Social Protection for All: An Agenda for Pro-Child Growth and Child Rights,"* argues that the single most remarkable shift in the global poverty reduction agenda of this new Millennium is the emergence of social protection as a top priority for most international organizations and development agencies. Furthermore, he explains why a social protection floor is a key element of pro-poor inclusive growth, and discusses how this relates to child rights.

Directly linked to the crisis and social protection, Nora Lustig's *"Rising Food Prices and Children's Welfare"* raises alarm on how world prices of food commodities have risen over the past few years and are a cause of major concern because high food prices bring significant and immediate setbacks for poverty reduction, nutrition, social stability, inflation and a rules-based trading system. Food prices are unique since food is unlike any other good. Food is essential for survival; it is the most basic of basic needs. Available evidence suggests that in the majority of countries, an increase in food prices is likely to result in an increase in overall poverty. The appropriate policy response is to have a package of social protection programs to help those who get hurt.

Other contributors to this volume called attention to specific, but fundamental issues, that need to be addressed for an equitable agenda for children. Paul Collier, in *"The Plundered Planet and The Bottom Billion: Why the mismanagement of nature matters for the world's most vulnerable,"* discusses the main findings of his recent publication *The Plundered Planet* as well as some of the ideas from his previous publication *The Bottom Billion*, and explains who the world's most vulnerable are and why, and how the mismanagement of nature matters for these populations.

Sheridan Bartlett, in *"Children in Urban Poverty: Can They Get More than Small Change?,"* highlights the plight of children living in urban poverty. It's widely recognized that the world is more than half urban; less widely acknowledged is the catastrophic extent of urban poverty or its implications for hundreds of millions of children. We are used to thinking of urban children as being better off than rural children in every way – better fed, better educated, with better access to health care and a better chance of succeeding in life. For many children, this is true. But for growing numbers, the so called "urban advantage" is a myth. Children growing up in urban poverty often remain invisible, not only uncounted but frequently unreached by any basic services: living without secure tenure; heavily exposed to toxics and pollutants; among the groups most at risk from disasters and the direct and indirect impacts of climate change; and, confined to small overcrowded homes with little opportunity for exploration or physical activity. It is crucial that policymakers understand that poverty reduction approaches developed to tackle rural poverty will not necessarily work in urban settings, as the nature of urban poverty is different from that of rural poverty.

Addressing child deprivations, however, must go beyond. In the late 1990s, when the development agenda opened to address poverty, major significant contributions were made. Many surveys and studies were done to understand the poor. Now we know who the poor are, their difficult conditions, voices, dynamics and concerns. However, looking at the poor only is unlikely to bring major change. The critical issue is to address inequality.

Ortiz and Cummins' comprehensive look at income distribution in 141 countries shows that global inequality is staggering. Using different estimation models, their analysis *"Global Inequality: Beyond the Bottom Billion,"* shows a world in which the top 20% of the population enjoys more than 70% of total income, contrasted by two paltry percentage points for those in the bottom quintile in 2007 under PPP-adjusted exchange rates. Using market exchange rates, the richest population quintile gets 83% of global income with just a single percentage point for those in the poorest quintile. While there is evidence of progress, it is too slow; it would take more than 800 years for the bottom billion to achieve ten percent of global income under the current rate of change.

The extreme inequality in the distribution of the world's income should make us question the current development model (development for whom?), which has accrued mostly to the wealthiest. Not only does inequality slow economic growth, but it results in health and social problems and generates political instability. Ortiz and Cummins show that for 94 developing countries, those countries in which levels of inequality have increased experienced slower annual per capita GDP growth over the same time period. Further, looking at crime rates and Gini indices across a sample of 138 countries, the authors find that countries with high levels of inequality tend to be much more violent. Inequality is dysfunctional, and there is a grave need to place equity, with a strong focus on redistribution, at the center of the development agenda. As an alternative, Ortiz and Cummins summarize the United Nations development agenda, which aims to strike the right balance between growth and equitable development progress.

Bill Kerry, Kate E. Pickett and Richard Wilkinson, in "*The Spirit Level: Why Greater Equality makes Societies Stronger*," explain why problems with social gradients (health, violent crime, and educational failure) are not caused by differences in material wealth, or by any kind of sorting or selection effects, but instead are due to social status differentiation itself - to the degree of hierarchy within a society. One of Wilkinson and Pickett's most significant contributions is the development of the International Index of

Health and Social Problems (IHSP). The composite index covers 23 OECD countries and includes the following indicators: homicides, imprisonment, infant mortality, life expectancy, math and literacy score, mental illness, obesity, social mobility, teenage births and trust. The authors discuss the impact of inequality on the most vulnerable, and offer ways to tackling inequality.

Alex Cobham, in *"We're all in this together: Why fighting inequality is central to development,"* highlights the gap between the ambition of the Millennium Declaration and the eventual form of the MDGs, mostly in three areas: sustainability, accountability and inequality. He discusses consequences of inequality to child poverty, and the opportunities and challenges in the process of identifying the post-2015 successor to the MDGs.

The prevalence of children and youth among the poorest world income quintiles is disturbing, as approximately 50% of children and youth are below the $2 a day international poverty line. This is due to high fertility rates in poor households. In 2011, the 7th billion child was born; the rate of population growth has increased drastically: in 1999 the world population was 6 billion, and it is expected to reach 8 billion in 2027. This is, the number of children and young people keeps rising massively and reducing poverty and inequality must be about a development agenda focused on children.

This equitable development agenda needs to move away from a shallow prioritization of growth rates accompanied by residual safety nets. The disconnect between economic policies and their social consequences has created a vicious circle of low employment for families and poor social progress for most. As many point out in this volume, reducing poverty and inequality will require socially-responsive macroeconomic policies, that is, focused on employment-generating growth and creating fiscal space for necessary social and economic investments; transformative social policies; enabling frameworks for peace/conflict prevention, good governance and human rights, as well as addressing systemic issues, such as the differential impact of globalization and inequalities among and within countries. How an equitable agenda would look in sectors like education, energy and mining, finance, health, housing, industry, labor, rural development, social protection, tourism, trade, transport and infrastructure, urban development, water and sanitation, can be found in Ortiz and Cummins in this volume.

Giovanni Andrea Cornia and Bruno Martorano provide country examples of this in their paper *"Policies for Reducing Income Inequality: Latin America During the Last Decade."* In most Latin American countries, income inequality rose steadily during the 1980s and 1990s, but declined from 2002 to 2007. Their paper analyzes the main factors explaining changes in income inequality, which are socially-responsive macroeconomic policies in tandem with progressive social policies, introduced in recent years by a number of left-of-centre governments which have come to power during the last decade. The paper tests econometrically the importance of all these factors on data for 18 countries from 1990 to 2007. The results suggest that a continuation of fiscally prudent distributive and redistributive policies, which have emerged in much of the region in the 2000s, should preserve most of the income inequality gains recorded in recent years.

For reference, Annex 1 presents data on multidimensional child poverty in selected countries, and Annex 2 a comprehensive list of income inequality in 141 countries.

Isabel Ortiz
Louise Moreira Daniels
Sólrún Engilbertsdóttir

Making the Case for Measuring Child Poverty
Alberto Minujin[2]

Children experience poverty differently from adults
The widely accepted monetary approach to identifying and measuring poverty is being challenged by other multidisciplinary approaches such as the child deprivation approach. Conventional poverty reduction strategies that concentrate only on generating economic growth to reduce poverty do not recognize that not only are these responses inadequate to address the multiple deprivations vulnerable households face, but also that children experience poverty differently from adults and that children have specific and different needs.

UNICEF acknowledges that children are vulnerable to certain types of deprivation; even short periods of deprivation can impact their long term development. "Children living in poverty experience deprivation of the material, spiritual, and emotional resources needed to survive, develop and thrive, leaving them unable to enjoy their rights, achieve their full potential or participate as full and equal members of society" (UNICEF, 2005). Child poverty is the poverty experienced during childhood by children and young people. It differs from adult poverty in that it has different causes and effects, and the impact of poverty during childhood has permanent effects on children (CHIP, 2004; UNDP, 2004).

The monetary measurement is an important measurement, but it does not capture how poverty affects children in physical, emotional and social ways. Additionally the monetary approach does not capture the multidimensional and interrelated nature of poverty as experienced by children, for example that malnutrition

---

[2]Alberto Minujin is Professor at The New School and at Columbia University, New York

can affect health and education which in turn may impact a child's long term development.

Measuring child poverty accordingly

There is no uniform approach for defining, identifying or measuring child poverty. The Bristol deprivation model was a groundbreaking effort aimed at measuring child poverty, which not only aims to measure the extent of child poverty but also the depth of poverty. The deprivation measures of child poverty are based on internationally agreed definitions based on child rights, namely adequate nutrition, safe drinking water, decent sanitation facilities, health, shelter, education and information.

UNICEF's Global Study on Child Poverty and Disparities_adopts both the Bristol model along with the monetary approach to measure child poverty. The Study also encourages countries to undertake qualitative studies to contextualise specific issues faced by countries.

The Young Lives project is another study that aims at highlighting the face of child poverty. This long term study seeks to improve our understanding of the causes and consequences of childhood poverty, tracking the lives of 12,000 children growing up in four developing countries over 15 years. The basis of this study is a questionnaire-based survey alongside in-depth research using participatory methods.

The monetary approach is also a useful model for measuring child poverty, but as indicated it is not adequate on its' own. The most common methodology in the monetary approach for measuring absolute poverty is through the creation of a national poverty line; most frequently $1 a day is used at the international level. According to a study by Deaton and Paxson (1997), using the absolute poverty model of $1 a day, they found that children made up a higher percentage of the income-poor than both adults and the elderly.

Inserting child poverty and the policy discourse

Child poverty is increasingly receiving the recognition that national priorities need to reflect stronger linkages between policies and children's needs. The major objective of measuring child poverty as distinct from other poverty measurements is to highlight the plight of children so that disadvantaged children are considered a priority, especially in the creation and implementation of poverty reduction strategies.

This multidimensional approach to child poverty has practical implications for policy advocacy and programs, such as:

- Influencing the nature of policy dialogue on poverty reduction. For instance, poverty reduction policies would need to incorporate a broader definition of poverty, in order to address how children experience poverty
- Influencing policy debates on social sector spending: For example in discussions on social and economic policy issues, would need to consider the returns to investing in children
- Influencing the design of indicators: the socio-economic and demographic indicators that capture information on children need to be enhanced.

National development plans including the Poverty Reduction Strategy Papers (PRSPs) outline the policy areas that a government considers of highest importance. Commonly such documents emphasize growth alone as the solution to alleviating poverty. It is therefore essential to re-direct the PRSP discussion so that it contributes to a sustainable reduction in poverty and it strengthens the rights of the child. In this regard it is essential to utilize sound techniques for measuring child poverty which in turn keeps poor children on the agenda.

The Global Study on Child Poverty and Disparities will provide relevant evidence and policy analysis on the situation of children living in poverty. This unique and valuable information should be used as powerful advocacy tools for placing children as a priority on the policy agenda at national, regional and global levels.

References

Deaton, A., and C. Paxton (1997). "Poverty among children and the elderly in developing countries." Research Program in Development Studies. Princeton.

Delamonica, E., Minujin, A., Davidziuk, A., and E.D. Gonzalez (2006). "Children living in poverty: Overview of definitions, measurements and policy." UNICEF Working Paper. New York.

Gordon, D., Nandy, S., Pantazis, C., Pemberton, S. and, P. Townsend (2003). *Child poverty in the developing world*. Bristol: The Policy Press.

UNDP (2004). "Dollar a day, how much does it say?" In Focus. Brasilia: International Poverty Centre for Inclusive Growth (IPC-IG).

UNICEF (2005). *State of the World's Children 2005 - Childhood under Threat*. New York: UNICEF.

Beyond Headcount: The Alkire-Foster Approach to Multidimensional Child Poverty Measurement

Sabina Alkire and José Manuel Roche[3]

I mproving multidimensional child poverty measurements
The Bristol multidimensional approach (Gordon et al. 2003) has contributed substantially to child poverty measurement, in expanding the income based approach. This model was the first measurement of the headcount of child poverty and is also aligned with the rights based approach and broad international consensus on what dimensions are essential for human development. While the measure improves upon income poverty, it does not account for the breadth, depth, or severity of dimensions of child poverty. The traditional income – FGT – measures in income poverty do account for these (see: Foster, Greer and Thorbecke, 1984). Also, the headcount cannot be broken down by dimension to uncover the components of child poverty in different regions or age groups or by gender.

A new methodology for multidimensional poverty measurement proposed by Alkire and Foster (2007) deals systematically with these issues and can be easily applied to child poverty measurement to enhance existing methodologies.

The Alkire and Foster methodology

Alkire and Foster's (2007) new methodology includes two steps: an identification method (ρk) that identifies 'who is poor' by considering the range of deprivations they suffer, and an aggregation method that generates an intuitive set of poverty measures ($M\alpha$) (based on traditional FGT measures) that can be broken down to target the poorest people and the dimensions in which they are most deprived.

---

[3]Sabina Alkire directs the Oxford Poverty and Human Development Initiative (OPHI), Oxford University
José Manuel Roche is Research Officer at Oxford Poverty and Human Development Initiative (OPHI), Oxford University

1) The *identification method* (ρk) identifies who is poor using two cutoffs.

- **First cutoff: whether a person is deprived in each dimension**. For example, Anna, who is nine years old, is mildly malnourished, has not received a dose of measles immunization, lives in a house with adequate sanitation facilities and does not attend school. If our poverty cutoffs are to be 'nourished, have received at least one dose of measles immunization, have adequate sanitation, and be attending school' – then Anna is deprived in three out of four dimensions. If we chose a different cutoff – for example having severe malnutrition – Anna would be deprived in only two out of four dimensions.

- **Second cutoff: the range of dimensions a person must be deprived in, in order to be considered poor**. In many situations we want to identify the poorest of the poor – people deprived in several aspects at the same time. To do this we might want to identify those who are deprived in at least three dimensions simultaneously. If so, Anna would be considered multidimensionally poor, as she is deprived in three dimensions. However, if we choose a cut-off of at least four dimensions, Anna would not be identified as poor. For simplicity in this example we have considered each dimension to be equally weighted – but different weights can be incorporated easily.

2) The *aggregation method* (Ma) determines the proportion of children who are poor and the average number (or weighted sum) of deprivations that poor children experience. It goes on to generate an enhanced headcount ratio that captures the breadth of deprivation. Because the headcount ratio is adjusted by dimension, an increase in the range of deprivations experienced by a poor child is reflected in the overall level of poverty. If data are cardinal, a related measure can reflect the depth and severity, as well as the breadth, of deprivation. These measures can be broken down by subgroup of the population (e.g. region, age, gender) and by dimension (e.g. education, access to drinking water, income), allowing useful comparisons between groups and identifying who is worst off and in which dimensions they are most deprived.

Informing policy

Decision makers need measures to identify whether multidimensional poverty is improving or worsening and how its dimensions differ among groups. The new methodology has been applied in a variety of contexts (see OPHI's Working Papers). Using the 2006 Multiple Indicator Cluster Survey in Bangladesh, Roche (2009) shows how this new methodology can improve upon previous measures of multidimensional child poverty. As this practical application illustrates, the new methodology can be used for a series of purposes including:

- Is this multidimensional measure significantly different from income and multidimensional headcount? What information does it include that others overlook? Does it add value – and if so, how? For example, Table 1 shows that the results of income poverty measures differ significantly from multidimensional measures of child poverty. Also, adjusting the headcount ratio by breadth of deprivation rearranges the ranking order of deprivation among regions. Going beyond headcount - matters.

Table 1. Ranking comparison according to different measures ($k=2$)

	1	2	3	4	5	6	7
Regions / Urban-Rural	Ranking WI	Ranking H	Ranking Mo	Dif. in rank order WI-Mo	Dif. in rank order WI-H	Dif. in rank order H-Mo	Average deprivations among the poor
Rural Rajshahi	1	3	3	-2	-2	0	2.63
Rural Dhaka	2	2	2	0	0	0	2.71
Rural Sylhet	3	1	1	2	2	0	2.89
Urban Rajshahi	4	10	10	-6	-6	0	2.61
Rural Barisal	5	5	4	1	0	1	2.77
Rural Khulna	6	7	9	-3	-1	-2	2.44
Rural Chittagong	7	6	5	2	1	1	2.81
Urban Barisal	8	12	12	-4	-4	0	2.72
Urban Sylhet	9	8	7	2	1	1	2.70
Urban Dhaka	10	4	6	4	6	-2	2.67
Urban Khulna	11	11	11	0	0	0	2.49
Urban Chittagong	12	9	8	4	3	1	2.75

Source: Roche (2009)
Note: WI: welfare index; H: headcount ratio; M_o: adjusted headcount ratio by breath of deprivation

- Breaking down by sub groups of population: for example, to compare deprivation by region, ethnicity, age, gender, urban versus rural areas, etc. This important property enriches understanding and facilitates targeting.
- Conducting sensitivity analysis of different cutoff decisions.
- Also, unlike the headcount, we can break down this measure by dimension. This is a powerful way to see 'at a glance' how the composition of poverty changes among groups. For example, Graph 1 shows that deprivation in access to drinking water accounts for an important percentage of child poverty in Barisal but very little in Chittagong and Rajshashi (Bangladesh), where lack of iodized salt contributes most. Therefore the same policies would not work equally well in both areas.

Figure 1. Percentage contribution of the dimension to the respective population level of M_0 (Equal weights and $k = 2$)

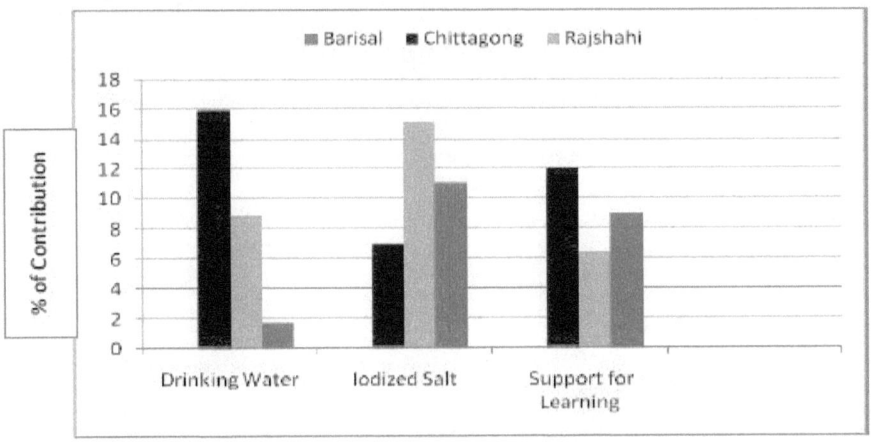

Source: Roche (2009)
Note: For simplification only few dimensions and regions are presented

- Comparing poverty over time: analysing how dimensions change over time is a powerful way of tracking a country's progress.

In summary, this intuitive methodology builds upon and goes beyond goes beyond headcount measures of multidimensional child poverty and can be used as a flexible tool to inform policy.

References

Alkire, S. and J. Foster (2007). "Counting and Multidimensional Poverty Measurement." OPHI Working Paper No. 7. Oxford, University of Oxford.

Delamonica, E., and A. Minujin (2007). "Incidence, Depth and Severity of Children in Poverty." Social Indicators Research, 82 (2), 361-374.

Foster, J., Greer, J. and E. Thorbecke (1984). "A Class of Decomposable Poverty Measures." Econometrica, 52 (3), 761-766.

Gordon, D., Nandy, S., Pantazis, C., Pemberton, S. and P. Townsend (2003). *Child poverty in the developing world*. Bristol: The Policy Press.

Roche, J. M. (2009). "Child Poverty Measurement: An assessment of methods and an application to Bangladesh." OPHI Workshop 'Multidimensional Measures in Six Contexts', 1-2 June, Queen Elizabeth House, University of Oxford.

UNICEF (2004). *The State of the World's Children 2005 - Childhood under Threat*. New York: UNICEF.

A Multidimensional Approach to Measuring Child Poverty

Sharmila Kurukulasuriya and Sólrún Engilbertsdóttir[4]

There is a growing consensus that children experience poverty in ways that are different from adults; and looking at child poverty through an income-consumption lens only is inadequate. The 2005 State of the World's Children presented the following definition of child poverty: "Children living in poverty experience deprivation of the material, spiritual and emotional resources needed to survive, develop and thrive, leaving them unable to enjoy their rights, achieve their full potential or participate as full and equal members of society." Using evidence from UNICEF's ongoing Global Study on Child Poverty in Disparities, this Brief illustrates the importance of looking beyond traditional methods of measuring poverty based on income or consumption levels, and emphasizes the importance of seeking out the multidimensional face of child poverty. This approach further recognizes that the method used in depicting child poverty is crucial to the policy design and implementation of interventions that address children's needs, especially among the most deprived.

A multidimensional approach

Growing up in poverty can be damaging to children's physical, emotional and spiritual development. However, child poverty is rarely differentiated from poverty in general and its special dimensions are seldom recognized. Child poverty differs from adult poverty in that it has different causes and effects, and the impact of poverty during childhood can have detrimental effects on children which are irreversible. Poverty impacts more acutely on children than on adults because of their vulnerability due to age and

---

[4]Sharmila Kurukulasuriya is a Poverty Specialist formerly at the Social Policy and Economic Analysis Unit (SPEA), Division of Policy and Practice, UNICEF

Sólrún Engilbertsdóttir is Policy Analyst at SPEA, Division of Policy and Practice, UNICEF

dependency. Poverty in childhood can cause lifelong cognitive and physical impairment, where children become permanently disadvantaged and this in turn perpetuates the cycle of poverty across generations. Investing in children is therefore critical for achieving equitable and sustainable human development.

The most commonly used method to measure poverty is based on income or consumption levels: which means that a person is considered poor if his/her consumption or income level falls below some minimum deemed level necessary to meet his/her basic needs. While such measures offer a broad understanding of populations living in poverty they provide a limited picture of child poverty and the actual deprivations children may face. In addition, they do not capture the disparities that may remain within countries; corrections for inequality are rarely made in monetary measures of poverty. For these purposes various social indicators often provide a more accurate picture of poverty. These indicators can capture the multidimensional and interrelated nature of poverty as experienced by children themselves, for example that malnutrition can affect health and education which in turn may impact a child's long term development.

UNICEF has long recognized the importance of adopting a multidimensional approach to measuring child poverty; in 2003 UNICEF supported Bristol University, UK in the development of a multidimensional child poverty measure. Multidimensional poverty measures gained increased attention in the past year with the release of the Multidimensional Poverty Index (MPI), developed by Oxford's Poverty and Human Development Initiative, which was featured in the 2010 Human Development Report.

UNICEF's Global Study on Child Poverty and Disparities, launched in 2007, and based on decentralised research and analysis in more than 50 countries looks at the linkages between child deprivations in eight critical dimensions; these are education, health, nutrition, water, sanitation, shelter, information and income/consumption. For a list of the indicators/thresholds for the dimensions of basic needs please refer to annex 1. In addition to reporting on income poverty, this Brief uses a methodology developed by Bristol University UK (Gordon et al.), which considers those who suffer from two or more deprivations as poor, and where each dimension is defined by thresholds – capturing moderate as well as severe deprivations. For example, the nutrition threshold for moderate deprivation includes "Children who are more than two standard deviations below the international reference population for stunting, wasting or underweight," and the nutrition threshold for severe deprivation are "Children who are more than three standard deviations below the international reference population for stunting, wasting or underweight" (see Global Study Guide and Child Poverty in the Developing World (Gordon et al.) for a complete list of these definitions). This Brief focuses on severe deprivations, as defining indicators in such severe terms leaves no doubt that living conditions are unacceptable.

The Global Study country analyses mostly use data from the Multiple Indicator Cluster Surveys and Demographic and Health Surveys, most commonly from 2005/6. In addition to the quantitative analysis, a number of countries have undertaken qualitative analyses to improve understanding of how poverty affects children in physical, emotional and social ways.

In 2005 the total number of children in the developing world was estimated 1.9 billion. This Brief draws upon data from 36 countries from seven regions, of the 52 countries that are participating in the Global Study, representing altogether coverage of 1.45 million children. The Brief focuses on multiple severe deprivations of children's basic needs in the 36 countries; and while it shows some aggregate figures for illustration, these should not be considered as regional or global estimates. Please refer to annex 1 for a comprehensive list of child deprivations of basic needs, for these 36 countries.

Child deprivation measure and the income measure
Out of the 1.45 million children included in this analysis representing 36 countries (Source: UNICEF Global Study on Child Poverty database):
- 51% experience at least two or more moderate deprivations of basic needs: 731,957 children;

- 38% experience at least two or more severe deprivations of basic needs: 553,049 children.

When measuring income poverty, the most commonly used indicator is $1.25 a day, where someone is considered poor if his or her income level falls below that level. It is generally assumed that the distribution of child poverty broadly conforms to this measure. In the graph below, the grey and white bars represent the percentage of children in each country that experience moderate and severe deprivations respectively, while the line represents the percentage of people in each country who are income poor according to the $1.25 a day poverty line (while recognizing that for some countries the data for income poverty and multidimensional child poverty are from different years).

In general the multidimensional child poverty measure conforms with the income measure, however there are also large differences; for example while 66 per cent of the population in Niger is considered income poor, 88 per cent of children experience two or more moderate deprivations and 84 per cent of children experience two or more severe deprivations. The reverse is evident in Philippines, where 23 per cent of the population is income poor while 15 per cent of children experience two or more moderate deprivations and only 2 per cent of children experience two or more severe deprivations National level analyses enriches one's understanding of the underlying reasons for these disparate poverty measure outcomes. This would include, for example, identifying who reaps the benefits of economic growth, tracking social sector investments, assessing the effectiveness of service delivery, analyzing employment trends etc. The following graph accentuates the importance of looking at both measures for policy purposes, as they can produce vastly different outcomes.

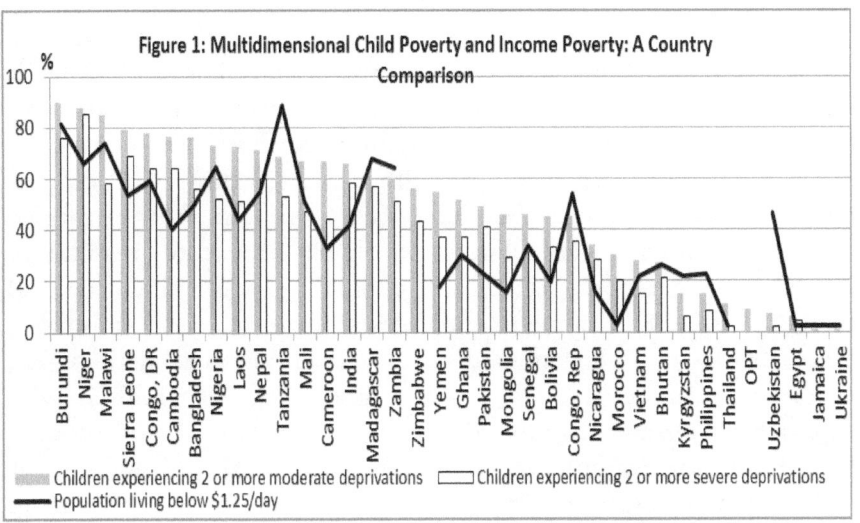

Figure 1: Multidimensional Child Poverty and Income Poverty: A Country Comparison

Children experiencing 2 or more moderate deprivations ▢ Children experiencing 2 or more severe deprivations
━━ Population living below $1.25/day

A commonly used international indicator of wealth is the per capita Gross Domestic Product (GDP) of a country. When looking at Uzbekistan, Vietnam, and India, which all have a GDP per capita in a similar range from US$ 2,190 – 2,573 (Source: World Bank 2006), one finds very different levels of child poverty. In Uzbekistan, Viet Nam, and India, 2%, 15%, and 58% of children experience 2 or more severe deprivations, respectively, and hence are considered poor. These differences emphasize the importance of looking beyond GDP and other such economic measures of poverty. Although these measures are important, they alone do not adequately capture the number of children experiencing severe deprivations of basic needs.

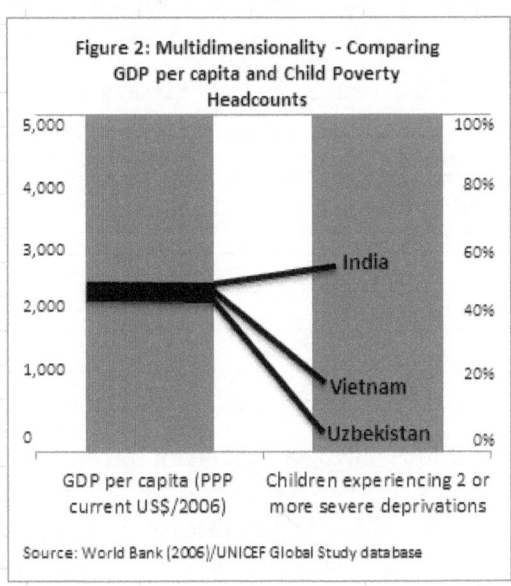

Figure 2: Multidimensionality - Comparing GDP per capita and Child Poverty Headcounts

GDP per capita (PPP current US$/2006)   Children experiencing 2 or more severe deprivations

Source: World Bank (2006)/UNICEF Global Study database

A comparable analysis focusing on eight countries whose population living below the international poverty line of $1.25 is in a similar range (from 44 per cent to 59 per cent) illustrate diverse child poverty headcounts. A preliminary analysis, looking at the percentage of children severely health deprived (those who did not receive immunizations against any diseases or who did not receive treatment for a recent illness involving an acute respiratory infection or diarrhoea) and health expenditures per capita (World Bank, World Development Indicators) in these eight countries, there seems to be a general tendency that countries with higher investments in health have a lower percentage of children who experience severe health deprivations. However, there are exceptions; for example, in Nepal per capita health expenditure is $18, which is similar to the $21 per capita health expenditure in Laos, however, severe health deprivations are 12 per cent in Nepal, while in Laos it is as high as 46 per cent of children. Hence, it is critical to not only understand per capita expenditure figures, but to also assess how the dollars are spent.

Table 1: Health deprivations and health expenditure	Population below $1.25/day)	Children experiencing 2+ severe deprivations	Children severely health deprived	Health expenditure per capita 2005 (current $US)
Laos	44%	51%	46%	US$ 21
Uzbekistan	46%	2%	4%	US$ 26
Bangladesh	50%	56%	17%	US$ 12
Mali	51%	47%	24%	US$ 28
Sierra Leone	53%	69%	33%	US$ 14
Republic of Congo	54%	35%	14%	US$ 43
Nepal	55%	60%	12%	US$ 18
Democratic Republic of Congo	59%	64%	31%	US$ 7

Additionally, we have not taken into account the vastly different health challenges a child living in Congo DR, for example, may be facing with a higher disease burden compared to a child living in for example Uzbekistan where less resources may be required to tackle child health challenges.

However, differences in disease burdens alone cannot explain the significant differences in health indicators for two neighboring countries, the Democratic Republic of Congo (DRC) and the Republic of Congo, where vastly different deprivation figures emerge. Some 31 per cent of children in DRC and 14 per cent of children (a figure similar to countries such as Nepal, Morocco and Nicaragua from our 36 country sample) in the Republic of Congo experience severe health deprivations.

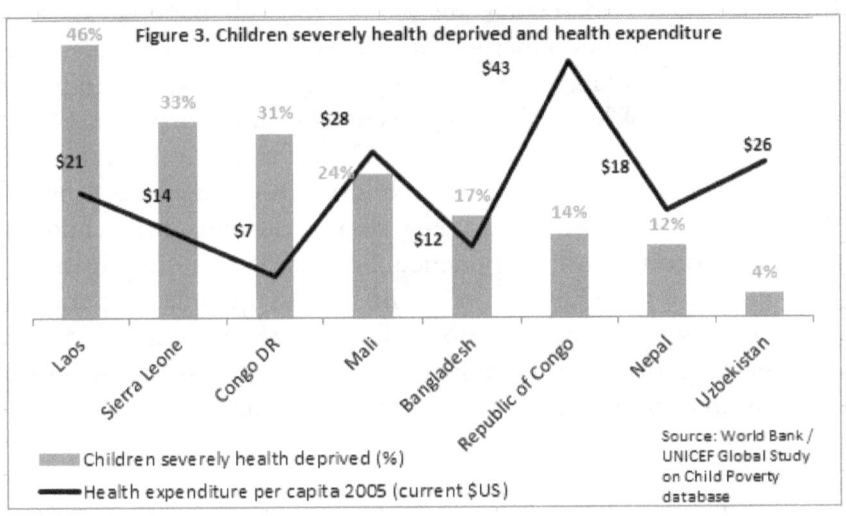

Figure 3. Children severely health deprived and health expenditure

Source: World Bank / UNICEF Global Study on Child Poverty database

Children severely health deprived (%)
Health expenditure per capita 2005 (current $US)

These figures may reflect the weight given to child health related services; for example, in the Republic of Congo health expenditure per capita in 2005 was $43, as opposed to $7 in DRC. It is also important to recognize that these are two vastly different countries; the Republic of Congo is classified as a lower middle-income country while DRC is a low income country that has been afflicted by a long and brutal conflict. It is therefore essential to strive towards a holistic understanding of the underlying reasons why certain child outcomes may emerge – using a multidimensional approach along with a comprehensive picture of the policy, socio-economic and institutional frameworks – which will enable the identification of the most effective and relevant policy responses needed to address these outcomes.

National averages: Inequities concealed

The analysis has thus far focused on national averages for the 36 countries in the sample. For certain middle-income countries, the deprivation approach to child poverty defined by severe thresholds, may not be adequate. For example, in Egypt four percent of children experience two or more severe deprivations and in Thailand 2 per cent of children experience two or more severe deprivations.

However, when undertaking analysis at the sub national level, a number of disparities emerge. In Thailand, great disparities are revealed when looking at severe deprivations by wealth quintiles and by ethnicity. While only two percent of children experience 2 or more severe deprivations on average, 23% of children from the Hill tribe are poor and zero percent of children from Laos and Chinese ethnicity are considered poor. Likewise, five percent of the children from the poorest quintile experience 2 or more severe deprivations, while none of the children from the richest quintiles experience severe deprivations. These numbers illustrate an important message; one needs to look beyond national averages to address intra-country inequities in order to reach the most deprived families.

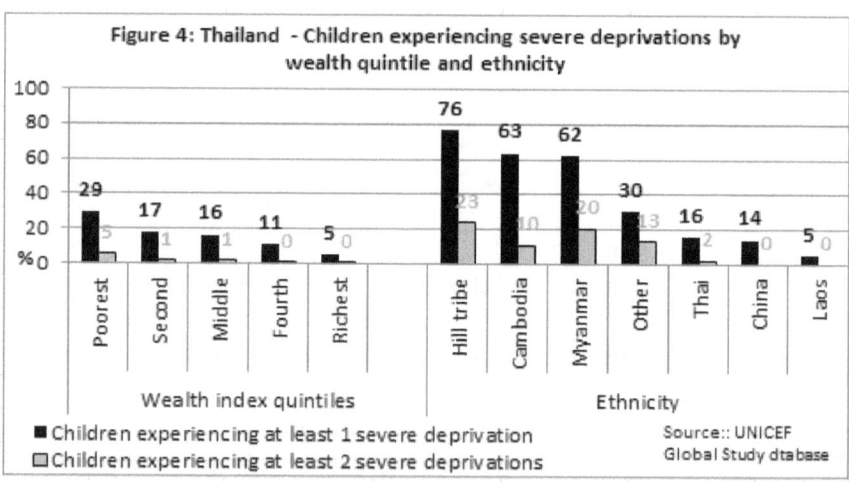

Figure 4: Thailand - Children experiencing severe deprivations by wealth quintile and ethnicity

Deprivation of emotional resources: Understanding poverty from a child's perspective

Multidimensional child poverty measures need to take spiritual and emotional deprivations into account; however quantifying emotional deprivation is a complex task and this dimension is often overlooked. A number of countries participating in the Global Study on Child Poverty and Disparities conducted qualitative research to gain insight into whether the data accurately reflected the plight of children living in poverty, as well as attempted to address how being deprived of basic needs affects their emotional well-being.

The Child Poverty Study in Bhutan found that 23 per cent of school aged children are severely deprived of education and the education analysis was further enriched by children's reflections:

"The worst thing that happened to me was the loss of my father [...] My mother and grandpa decided to send me to a school. I was so excited, but on reaching the school for admission, the headmaster did not accept me, as I could not present my health card. My health card got burnt down along with my house. That day onwards, I gave up the hope for getting educated. My mother sent me here in Bumthang to work as a domestic worker. At least, I am free from the stepfather's cruel treatment. I am quite happy here." - 10 year old girl

"When I was about seven, I was in the village looking after the cattle. Those were the most difficult part of my life. I had to walk in the forests without any slippers looking after the cattle. My father always promised me that he would send me to school, but he never did that. When he got a work in Bumthang, he even bought me school uniform to get admitted in Wanduecholing School, but by that time I was considered too old for the school." - 14 year old boy

The Kosovo Child Poverty Study team carried out a qualitative study using focus group discussions and a psychological test. The focus population of children included Albanian, Serbian and minority communities. At the heart of the study findings were the children's clear recognition that poverty is damaging, both personally and socially; and an acute awareness that some minority children have experiences that vary significantly from those of other children:

"Sometimes poor children don't know how to write while the rich ones know how to write. Children who don't know how to write are yelled at by the teacher. The teacher beats them with a stick. There are cases when the teacher throws pupils out of class when they did not know how to write, and tells them not to

come back without their parents." - 9 year old Ashkali boy

These qualitative studies are a useful, powerful and integral part of the analysis in understanding how poverty affects children's emotional well-being. It is critical that these qualitative analyses are undertaken in conjunction with routine quantitative analyses in order to verify and enrich policy makers understanding of child well-being.

Policy implications

The Brief has demonstrated that child poverty based on two or more severe deprivations varies markedly from using a single income/consumption poverty measure: child well-being is not only dependent on accessing a certain level of household income; it is also about access to adequate nutrition, education and so forth. Helping families move out of poverty means moving beyond solely increasing incomes, to aiming for greater social investment in general, as well as monitoring of progress and impact.

Initial analysis suggests that countries that have a range of policies in place to support families with children generally have lower severe child deprivation rates, as is evident in Kyrgyzstan, where 22% of the population is living below $1.25 and six percent of children experience 2 or more severe deprivations. This is in part due to Government commitment to social service delivery and some of the benefits of the Soviet era are still evident, such as high education levels. There are various policies and programs in place that address child well-being, for example the "Unified Monthly Benefit" for children from poor families, primary and secondary education is free, the proportion of public expenditure for health services for the poor has increased, social benefits are provided to disabled children and so forth. However, these social safeguards are inadequate and insufficiently targeted as evidenced by 13% of children in the Batken region experiencing 2 or more severe deprivations as opposed to one percent in the Chui region (National Study on Child Poverty and Disparities in the Kyrgyz Republic, 2009).

Policy design and implementation are key factors in ensuring that children benefit from policies aimed at increased child well-being.

These policies may include, among others: free/low cost basic health care services, maternity benefits and the availability of low-cost childcare that enables both parents to work. National priorities need to reflect strong linkages between these policies and child well-being. Social protection measures are increasingly gaining recognition as successful tools in reducing child poverty as these measures commonly address social vulnerability and take into account the inter-relationship between exclusion and poverty.

The analysis has also indicated that a high GDP per capita is not necessarily directly associated with low levels of child poverty, and likewise a low GDP per capita is not necessarily associated with high levels of child poverty. Looking at countries with similar levels of GDP we see highly disparate rates of child poverty which can be explained by varied investments and policies that benefit children. For example, both Tanzania and Uzbekistan - which are low income economies, who have historically prioritised social investments - post far better child well-being indicators than their GDP would imply. On the other hand Tanzania also provides a case in point that social investments need to be complemented with income enhancing policies, as demonstrated by the extremely high rate (89%) of people living below the $1.25 poverty line.

Children suffering from two or more severe deprivations often experience cumulative disadvantages and special attention needs to be paid to these children and their families. This paper emphasizes the importance of gaining a holistic understanding of the underlying reasons to these poor child outcomes. This paper also opens up opportunities for further analysis, with the primary hypothesis that countries that implement holistic policies/strategies that address the multidimensionality of child poverty are likely to be more successful in advancing children's rights and well-being rather than countries with piecemeal strategies.

References

Delamonica, E., Minujin, A., Davidziuk, A., and E.D. Gonzalez (2006). "Children living in poverty: Overview of definitions, measurements and policy." UNICEF Working Paper Series. New York.

Fajth, G. and K. Holland (2007). "Child Poverty: A perspective." UNICEF DPP Working Papers. New York

Gordon, D., Nandy, S., Pantazis, C., Pemberton, S. and P. Townsend (2003). *Child poverty in the developing world*. Bristol: The Policy Press.

UNDP (2004). "Dollar a day, how much does it say?" In Focus - International Poverty Centre for Inclusive Growth (IPC-IG), Brasilia.

UNDP (2010) Human Development Report. *The Real Wealth of Nations: Pathways to Human Development.*

UNICEF (2005). Global Study Guide on Child Poverty and Disparities. New York: UNICEF. Available at www.unicefglobalstudy.blogspot.com

UNICEF (2005). *State of the World's Children 2005 - Childhood under Threat*. New York: UNICEF.

UNICEF (2009). Child Poverty Network Consolidated Reply – "Undertaking Qualitative Research as Part of the Global Study on Child Poverty and Disparities."

UNICEF (2010). "Child Poverty and Disparities in Bhutan: Towards Betterment of Child Well Being and Equity." Thimphu: The Centre for Bhutan Studies. *Not yet published.*

UNICEF (2010). Child Poverty and Disparities in Egypt Report: Building the Social Infrastructure for Egypt's Future.

UNICEF (2010). Child Poverty and Disparities in Thailand Report.

World Bank (2005). World Development Indicators. Health Expenditure per capita (current US$).

World Bank (2006). World Development Indicators. GDP per capita (current $US).

World Bank (2006). World Development Indicators. GNI per capita (current international $).

World Bank (various years). World Development Indicators. Poverty headcount ratio at $1.25 a day (PPP) (per cent of population).

The Dynamics of Poverty
Deepa Narayan[5]

Moving out of Poverty
Moving out of Poverty, a large-scale, 15-country comparative study, is unique among other poverty studies as it puts conventional assumptions about poverty aside and relies on the ratings and perspectives of the poor themselves. This work reveals three key issues:

- **Poverty is multidimensional**: it includes not only economic well-being, but also social well-being, issues of dignity, freedoms, democracy, equality, empowerment and aspirations, to name a few. Understanding poverty in such a way differs from definitions from orthodox studies, which typically focus on people who live below an income poverty line.

- **Poverty is a dynamic phenomenon**: Many previous studies around the world, whether qualitative or quantitative, are snapshots; they focus at one point in time, which in turn implies that poverty reduction strategies are based on these snapshots. This study shows that poverty is a situation not a characteristic of the poor as there is much movement up and down. In addition the factors leading to upward movement are different from those related to downward movement. This necessitates different policies.

- **Variation is greater within country than across countries**. While national level studies are useful, the study reveals that poverty mobility varies more within a country rather than across countries. This was true for other important measures such as the responsiveness of local democracy. Hence it is important to understand local dynamics in different types of communities within a country.

---

[5]Deepa Narayan is former Senior Advisor in the Poverty Reduction and Economic Management Network of the World Bank

Principles and methods to engage with the poor

The *Moving Out of Poverty* study is a follow-up to the earlier *Voices of the Poor* study. Its purpose is to explore from the bottom up how people move out of poverty. The study focuses in depth on 500 communities and is not nationally representative. Principles that guided the work: (i) each individual is the expert on her or his own life. The analysis gives primacy to the voices of 60,000 people, living primarily in rural communities, who shared their life experiences and insights, and (ii) local context matters. Individuals and households were located in their community contexts, and goes beyond the exclusive focus on individual or household characteristics that is often typical of poverty surveys.

In order to really capture poor people's own perspectives and definitions of poverty and prosperity, researchers developed a tool called the Ladder of Life. In group discussions, participants built a 'Ladder of Life,' or a continuum describing degrees of poverty and well-being, and then decided where in this continuum specific households in their community stood in 2005 (the time of the study) and 10 years previously. Asking participants to establish where households stood both in 1995 and in 2005 allowed the authors to see such mobility, and to categorize households in terms of their poverty mobility as: movers (poor in 1995, non-poor in 2005), chronic poor (still poor since 1995), never poor, and fallers (non-poor in 1995, poor in 2005). An example of 'ladder of life' in a village in Andhra Pradesh has as the poorest the landless laborers, and the wealthiest, landlords, with four categories (steps) in between those extremes. Often people's own poverty line was higher than the official poverty line.

This tool allowed the authors to gain an overall picture of mobility in and out of poverty in each community, using community poverty lines. The overall results draw upon individual life stories, focus group discussions and household interviews.

Poverty dynamics

In spite of the many obstacles poor people confront, many do escape poverty. Poverty is a condition and not a characteristic. Across the studied communities in the world, close to half the population is moving up or down, often with the same people falling and rising at different times. There is great variation across countries, with the highest falling rates in Africa. But worldwide, 23% moved out of poverty while almost the same number -- 22% -- fell into poverty. Just by stopping the falling we can dramatically affect poverty rates.

This analysis of poverty mobility also reveals that similar net reductions in poverty in the different study regions can mask very different poverty dynamics. For instance, in West Bengal about 30% of those who began in poverty moved out, while only about 17% of the initially poor moved out of poverty in Andhra Pradesh. But the net reduction in poverty was only four percentage points larger in West Bengal, because 21.1% of the non-poor there moved into poverty, and in Andhra Pradesh, this movement was only half as large. Thus, the dynamics of the non-poor matter for poverty reduction as well. In Malawi, the authors found that falling rates among rural communities were high enough to cancel out the upward movement. The main reasons across countries for falling into poverty were health shocks and declines in local economic prosperity.

Moving in and out of poverty
The study shows that the reasons for moving out of poverty and for falling into it are different, and need to be analyzed. These reasons are shown on the figure on the next page.

- **Strong aspirations and individual initiative drive efforts to improve their own situation** and lay the foundation for a better future for themselves and their children. 77.5% of people cite "individual initiative" as the main reason for moving out of poverty. Empowerment is thus a major factor in poverty reduction. Regression analyses also highlighted the importance of empowerment in moving out of poverty even after controlling for many other factors. Despite social, political and economic barriers that poor people are often faced with, they take many risks in an active search for opportunities to improve their welfare.

Figure 1. Reasons for falling into and moving out of poverty

Gambling, drugs, and alcohol are rarely cited as reasons for falling

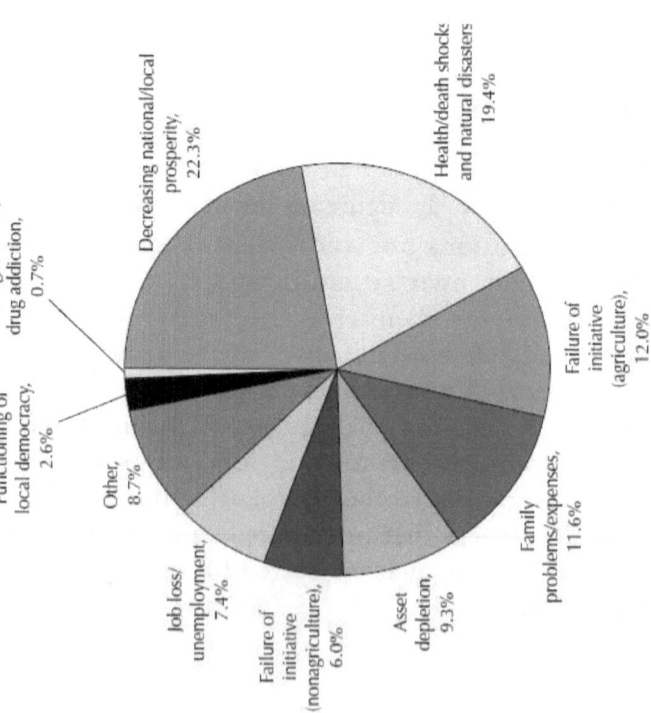

Source: Authors' analysis of household survey; all study regions; *N* = 3,661 (all four mobility groups).

Note: Figures are percentages of reasons cited by respondents in all mobility groups when asked to name the top three reasons for their downward movement.

Movers most frequently cite initiatives as reasons for their move out of poverty

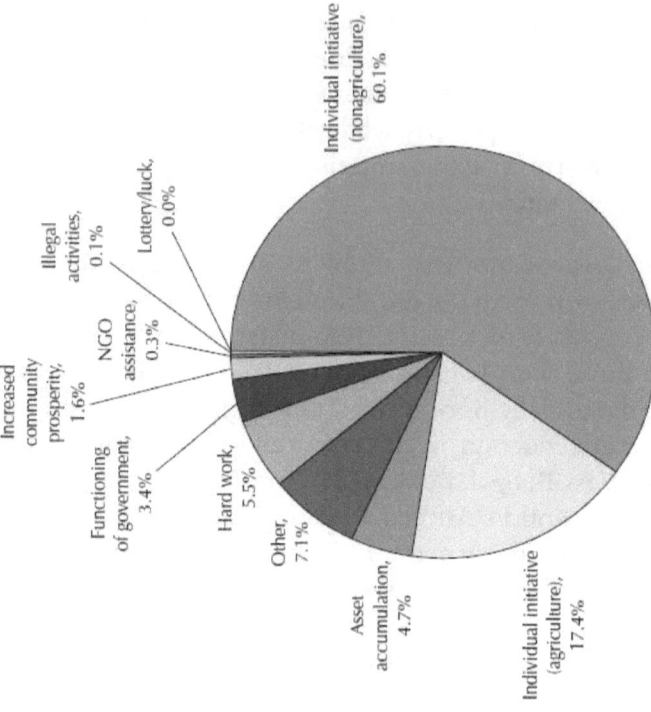

Source: Authors' analysis of household survey; all study regions; *N* = 3,991 movers.

Note: Figures are percentages of reasons cited by movers when asked to name the top three reasons for their movement out of poverty. "Individual initiative (nonagriculture)" includes finding jobs, investing in business, adding new sources of income, and migration.

- **Poor people frequently confront exclusionary markets and lack resources**. Despite the micro-credit revolution, poor people remain starved for credit and excluded from other financial services. Micro credit alone cannot pull people permanently out of poverty.
- The extent of downward mobility reveals that **vulnerability and insecurity** are key issues. Participants identified those households on the first and second step immediately above the community poverty line as the most vulnerable. Often, this group has no savings or assets to fall back on. The figure below shows the net poverty reduction rates in five countries with high falling rates versus the poverty reduction rates if no one had fallen into poverty.

Figure 2. Dynamics of poverty reduction

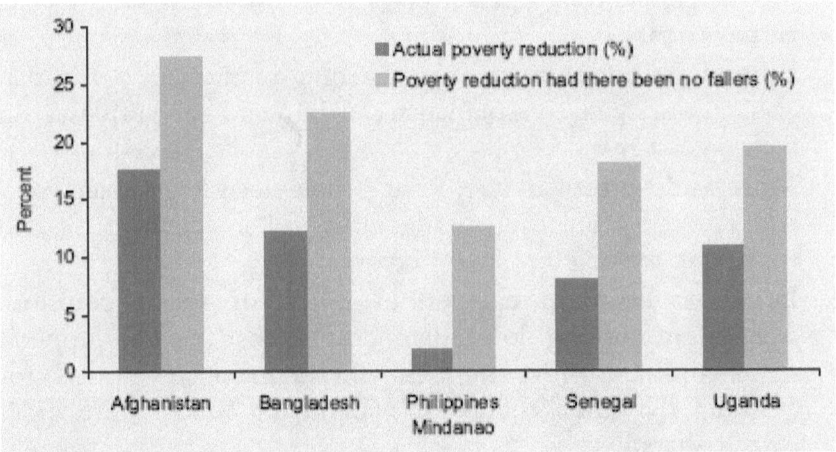

Source: Calculations from the Ladder of Life community mobility matrixes, Narayan et al. (2009).

Policy implications emerging from Moving Out of Poverty

New strategies are needed, with particular focus on vulnerability, to increase people's resilience, first, by helping them reach an asset threshold that would allow them to survive shocks such as illness, crop failure, and food and fuel price increases. Second, poverty can be dramatically decreased through social protection measures, including social and health insurance programs as well as cash transfers that help people deal with shocks, particularly ill health, one of the most frequent triggers for descent into poverty. Narrowly based targeting when large numbers are poor is ineffective. All development agencies should concentrate resources in a geographic area before moving to the next rather than scatter resources over large areas.

Some of the policy recommendations that arise from *Moving Out of Poverty*:

- **Location matters, and so does connectedness**: The provision of quasi-public goods like permanent roads, physical market spaces, irrigation waterways, telephone networks, electricity and cheap, reliable transport is a powerful lever for increasing economic opportunity;
- **Fair access to markets is key**: Expanding opportunities for the poor requires an analysis of the business climate not only for large, formal producers, but for tiny and small entrepreneurs;
- **Liberalization from below**: Opening markets in a way that even poor, small entrepreneurs can buy and sell surpluses on their own terms;
- **More and better finance**: Poor people need larger loans, new and innovative financing arrangements for small enterprise, and support in making best use of credit;
- **Local government can either block or spur economic dynamism**: Strong local democracies that ensure property rights and a positive business environment are critical for ensuring that the benefits of opening up markets are more equally shared.

References

Dudwick, N., Hull, K. and E. Tas (2009). "A Note on Vulnerability: Findings from Moving Out of Poverty." PREM Notes – Poverty No. 132. World Bank.

- **Moving Out of Poverty Series**

Narayan, D. (2009). *Moving Out of Poverty: The Promise of Empowerment and Democracy in India*. Palgrave Macmillan.

Narayan, D. and P. Petesch (2007). *Moving Out of Poverty: Cross-disciplinary Perspectives on Mobility*. Palgrave Macmillan.

Narayan, D., and P. Petesch (2009). *Moving Out of Poverty: Rising from the Ashes of Conflict*. Palgrave Macmillan.

Narayan, D., and P. Petesch. (2005). "Moving out of Poverty: Understanding Freedom, Democracy and Growth from the Bottom-Up." Methodology Guide. World Bank.

Narayan, D., Pritchett, L. and S. Kapoor (2009). *Moving Out of Poverty: Success from the Bottom Up*. Palgrave Macmillan.

- **Voices of the Poor Series**

Narayan, D. and P. Petesch (2002). *Voices of the Poor: From Many Lands*. New York: Published for the World Bank, Oxford University Press.

Narayan, D., Patel,R., Schafft, K., Rademacher, A. and S. Koch-Schulte (2000). *Voices of the Poor: Can Anyone Hear Us?* New York: Published for the World Bank, Oxford University Press.

Narayan, D., Chambers, R., Shah, M.K., and P. Petesch (2000). *Voices of the Poor: Crying Out for Change*. New York: Published for the World Bank, Oxford University Press.

The Changing State of Global Poverty
Laurence Chandy and Geoffrey Gertz

Tracking global poverty
Official estimates of global poverty (based on levels of consumption) are compiled by the World Bank and stretch back 30 years. The Bank's most recent estimate is for the year 2005, when 1.37 billion people were believed to be living under the international poverty line of $1.25 a day.

Given the high, sustained economic growth achieved throughout most of the developing world over the last six years, there is reason to believe poverty has declined dramatically since 2005. By combining the most recent national survey data with up to date estimates of private consumption growth for 119 developing countries, we generate global poverty estimates that apply right up to the present day.

We estimate that between 2005 and 2010, the total number of poor people around the world fell by nearly half a billion people to under 900 million in 2010. This means that the prime target of the Millennium Development Goals – to halve the rate of global poverty by 2015 from its 1990 level – was probably achieved around three years ago. Whereas it took 25 years to reduce poverty by half a billion people up to 2005, the same feat was likely achieved in the six years between then and now. Poverty reduction of this magnitude is unparalleled in history; never before have so many people been lifted out of poverty over such a brief period of time.

Using consumption forecasts for the next few years, we estimate that extreme poverty could fall to under 600 million people by 2015.

[6]Laurence Chandy is a Fellow at the Brookings Institution
Geoffrey Gertz is a Research Analyst at the Brookings Institution

Poverty reduction in all parts of the world

Unlike during previous decades, such as the 1980s (when the poverty rate increased in Africa) and the 1990s (when it increased in Latin America and the former Soviet Union), poverty reduction is currently taking place in all regions of the world. As expected, the greatest reduction has occurred in Asia, home to some of the largest and most dynamic emerging economies. A less rapid but perhaps more surprising change is the one taking place in Sub-Saharan Africa. The region finally broke below the symbolic threshold of a 50% poverty rate in 2008 and its number of poor people has begun falling for the first time on record.

A similar pattern emerges at a country-level, with many countries sharing in the overall pattern of success, but the biggest reductions in poverty attributable to a few big-hitting counties. The two developing giants, India and China, are alone responsible for three-quarters of the reduction in the world's poor expected over the period 2005-2015. Other countries home to large poor populations—Bangladesh, Ethiopia, Pakistan, Vietnam, Indonesia and Brazil—will see tens of millions of their citizens escape poverty over this period. And a number of African countries, including Nigeria, South Africa, Mozambique, Ghana and Tanzania, follow closely behind.

Changing composition of global poverty

The global poverty landscape is quickly being redrawn. Between 2005 and 2015, Asia's share of global poverty is expected to fall from two-thirds to one-third, while Africa's share more than doubles from 28% to 60%. Poverty will thus increasingly be seen as an African problem, despite the progress the continent is now making.

With the graduation of some of the world's biggest developing countries into middle income-country (MIC) status, poverty is no longer concentrated in low-income countries (LIC). According to our estimates, the share of the world's poor residing in LICs hit a low of 33% in 2009 and will remain below 50% until after 2015.

Figure 1. Share of world's poor by country category

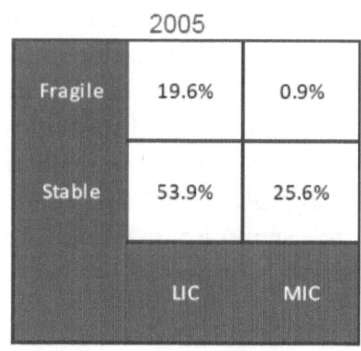
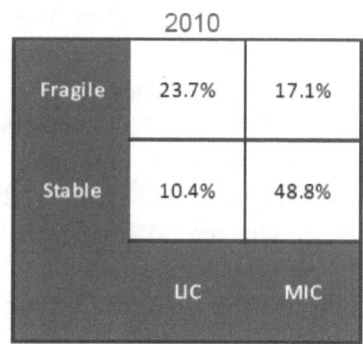

Source: Chandy and Gertz (2011b).

Meanwhile, poverty is becoming increasingly concentrated in fragile and conflict-afflicted states. Countries that remain locked in fragility are unsurprisingly not recording the same feats of poverty reduction achieved by stable countries. Whereas only 20% of the world's poor lived in fragile states in 2005, this share is now over 40% and will exceed 50% by 2014.

Implications for organizations committed to the wellbeing of children

These trends have three important implications for UNICEF and other organizations devoted to the welfare of children.

First, in order to successfully target the world's poorest children organizations such as UNICEF must update their policies and programming to reflect the new reality.

At one level, this is a simple matter of determining how resources should be allocated: for instance, there may be less demand for resources in countries where extreme poverty is falling rapidly or has already been eliminated, freeing up funds and expertise to be devoted to Sub-Saharan Africa where the numbers of poor children remain high.

At another level, however, a more qualitative change in the way development interventions are approached is justified.

In 2005, more than half the world's poor lived in stable, low-income countries. Development programs, including those for children, could therefore be designed around the typical needs and circumstances of these sorts of countries. While this approach remains relevant for some countries, its broader application can no longer be justified as 90% of the world's poor live in different settings today.

Yet such an admission poses a dilemma. One of the reasons the stable low-income paradigm has persisted is because it characterizes an environment in which development agencies and NGOs feel most comfortable and have the most experience. Specifically, the role of external actors in helping the poor in stable low-income countries is well understood and the standard tools of foreign aid – financial and technical assistance – are well suited to them.

The same cannot be said for other environments. Middle-income countries do not face the same financial constraints as low-income countries do, which makes the case for financial assistance less compelling. As for fragile states, many of the development challenges they face are strictly political, as opposed to technical. Technical assistance is hard to justify if existing technical know-how is deliberately underemployed. Moreover, external actors are less likely to find willing and reliable partners with which to work in fragile states.

Organizations such as UNICEF have experience working in many different country settings. But the changing poverty landscape will force them to adapt the way they work to better suit the challenges of helping children in middle-income countries and fragile states, where the role of external actors is less straightforward.

Second, given the different poverty trends found throughout the world, interventions for children should be informed by a dynamic, forward-looking perspective, addressing the world as it is today while anticipating future needs.

Our poverty forecasts suggest that many of the children who are extremely poor today live in households that may soon enjoy higher incomes and represent the last generation who will be born into extreme poverty in their country. This is characteristic of children in a number of emerging economies, where poverty is still prevalent but is falling rapidly. In these countries, the case for immediate palliative measures to support poor children today is beyond doubt. But the needs of tomorrow will differ markedly, and may include social safety nets to prevent households that have broken out of poverty from slipping backwards, or targeted interventions aimed at discriminated minorities or sub-national regions that could miss out on the rising living standards enjoyed by others.

Poor children born in other parts of the world are likely to remain destitute into adulthood meaning that their offspring will likely be born into another cycle of poverty. This is the case for children living in countries where poverty rates are high and are expected to remain elevated into the future. Here, the need is for large scale, long-term programs aimed in many cases at entire populations, which can provide for children's basic needs in education, health, nutrition and social protection. The design of these programs should be focused on maximizing sustainability: keeping costs low on the assumption that government revenues are unlikely to increase significantly, using simple approaches that are easily scalable and can operate with limited capacity, and supported by efforts to strengthen the institutions on which they depend.

Third, serious consideration should be given to rolling out cash transfers to support the poorest families and their children.

Our results indicate that providing every person in the world with a minimum income of $1.25/day—in other words guaranteeing the right not to live in absolute poverty—is rapidly becoming feasible. In 2005, supplementing the income of each poor person in the world to bring their daily income up to $1.25 would have cost $96 billion, or 80% of the total volume of foreign aid disbursed that year. In 2010, with poverty less widespread and larger global aid volumes, the cost of such a global safety net would be just $66 billion, or slightly more than half of all official aid. Moreover, conditional transfers which encourage families to keep children in school and ensure they receive regular medical care can compound the development impact of a global safety net.

While the logistics of distributing cash to poor populations would not be without challenges, recent advances in biometric identification technologies—such as fingerprint and iris scanning— have greatly expanded the promise of implementing large-scale welfare programs in poor countries.

References

Chandy, L. and G. Gertz (2011a). "Poverty in Numbers: The Changing State of Global Poverty from 2005 to 2015." The Brookings Institution.

Chandy, L. and G. Gertz (2011b). "Two Trends in Global Poverty." The Brookings Institution.

Chen, S. and M. Ravallion (2008). "The Developing World is Poorer than We Thought but No Less Successful in the Fight against Poverty." World Bank Policy Research Working Paper #4703.

Kenny, C. (2011). *Getting Better: Why Global Development Is Succeeding—And How We Can Improve the World Even More*. New York: Basic Books.

Hanlon, J., Barrientos, A. and D. Hulme (2010). *Just Give Money to the Poor: The Development Revolution from the Global South*. Sterling: Kumarian Press.

Escaping Poverty Traps – Children and Chronic Poverty

Caroline Harper, Hanna Alder and Paola Pereznieto[7]

Chronic poverty and development

The last five years saw unprecedented global wealth creation; yet, the number of people living in chronic poverty—extreme poverty that persists for a long time—has *increased.* Between 320 and 443 million people are now trapped in chronic poverty, which many times is also transmitted inter-generationally to their children. The Millennium Development Goals target to halve global poverty by 2015 fails to account for the many who will remain trapped in poverty for some duration of time. The MDGs can only be achieved if chronic poverty is effectively tackled, particularly in sub-Saharan Africa and South Asia, and if the target is extended to 2025 to enable national governments and international organisations to make the necessary political commitments and resource allocations and implement necessary policies.

Whichever way one frames the problem of chronic poverty – as human suffering, as vulnerability, as a basic needs failure, as the abrogation of human rights, as degraded citizenship – widespread chronic poverty occurs in a world that has the knowledge and resources to eradicate it. Tackling chronic poverty is therefore *the* global priority for our generation and is vital if our world is to achieve an acceptable level of justice and fairness.

---

[7]Caroline Harper is Associate Director of the Chronic Poverty Research Centre and a Research Fellow at Overseas Development Institute, UK

Hanna Alder is Programme/Research Officer at Overseas Development Institute, UK

Paola Pereznieto is Research Fellow in the Social Development Programme at Overseas Development Institute, UK

The drivers of chronic poverty

Chronic poverty is distinguishable by its duration and multidimensionality. Chronically poor people always or during long period of their lives live below a poverty line, and their situations are usually defined by structural and social inequalities influenced by multiple discriminations. This is different from the transitorily poor, who move in and out of poverty, or only occasionally fall below the poverty line. The chronically poor are not a distinct group; most of them are 'working poor,' with a minority unable to engage in labour markets. They include people who are discriminated against or socially marginalised, frequently because they are members of ethnic, religious, indigenous, nomadic and caste or class groups. They are also migrants and bonded labourers; refugees and internally displaced; disabled people; those with ill health; and the young and old. In many contexts poor women and girls are the most likely to experience lifelong poverty.

Yet, despite this heterogeneity, five main traps underpin chronic poverty:

1. **Insecurity:** The chronically poor frequently live in insecure environments with few assets or entitlements to cope with shocks and stresses.
2. **Limited citizenship**: Chronically poor people have no meaningful political voice and lack effective political representation.
3. **Spatial disadvantage:** Remoteness, certain types of natural resource base, political exclusion and weak economic integration can all contribute to the creation of intra-country spatial poverty traps.
4. **Social discrimination:** Chronically poor people often have social relations of power, patronage and competition that can trap them in exploitative relationships or deny them access to public and private goods and services. These are based on class and caste systems, gender, religious and ethnic identity, age and other factors.
5. **Poor work opportunities:** Where there is limited or unevenly distributed economic growth, work opportunities are limited and people can be exploited. Such work allows day-to-day

survival but does not facilitate asset accumulation or fund children's education.

Children are disproportionately affected by chronic poverty

Chronic poverty has serious consequences for children, not least the strong likelihood of suffering a premature death from easily preventable health problems, or lifelong ill health due to deprivations. The durable nature of chronic poverty combined with lower levels of assets result in decreased resilience to shocks and weaker springboards for escaping poverty. The long-term impact that chronic poverty has when experienced in childhood and the potential for intergenerational transmission that adds to its injustice and to the intractable nature of this issue. Intergenerational transmission of poverty occurs through different channels in different contexts. For instance, low levels of *in utero* and child nutrition resulting from poor maternal and child health lead to long term physical and mental stunting. Low levels of parental education and income serve to limit the potential for children's education and low parental income is also a key driver to early marriage and early childbirth, themselves determinants of higher than average maternal death and injury and lifelong resultant illness among girls and young women. Poor parents have poor children, and those children are more likely to grow up as poor adults because of the structural, social and health limitations faced as children.

Additionally, child poverty has strong gender dimensions, and social institutions many times play a role in leading to and perpetuating chronic poverty, vulnerability and discrimination over the course of childhood and into adulthood for girls. The chronically poor are more likely to experience higher levels of vulnerability to multiple discriminations, all of which compound and contribute to the severity and duration of the experience of poverty and increase the impact on life-course potential. Girls' vulnerabilities in relation to poverty dynamics are different to those of boys; more than 100 million girls aged 10 to 19 are expected to marry between 2005 and

2015[8], increasing the risk to the known dangers of early pregnancy and forgone educational opportunities. 60,000 to 70,000 girls aged 15 to 19 die from complications of pregnancy and childbirth every year (WHO, 2008d, in Temin et al., 2010). Women under 20 giving birth face double the risk of dying in childbirth compared with women over 20, and girls under age 15 are five times as likely to die as those in their 20s[9].

Meanwhile, it is estimated that more than 130 million girls and women alive today have undergone female genital mutilation (FGM) or cutting (FGC), which among other issues can lead to life threatening and lifelong health problems (UN, General Assembly, 2006). Moreover, young women are particularly vulnerable to coerced sex and are increasingly being infected with HIV and AIDS (UNIFEM, 2010). Further, two thirds of the 137 million illiterate young people in the world are women (UNFPA, 2007), and in 2007 girls accounted for 54% of the world's out-of-school population (UN, 2009). In many cases, these overlapping and intersecting experiences of deprivation and vulnerability, foregone human development opportunities and abuse or exploitation serve to perpetuate and intensify poverty of girls and women over the life-course.

Childhood, adolescence and early adulthood are critical in determining life-course potential. Physical and neurological development and social, educational and work skills attainment are all decisive development and learning acquisitions. Yet this key period remains for many children one of deprivation, danger and vulnerability, resulting in a significant lack of agency and critical development deficits, which often have long-term detrimental life-course consequences.

---

[8]Based on girls aged 10 to 19 in developing countries, excluding China, projected to marry before their 18th birthday (Clark, 2004)
www.unfpa.org/swp/2005/presskit/factsheets/facts_child_marriage.htm
[9]www.wpf.org

Addressing chronic poverty

The following five key policy responses presented in the second chronic poverty report (2008) refer to the five main traps that underpin chronic poverty although it should be noted that they do not map neatly one-for-one against each trap, but rather create an integrated policy set that respond to the multiple, overlapping causes of chronic poverty:

- **Social protection:** Publicly provided social protection, and particularly social assistance, plays a vital role in reducing insecurity and increasing opportunities for the chronically poor to engage with the growth process.

- **Public services for the hard to reach:** Making available reproductive health services and post-primary education can break the intergenerational transmission of poverty and have a dramatic effect on the prospects of chronically poor households.

- **Building individual and collective assets:** Asset holdings increase the personal (and collective) agency of the chronically poor. The more assets – psychological, as well as physical and social – a household possesses, the more leverage it has in social networks and transactions, as well as in formal financial markets.

- **Anti-discrimination and gender empowerment tools:** Tackling social discrimination promotes a just social compact and increases the economic opportunities of the chronically poor. Powerful policy levers in areas such as legal rights, political representation, economic resources and attitudes and perceptions will facilitate the transformative social change necessary to enabling gender empowerment.

- **Strategic urbanisation and migration:** Chronic poverty remains mainly a rural phenomenon although urban chronic poverty can be particularly harsh, because chronically poor people do not access the benefits of urbanisation, and cannot seize the opportunities offered by migration. Chronically poor people need to be given the chance to migrate, through education and antidiscrimination policies.

Bringing services to the chronically poor is certainly a challenge but it is worth keeping in mind that interventions in reproductive health, education, nutrition and social protection complement each other, forming a virtuous circle of social and economic development. What can be done in each of these five policy areas partly depends upon country context. Although country context influences the chances of ending chronic poverty, it certainly does not determine it.

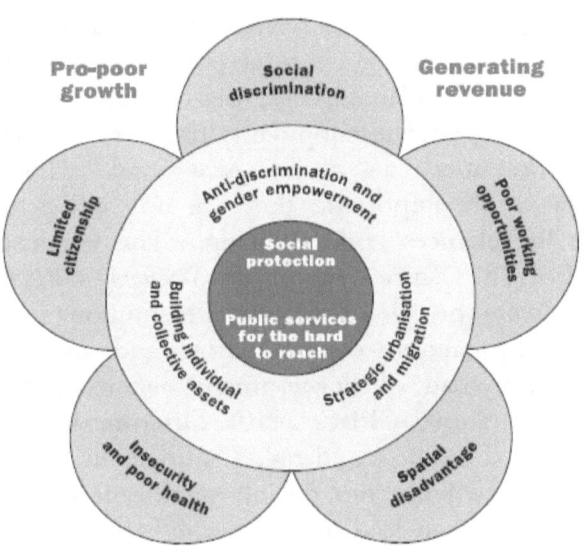

Additionally, policy change must include the chronically poor themselves as the leading actors in overcoming their poverty. To date, when their existence is recognised at all, the chronically poor are perceived both by policymakers and in the popular imagination as dependent and passive. The fact is that nothing could be further from the truth. Most people in chronic poverty are striving and working to improve their livelihoods and the prospects for their children, in very difficult circumstances they have not chosen (CPRC, 2008). They need real commitment from decision-makers, matched by actions and resources, to support their efforts and overcome the obstacles that trap them in poverty and deny them citizenship.

Tackling child chronic poverty

Fundamentally progressive social change is essential for tackling chronic poverty. Existing social orders (caste, age, gender, race and class relations etc.) underpin and perpetuate social discrimination, poor work opportunities and limited citizenship that stop the poorest from improving their circumstances.

Chronically poor people do not just need 'good policies' they need societies that give them a voice and facilitate their human rights. Achieving this is the most difficult part of the policy and political agenda – social and cultural relationships and practices are often entrenched. Policies to end chronic poverty have a particular focus on childhood as explained, because of the implications of life course and inter-generational poverty transfers. Tackling poverty in childhood requires a *specific focus* and whilst household improvements are important, they are not sufficient to improve children's life chances and wellbeing. This is illustrated by the Chronic Poverty Centre's report on *Stemming Girls Chronic Poverty* which highlights the role of five social institutions in particular that perpetuate inequalities, discrimination and exclusion, in turn generating a myriad of development deficits and physical and psychological trauma (CPRC, 2010). Discriminatory family codes, son bias, limited resource and rights entitlement, physical insecurity and restricted civil liberties are all significant barriers to human development and can lead to and perpetuate chronic poverty and vulnerability over the course of childhood and adulthood, and potentially inter-generationally.

Six key recommendations for action to more effectively tackle chronic poverty and promote progressive social change are:

1. **Develop and enforce context-sensitive legal provisions to eliminate gender discrimination in the family, school, workplace and community**: The harmonisation of national legal frameworks with international commitments (CEDAW) and of local customs and codes with more formal legislative approaches combined with the introduction of reforms such as a ban on sex-selective abortion or the prevention of gender-based-violence.

2. **Support measures to promote children's, and especially girls' right, to be heard and to participate in decisions in areas of importance to them:** Empowerment programmes supported by mentors to promote girls' voice and agency combined with educational programmes for boys and young men to challenge aggressive understandings and practices of machismo.

3. **Invest in the design and implementation of child- and gender-sensitive social protection:** Initiatives to promote girls schooling, cash transfers, social health insurance and health fee exemptions, asset transfers and public works programmes designed to target female time poverty are all forms of social protection that can be a powerful tool to mitigate the worst effects of both economic and social risks and to promote pathways out of poverty.

4. **Strengthen services for girls who are hard to reach, because of both spatial disadvantage as well as age- and gender-specific socio-cultural barriers:** Initiatives aimed at promoting girls' access to and use of existing services need to focus on innovative and gender-sensitive means of extending programmes such as microfinance and reproductive health services and on bringing services to girls where possible.

5. **Support measures to strengthen girls' and young women's individual and collective ownership of, access to and use of resources:** A collective approach, supported by strong mentors is needed to promote information sharing, self-esteem, capability development and social capital to help girls gain confidence with and through each other and to develop a sense of agency.

6. **Strengthen efforts to promote girls' and women's physical integrity and control over their bodies, especially in conflict and post-conflict settings:** Educational and empowerment programmes that raise girls' and young women's awareness of their right to be protected from violence, efforts to counter the culture of impunity surrounding gender-based violence in conflict and post-conflict settings and efforts to involve girls and young women in age- and gender-sensitive disarmament, demobilisation and reintegration programmes are all vital.

References

Chronic Poverty Research Centre (CPRC) (2008). *The Chronic Poverty Report 2008-9: Escaping Poverty Traps*. Manchester: Chronic Poverty Research Centre.

Chronic Poverty Research Centre (CPRC) (2010). *Stemming Girls Chronic Poverty: Catalysing development change by building just social institutions*. Northampton: Belmont Press Limited.

Chronic Poverty Research Centre (CPRC) (2010). *Tackling chronic poverty: Key messages for policy makers*. Working Paper.

Temin, M., Levine, R. and S. Stonesifer (2010). *Start with a Girl. A New Agenda for Global Health*. Washington, DC: Center for Global Development.

UNIFEM (2010). Annual Report 2009-2010. New York: UNIFEM

United Nations (UN) General Assembly (2006). "In-Depth Study on All Forms of Violence against Women." Report of the Secretary-General. A/61/122/Add.1. 6 July.

UNFPA (2007). *Framework for Action on Adolescents and Youth: Opening Doors with Young People*. New York: UNFPA

United Nations (UN) (2009). *Millennium Development Goals Report 2009*. New York: UN.

Can the MDGs Provide a Pathway to Social Justice?
The Challenge of Intersecting Inequalities
Naila Kabeer[10]

The fundamental values of the MDGs
A decade ago, 189 of the world's leaders came together to sign the Millennium Declaration and to commit themselves on our behalf to co-ordinated action on one of the more pressing and durable problems that the world faces: the problem of extreme poverty. The Declaration was based on a set of fundamental values which together spelt a firm commitment to social justice as the guiding spirit of all these efforts. These values included:

- **Freedom:** men and women have the right to live their lives and raise their children in dignity, free from hunger and free from fear
- **Equality:** the equality of rights and opportunities of men and women must be assured
- **Solidarity:** those who suffer or who benefit least deserve help from those who benefit most
- **Tolerance:** human beings must respect one another in all their diversity of belief, culture and language. Differences within and between societies should be cherished as a precious asset of humanity.

The Declaration was subsequently translated into eight Millennium Development Goals in order to provide an agenda for action. These included halving extreme poverty and hunger by 2015, assuring adequate health and education for all, promoting gender equality and strengthening the spirit of international co-operation.

---

[10]Naila Kabeer is Professor of Gender and Development at the School of Oriental and African Studies (SOAS), University of London

The unequal pace of MDG progress and how it relates to children

With five years to go, the world leaders have gathered together again to celebrate what has been achieved and to take stock of what has not. That there have been gains is undeniable. But in the necessary translation of the declaration into goals, we lost sight of the fundamental values of the Declaration and its vision of social justice. The focus of the MDGs on 'average' measures of progress fails to capture the unequal pace of this progress and the systematic exclusion of certain groups in society.

Figure 1. Ratio of indigenous to non-indigenous infant mortality rate, 2000-02, selected Latin American countries

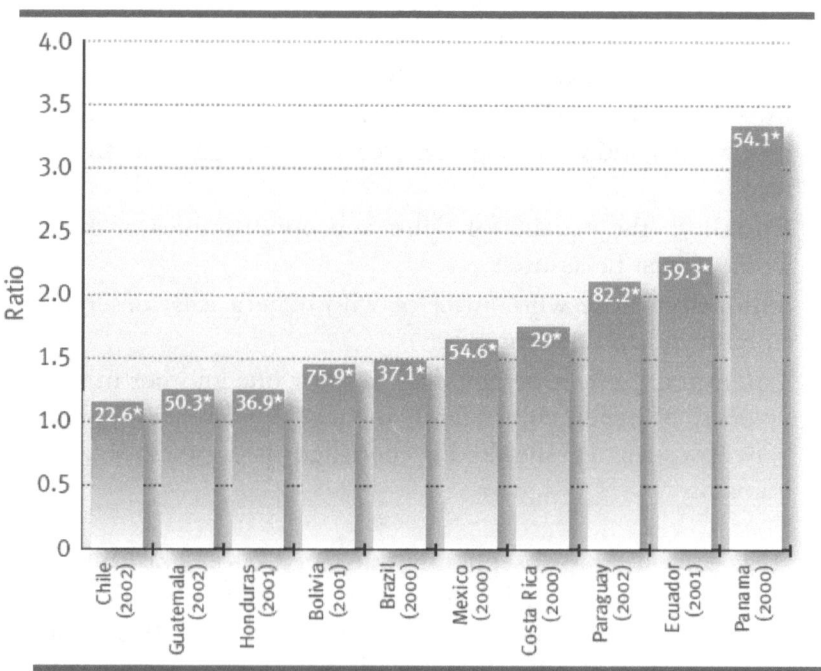

Source: Del Popolo, F. and Oyarce, A. (2005).

A report funded by the MDG Achievement Fund focuses on precisely these groups. In almost every society, in every region of the world, both rich and poor, there are certain groups of people who face systematic social exclusion as the result of the intersecting inequalities that characterise their lives. These include:

- Cultural inequalities: forms of discrimination and devaluation that treat members of these groups as of lesser status and worth than others
- Spatial inequalities: such groups frequently live in places that make them harder to reach or easier to ignore
- Economic inequalities: they are at the receiving end of an unfair distribution of assets and opportunities
- Political inequalities: they are deprived of voice and influence in the decisions that affect their lives and their communities.

Each of these inequalities is a source of injustice in and of itself but it is their mutually reinforcing interaction that explains the persistence of social exclusion over time and its resistance to 'business as usual' approaches to the MDGs. Caste, race, ethnicity, language and religion are among the most common markers of exclusion. And as elsewhere in society, gender cuts across all these so that women and girls from marginalised groups generally fare worse than men and boys.

That these injustices begin in the earliest years is evident from some of the examples relating to children cited in the report:
- In India, despite overall declines in child mortality, it is over 90 per 1000 live births among dalit caste and tribal groups compared to 59 among the better off castes
- Infant mortality rates among indigenous groups in Latin America are much higher than those for non-indigenous groups: in the early 2000s, it was 1.5 times higher in Brazil and Mexico, 2 times higher in Ecuador and over 3 times higher in Panama.
- In Nigeria, the predominantly Hausa-Fulani northern states have much higher levels of poverty and child and maternal mortality than the predominantly Yoruba/Igbo southern states. The interaction between class, ethnicity, gender and location in Nigeria means that a poor rural Hausa girl living in the north is at the bottom of the distribution of educational opportunities in her country
- In China, malnutrition was (2005) considerably higher in the western provinces where its ethnic minorities are concentrated

than in the eastern provinces: there were 12.5% underweight children in the former compared to 5.8% in the latter.

Figure 2. Prevalence of child malnutrition by residence, Nigeria

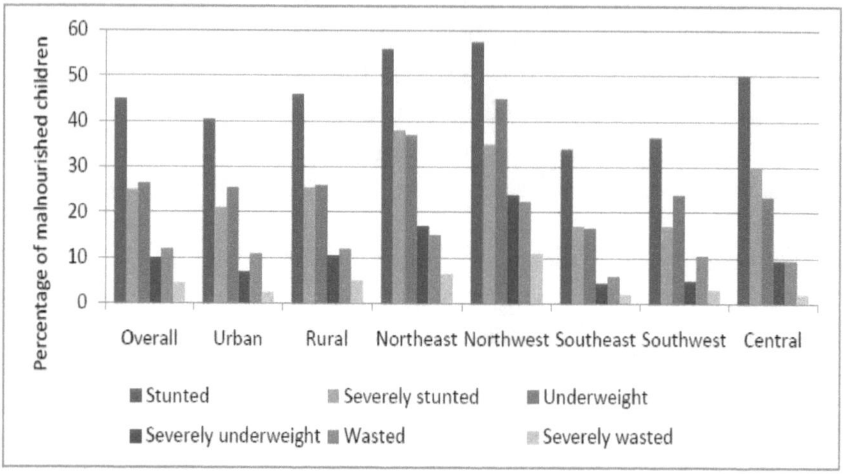

Source: Omilola (2010).

Social exclusion, MDG progress and effective policies

Social exclusion matters because it undermines progress on the MDGs and betrays the promise of social justice contained in the Millennium Declaration. It slows down the rate at which a given level of economic growth translates into poverty reduction. Indeed, by disadvantaging certain groups from childhood, it contributes to the inter-generational cycle of poverty. It has tragic personal consequences: it undermines people's sense of self worth and agency. It is associated with despair, depression, substance abuse and criminal activity. And it can have profound consequences for the fabric of society: the grievances associated with social exclusion lie behind many examples of civil conflict in the world today.

In answer to the question posed by our report, the MDGs *can* provide a pathway to social justice but *only* if attention is paid to the social, cultural and political dimension of policies as much as to their technical and economic dimensions. We have to go beyond business as usual approaches, we have to make the additional effort. Here we can learn from the countries that have made progress on the inequality front – many of the countries in Latin America with some of the most historically entrenched inequalities have managed to make such progress. So have countries like Malaysia. India stands out for its persistent attempts – not always successful – to name and tackle social exclusion. And South Africa has made major strides in its efforts to reverse the inequalities of the past. These countries, along with successful examples from elsewhere, highlight the importance of certain policies:

1) **Comprehensive information policies**. The level of disaggregation of the information base from which we plan and measure progress on development goals obviously has powerful equity implications. But information and knowledge has other value as well. It can help to address long-standing prejudices and build more tolerant societies. And it is a critical resource for excluded groups to understand and act on their rights and entitlements.

2) **Strengthening the resource base of marginalized groups**. This can be achieved through a variety of measures: protecting customary land rights, land reform, asset transfers, establishing user rights to natural resources, promoting residential security, inclusive financial systems.

3) **Investment in infrastructure and area-based development**. This can help to address the spatial disadvantages of marginalized groups and improve their connectivity with the rest of society.

4) **Improving the outreach, quality and relevance of basic social services**. Financial access is important but so too are questions of location and availability, language, attitudes and behaviour and provision for voice and accountability.

5) **Comprehensive social protection systems**. This are necessary not only to underwrite basic livelihood security in an increasingly uncertain world but also to dissolve the relations of fear and dependency that reproduce social exclusion in many contexts

6) **Finally, group-based exclusion requires group-based solutions**. Building the capacity of excluded groups to come together around their shared needs and interests, their capacity to make alliances with others in society concerned with social justice and their capacity to participate in the collective

decisions that affect their lives can provide a strong bottom up pressure for more inclusive approaches to the MDGs.

However, direct action to promote social justice through the MDGs is not enough. It will need to be reinforced by action on other fronts in order to create the necessary enabling environment to sustain gains beyond 2015. Broad-based, employment-centred economic growth can make a powerful contribution to sustaining gains on the 'economic' MDGs while redistributive fiscal policies can support gains in relation to the 'social' MDGs. Strengthening formal and grassroots democratic processes is essential if the institutions of society are to embody a shared vision of freedom, equality, solidarity and tolerance among all citizens.

And finally we need to pay more serious attention to MDG8 and the principles of international solidarity: those countries and groups that have benefited most from progress on the global front have a responsibility towards those countries and groups who have benefited least. This requires genuine international partnerships based on the principle of mutual respect and responsibility. This is an ambitious agenda, easy to declare, hard to do. It is one of the challenges that we carry with us into the post MDG world.

References

Del Popolo, F. and A. Oyarce. (2005). "América Latina, Población Indígena: Perfil Sociodemográfico en el marco da la Conferencia Internacional sobre la Poblacion y el Desarollo y de las Metas del Milenio", *Notas de Población* 79. Santiago de Chile: CELADE

Kabeer, N. (2010) "Can the MDGs provide a pathway to social justice? The challenge of intersecting inequalities," MDG Achievement Fund and IDS, Sussex.

Kabeer, N. (Podcast): the importance of putting the issue of social exclusion and inequality firmly at the centre of the fight against poverty and all efforts to achieve the Millennium Development Goals www.ids.ac.uk/go/naila-kabeer-podcast

Omilola, B. (2010). "Patterns and Trends of Child and Maternal Nutrition Inequalities in Nigeria." IFPRI Discussion Paper 00968.

United Nations MDG Achievement Fund: an inter-agency initiative that supports national efforts to eradicate poverty and inequality and achieve the MDGs www.mdgfund.org

Rethinking Poverty
Jomo Kwame Sundaram[11]

Rethinking Poverty Eradication

The 2010 UNDESA *Report on the World Social Situation* seeks to contribute to rethinking poverty and its eradication. It affirms the urgent need for a strategic shift away from the market fundamentalist thinking, policies and practices of recent decades towards more sustainable development- and equity-oriented policies appropriate to national conditions and circumstances. Some of the key messages are as follows:

- **The number of people living on less than \$1.25 a day declined globally from 1.9 billion in 1981 to 1.4 billion in 2005** according to the World Bank. This decline is largely due to rapid growth in China. However, the absolute number of people living in poverty actually went up during this period in many countries in sub-Saharan Africa, Latin America, the Middle East and Northern Africa, as well as Central Asia.

- **The global financial, food, and fuel crises, as well as the ongoing effects of climate change threaten efforts** to greatly reduce extreme poverty, undermining some gains achieved since the 2000 Millennium Summit. The negative economic and social impacts of these crises threaten the lives of people living in poverty and call into question the sustainability of global poverty reduction.

- **The experience of poverty is multidimensional**. A wider definition of poverty, adopted by the 1995 World Summit for Social Development, includes deprivation, social exclusion and lack of participation. Using this broader definition, the situation today may be even more deplorable than a monetary income poverty line would suggest.

---

[11]Jomo Kwame Sundaram is United Nations Assistant Secretary-General for Economic Development in the United Nations Department of Economic and Social Affairs

- **Experience has shown that current conventional policy approaches to poverty eradication are insufficient and require serious rethinking by policy makers**. The challenges to reducing global poverty remain formidable, numerous and complex, and have been exacerbated by the economic crisis. We need to prioritize sustainable development and structural transformation - involving sustained growth, employment and incomes, with inclusive development which benefits people living in poverty.

Figure 1. Global and regional trends in extreme poverty, 1981-2005

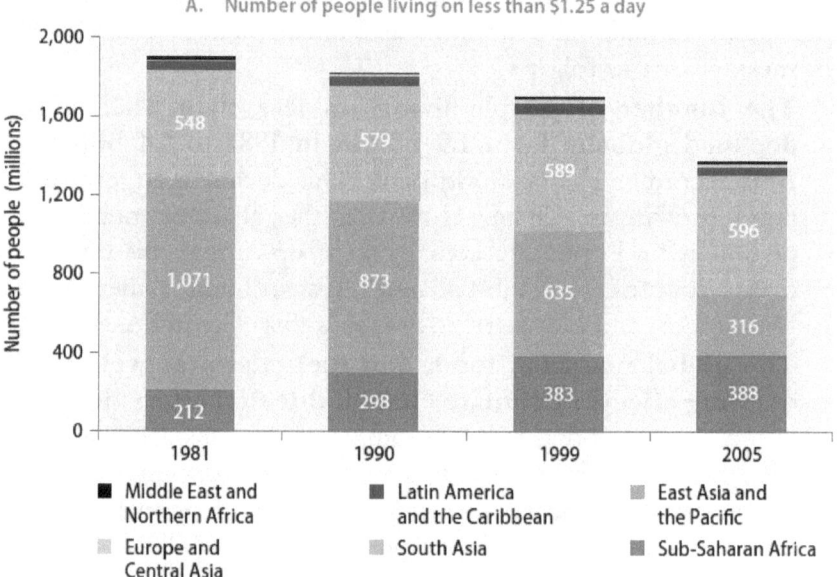

A. Number of people living on less than $1.25 a day

Source: United Nations (2010).

Global poverty trends and distribution patterns over the last 20 years

World leaders agreed in 2000 to halve the number of people living on less than a dollar a day by 2015. There has been some success in reducing global poverty levels. According to the World Bank, the number of people living on less than $1.25 a day in developing countries declined from 1.9 billion to 1.4 billion between 1981 and 2005, at 2005 purchasing power parity. In addition, the proportion of people living in extreme poverty dropped from 52.0 to 25.7 per cent during this period.

Many analysts have noted shortcomings in making these estimates. The main problem concerns the intrinsic worth of the poverty line as a meaningful measure of poverty. Evidence suggests that such poverty lines misrepresent the actual extent of poverty. For instance, global poverty is said to have declined while global hunger is said to have increased while the poverty line is supposed to be principally determined by the money income needed to avoid being hungry. Also, the new World Bank line is not based on the United States rate of inflation; had it been taken into account, the original $1.08 a day would have become $1.45 a day for 2005, with obvious implications for the corresponding estimates of people in poverty, and hence, for the achievement of the Millennium Development Goals poverty target by 2015.

Additionally, the distribution of people living in poverty within and across regions has changed. While 57 per cent of the world's extremely poor lived in East Asia and the Pacific in 1981, the sub-region was home to only 23 per cent of the global poor in 2005. In contrast, the share of the world's extremely poor people increased in South Asia, from 29 per cent in 1981 to 43 per cent in 2005, and more than doubled in sub-Saharan Africa, from 11 per cent to 28 per cent between 1981 and 2005. The changing regional distribution of poverty reflects broad changes in economic performance.

Trends in inequality should also be considered. Not only are there wider income gaps between rich and poor countries, but within-country income inequalities have also increased in the majority of countries during this period: between the early 1980s and 2005, income inequality rose in 59 out of 114 countries for which data are available, and declined in 40 countries.

A need for rethinking policy approaches
Although the current monetary poverty-line approach provides a useful definition of absolute poverty and allows for various types of comparison, it nonetheless has considerable shortcomings that could be overcome by multidimensional poverty measurement. The

economic crisis has served as a reminder that poverty is not an attribute of a fixed group, but rather a condition that all vulnerable persons risk experiencing at some point in life. It is essential for people to be healthy, educated, well housed and fed to be more productive and to contribute, in turn, to society. Approaches to poverty reduction should therefore be developmental and holistic, integrating economic and social policies to achieve people-centred development outcomes.

Figure 2. Ratio of under-five mortality rate for the bottom quintile to that for the top quintile, selected developing countries, late 1980s and mid to late 1990s

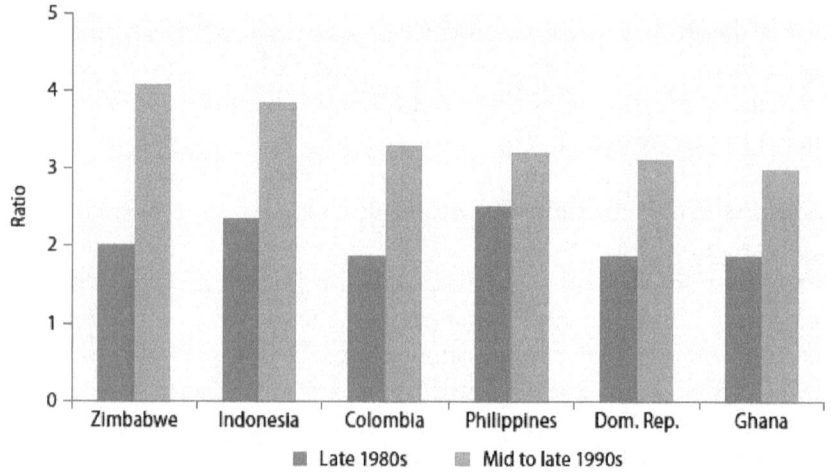

Source: World Health Organization, Regional Office for the Western Pacific (2002).

The report critically examines the conventional policy framework and popular poverty reduction programmes in the context of persisting poverty, rising inequality and, until very recently, lacklustre growth performance in many developing countries. There are many arguments that question current approaches based on pro-cyclical macroeconomic policies accompanied by microeconomic interventions targeted at the poor, and emphasize the need for governments to play a developmental role. This would entail an integrated approach to economic and social policies designed to support inclusive output and employment growth as well as to reduce inequality and promote justice in society. Poverty, and its reduction, always occurs within a macroeconomic context.

Countries that adopted stabilization measures and structural adjustment programmes generally experienced declines in average economic growth and increases in inequality and poverty during the 1980s and 1990s, especially in Africa and Latin America. In general, macroeconomic stabilization measures led to declines in public investment and increased the volatility of economic growth and employment. The mixed record of poverty reduction calls into question the efficacy of conventional approaches involving economic liberalization and privatization. Reductions in public investment in health, education and other social programmes disproportionately affected people living in poverty. They were also adversely affected by increased output volatility, especially since unskilled workers tend to be the first to lose their jobs, and because job recovery lags behind output recovery.

There are grave concerns that targeting is not only expensive, but also excludes many of those who are deserving. Furthermore, many poverty programmes favoured by some donors have not been very effective in actually reducing poverty although some of them have undoubtedly served to ameliorate the crushing burdens of poverty, especially during times of crisis.

Key policies for poverty reduction include:

- **Macroeconomic policies focused on the stability of real output, incomes and employment**: It is necessary to relax unnecessarily stringent fiscal and monetary restrictions and enable countries to use counter-cyclical fiscal and monetary policy to boost employment and incomes, as well as to reduce poverty. This is an urgent need in the current crisis. It is important that macroeconomic stabilization not be limited to controlling inflation, trade and fiscal deficits. Fiscal policy can play an important counter-cyclical role, if resources are accumulated during boom periods and used to fund expansionary policies during downturns. Monetary policies can be supportive by accommodating countercyclical measures and development activities, especially by including measures to promote employment and reduce poverty.

- **Social policy focused on the determinants of asset and income inequality as well as poverty**: Social policy and spending are key to breaking the intergenerational transmission of inequality and poverty. Experiences in many countries have shown that employment and universal social policies are central to poverty reduction. Expansion of social protection programmes (e.g. a social protection floor) is essential to protect society's more vulnerable members against livelihood shocks and risks, enhance the social status and rights of the marginalized and protect workers against ill health, unemployment and destitution, in an integrated package. The current global crises and their impacts on workers in developed and developing countries alike further underscore the importance of providing a social protection floor for the poor as well as the non-poor. While there has been progress in advancing education and health in developing countries over the last decade, serious gaps remain. There are important disparities in access between children in rich and poor households and in urban and rural areas, among others. Public social expenditures, in particular on education and health, are critical for supporting investment in human resource development. Public social expenditures should be safeguarded and even increased – counter-cyclically – in the current crisis.
- **Promotion of participation, inclusion and voice of poor people**: The importance of participation for poverty reduction and social integration policies is based on the fundamental premise that people, including people living in poverty, have the right to influence decisions that affect their lives. It is crucial to remove barriers to participation and to promote the social inclusion and voice of poor people

References

United Nations (2010). *Rethinking Poverty: Report on the World Social Situation 2010*. New York: UNDESA.

Combating Poverty and Inequality: Structural Change, Social Policy and Politics
Sarah Cook[12]

Interconnections among economic development, social policy and politics

UNRISD's recent publication, *Combating Poverty and Inequality*, attempts to explain how poverty reduction depends crucially on the interconnections among economic development, social policy and politics. It emphasizes that poverty and inequality cannot be addressed by narrow approaches to social protection or by economic growth alone. Instead, there is a need for new directions in macroeconomic policy and structural change to generate decent employment. Some of the key messages are as follows:

- **Poverty reduction requires growth and structural change that generate productive employment**: Employment represents a channel through which additional income generated by growth can be widely distributed throughout a population. Where poverty has been reduced successfully and sustainably, governments used policy interventions to facilitate employment-centred structural transformations of their economies.

- **High levels of inequality are an obstacle to poverty reduction**: Poverty and inequality are part of the same problem. High levels of inequality make it difficult to reduce poverty even when economies are growing; and poor countries are generally more unequal than rich ones. Inequality manifests itself in relation to wealth and income status, health and education outcomes, gender and ethnicity, as well as access to employment and social services.

---

[12]Sarah Cook is Director of United Nations Research Institute for Social Development (UNRISD)

- **Comprehensive social policies are essential for successful poverty reduction**: For social policy to be effective as a transformative instrument against poverty and inequality, it must transcend its residual role of safety net and engage with broad public policy issues of distribution, protection, production and reproduction.

- **Politics matters for poverty reduction**: The protection of civil rights, active and organized citizens, and political parties that effectively engage the poor and other disadvantaged groups are all important for sustained progress towards poverty reduction.

- **There are many paths to poverty reduction**: Most countries that have successfully reduced poverty adopted heterodox policies that reflected their national conditions, rather than fully embracing market-conforming prescriptions. Countries and peoples must be allowed the policy space to adopt different models of development where aspects of livelihood and food security, land reform, cultural rights, gender equity, social policy and associative democracy figure prominently.

Figure 1. Global and regional trends in extreme poverty, 1981-2005. Number of people living on less than $1.25 a day

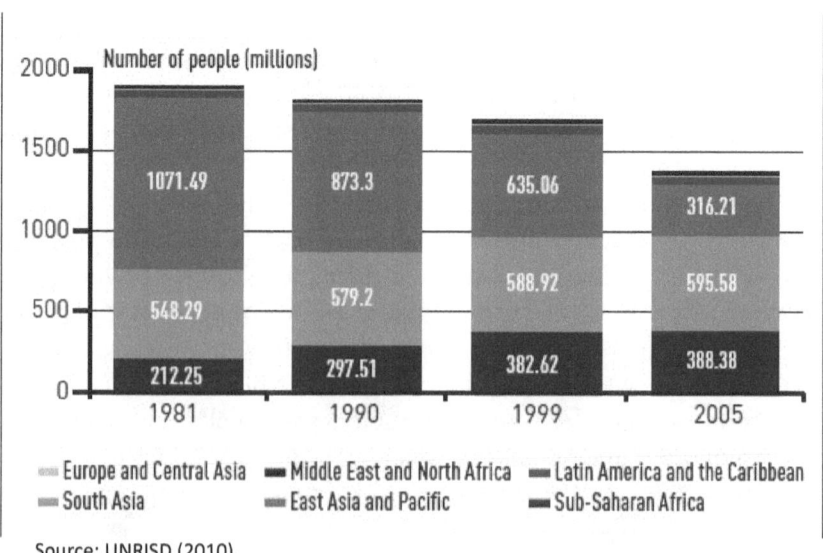

Source: UNRISD (2010).

Persistence of poverty and inequality despite being high in the international development agenda

Poverty reduction is a central feature of the international development agenda. A number of key social development objectives were agreed by world leaders at the Millennium Summit, with the goal of significantly reducing poverty by 2015. Yet, even if the global poverty rate is halved by 2015, as the latest United Nations progress report on the MDGs suggests, about one billion people will still be mired in extreme poverty. Income and wealth inequality have increased in most countries, as have inequalities based on gender, ethnicity and region. This persistent poverty in some regions, and growing inequalities worldwide, are stark reminders that economic globalization and liberalization have not created an environment conducive to sustainable and equitable social development.

Combating Poverty and Inequality argues that many contemporary approaches to poverty reduction treat poverty and inequality as residual outcomes of wider growth processes that can be addressed through discrete and targeted policy interventions. These approaches fail to consider key institutional, policy and political dimensions that may be both causes of poverty and inequality, and obstacles to their reduction. They are weakly related to a country's system of production or macroeconomic policies. This has been the case with three of the dominant approaches to poverty reduction in the past decade, including the IMF– and World Bank–led Poverty Reduction Strategy Papers (PRSPs), the introduction in many countries of targeted poverty reduction and social protection programmes, and the UN–led Millennium Development Goals. Current approaches have increasingly focused on "targeting the poor." However, when a substantial proportion of a country's population is poor, it makes little sense to detach poverty from the dynamics of development.

Figure 2. Global patterns of inequality over time, 1963-2002

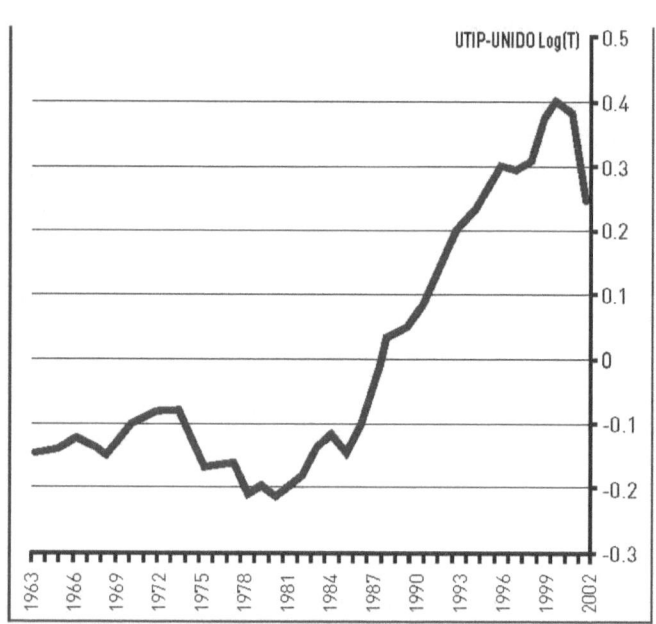

Source: Kum (2008).

In short, poverty remains a major challenge because current dominant approaches go against the evidence that a fall in poverty generally results *not from policies aimed at poverty, but from long-term processes of structural transformation.* Shortcomings of such approaches to poverty reduction are a source of widespread concern.

Successes in reducing poverty and inequality

For countries that have been successful in increasing the well-being of the majority of their populations over relatively short periods of time, progress has occurred principally through *state-directed strategies that combine economic development objectives with active social policies* and forms of politics that are complementary and synergistic and that elevate the interests of the poor in public policy. Poverty outcomes are shaped by complex interconnections of ideas, institutions, policies and practices in the social, economic and political spheres.

The report does not dispute the importance of economic growth, but argues that it is the nature and pattern of growth that has critical implications for poverty and inequality.

Employment represents one critical channel through which the benefits of growth can be widely distributed throughout a population. Where poverty has been reduced successfully and sustainably, *governments used policy interventions to facilitate employment-centred structural transformations* of their economies. The Republic of Korea, for example, invested substantially in infrastructure, channelled credit to specific productive activities and pursued well-managed industrial and agricultural policies as well as social policies that improved the skill levels and welfare of the population.

Another feature of countries that have transformed their economies and reduced poverty relatively quickly is that *social policy has been an integral part of their development strategies.* Evidence demonstrates that a number of welfare policies are feasible and affordable for countries at fairly low levels of income. Successful countries have tended to invest substantially in education and skills development, as well as in health and social protection. In fact, the most significant reductions in poverty have occurred in countries where social policies have been aimed at broader goals, including enhancing productivity, promoting social cohesion or national building. In these circumstances, social policies tend to be comprehensive and move towards universal coverage. The report argues that there are three critical elements to a sustainable and inclusive development strategy:

- Patterns of growth and structural change (whether in the agricultural, industrial or service sectors) that generate and sustain jobs that are adequately remunerated and accessible to all, regardless of income or class status, gender, ethnicity or location;
- Comprehensive social policies that are grounded in universal rights and that are supportive of structural change, social cohesion and democratic politics; and

- Protection of civic rights, activism and political arrangements that ensure states are responsive to the needs of citizens and the poor have influence in how policies are made.

Reducing inequality essential for poverty reduction

Evidence suggests that there is a two-way causal relationship between poverty and inequality, indicating the importance of addressing inequality for poverty reduction. Moreover, the international human rights framework commits governments to uphold equity in civil and political rights and to take steps to progressively achieve this. High levels of inequality serve as an obstacle to poverty reduction because they make it harder to incorporate the poor and socially marginalized groups in the growth process; limit the size of the domestic market and prospects for sustained growth; may cause crime levels to rise and plunge societies into conflict; and encourage the emergence of institutions that lock the poor into poverty traps.

Since reducing inequality has value in its own right, and also yields substantial benefits in poverty reduction and growth, we suggest a number of mutually supportive redistributive policies that countries can adopt:

- Land reform, especially in highly unequal economies where the poor depend substantially on land for their livelihoods;
- Fiscal reforms that improve tax administration, prevent tax evasion and avoidance, and limit opposition to progressive taxation and redistribution;
- Income-generating employment opportunities; and
- Expenditure-related policies that enhance the welfare of lower income and excluded groups.

Strategies for socially inclusive structural change

Substantial and sustained poverty reduction requires growth and structural change that generates productive employment, improves earnings and contributes to the welfare of the population. Many believe that employment is a by-product of economic growth; however this report argues that economic growth or industrialization per se will not lead to sustained improvements in employment. Structural change can have many trajectories: situations of stalled industrialization and dualistic labour markets as in many Latin American and middle-income countries; service-led growth paths or those dominated by agriculture; and those that are determined by mineral wealth. We find that growth paths that are driven by low-productivity activities, where structural change is stuck in the primary sector, have produced highly segmented and unequal labour markets, and the poor are often locked out of dynamic growth sectors.

Policy is crucial for generating structural change that realizes better quality employment and poverty outcomes. Governments can achieve employment-centred, socially inclusive structural change through:

- Avoiding pro-cyclical policies during periods of slow growth;
- Pursuing well managed industrial and agricultural policies such as subsidies, tax credits, extension services and land redistribution;
- Stimulating and maintaining an adequate level of labour demand;
- Public investment in infrastructure and skill levels of the population; and
- Reducing vulnerability to commodity price and interest rate shocks.

Macroeconomic policy, financial institutions, the international structure of production, the nature and composition of households, gender dynamics and social policy all influence employment outcomes and the potential for opportunities to translate into real differences in people's lives.

Social policy impact on poverty and inequality in low-income countries

Social policy can contribute to economic growth as well as social welfare, and is an integral part of the growth strategies of countries that have experienced far-reaching structural change and reduced poverty rapidly. The report argues that although structural constraints matter, there are no prerequisites for social and economic policies that seek to eradicate poverty. Nor are there stages of development through which countries must inevitably pass when introducing social policy. Typically, a fall in poverty has had less to do with policies aimed at poverty per se than those aimed at much wider social objectives. Indeed, in a number of countries that have successfully dealt with poverty, such as in the Nordic and East Asian countries, its alleviation was just one of the several goals prompting the introduction of social policies.

Additionally, the most significant reductions in poverty have occurred in countries with *comprehensive social policies that lean towards universal coverage.* When poverty is widespread, targeting the underserved is unnecessary, administratively costly, and fraught with problems such as asymmetries of information, distortion of incentives, and moral hazard. There are other numerous reasons to invest in public, universal social protection policies in developing countries, since they:

- Protect people from income loss throughout the lifecycle, in times of economic transition or crisis;
- Enhance the productive capacities of individuals, groups and communities;
- Reinforce the progressive redistributive effects of economic policies; and
- Facilitate the reproduction of labour and society and reduce the unpaid care burden which is often on women.

Child well-being is affected by the unpaid care work that goes into sustaining families, households and societies on a daily basis. It is estimated that if such work, performed mostly by women, were assigned a monetary value, it would constitute 10 to 19 per cent of a country's GDP. The need to address care through public policy is now more urgent than ever. In times of crisis, care responsibilities are shifted back onto families, with women and girls often acting as the ultimate safety net. Many developing countries are experimenting with new ways of responding to care needs in their societies.

One of the emerging examples is child-centred cash transfer schemes. While these transfers are not meant to pay for care, many of them are explicitly targeted on primary caregivers and facilitate the care work they do by allowing them to purchase essential inputs or to buy-in care substitutes (by drawing on family members or informal carers). Despite their limitations, positive effects on child development are evident from these schemes, including improvements in primary and secondary school enrolment and attendance rates, food consumption and height, as well as school drop-out rates and child labour. Investing in good quality and accessible early childhood education and care services constitutes another useful strategy to ensure that all children, regardless of social class and background, receive adequate care, and to assist those who usually care for them to engage in income-earning work (or education, etc.). This would also represent a useful strategy for generating new forms of employment.

Universal social policies are feasible and affordable for countries at fairly low levels of income. ILO estimates suggest that a basic social protection package (pensions for the elderly and disabled, child benefits and essential health care) for low-income countries such as Bangladesh, Kenya or Pakistan, would cost about ten percent of GDP. That is less than the average amount spent on social protection in Eastern Europe, Central Asia and some Latin American countries, and is far below the OECD average of about 17% of GDP. Moreover, there are a number of instruments that can finance social policy in developing countries: from domestic taxation and social insurance schemes to external aid, rents from mineral resources, and remittances, to name a few.

Taking politics and power relations into account in order to reduce poverty and inequality

Power relations are at the centre of development. The interests of the political arena and how these translate to policy determine all successful attempts at significant poverty reduction. Poverty reduction requires effective and accountable states, institutionalization of rights, sustained public engagement, expansion of the bargaining power of the poor and those who represent them, and pacts that are structured around issues of employment, welfare and growth.

Democracies are able to deliver outcomes that are beneficial to the poor under the following circumstances:

- When rights are institutionalized, allowing the poor to exercise political choice, build alliances with others and hold leaders to account;
- When social groups with strong ties to the poor demonstrate capacity for organization and mobilization;
- When social groups create links with actors involved in policy making (leading, at times, to social pacts); and
- When they are able to transcend or reconcile horizontal divisions.

Moreover, poverty is reduced when economic and social policies, institutions and political arrangements are mutually supportive. The pursuit of a set of policies in one domain, while neglecting the others may undermine the full realization of the benefits from the chosen policy.

References

UNRISD (2010). *Combating Poverty and Inequality: Structural Change, Social Policy and Politics.*
The Millennium Development Goals Report 2010.

UNICEF, Economists and Economic Policy:
Bringing children into development strategies
Richard Jolly[13]

From as early as 1947, UNICEF recognized the importance of economic policy for children and has sought the help of development economists in mapping out what this might involve. Indeed, at least two Nobel Prize winners in economics have contributed ideas and advice to UNICEF – and with the recent participation of Joe Stiglitz the number is raised to three.[14]

This may come as a surprise to many members of the economic profession, who are often unaware of children's issues and, when aware, tend to think of the issues as primarily those of calculating the rates of return on education or finding the resources needed to pay for health, education and other social services.

Long history of policy engagement

The early years
The first encounter came in 1947. Maurice Pate, UNICEF's first executive director, approached David Owen, head of the UN's Economic Affairs Department, with the request that one of the economists in his department might undertake a study on children and economic development. UNICEF was about to be transformed from a UN emergency agency for children to one dealing with children's long-run needs. David Owen passed the request to Hans Singer in the development section of his department. Hans was busy at the time working on his study of the long-run terms of trade and put the request to the side. Hans has even had the frankness in

---

[13]Sir Richard Jolly is Research Associate at the Institute of Development Studies (IDS) and former Assistant Secretary General UNICEF
[14]The three are Jan Tinbergen, Amartya Sen and Joseph Stiglitz

an interview to confess that when first given this request he didn't see any connection between children and development.

But shortly afterwards, Hans went to Harvard to visit his old professor Schumpeter. While there, he heard a lecture given by Nevin Scrimshaw, at the time a young nutritionist at MIT. The lecture was reporting research on malnutrition among pregnant women and young children and the long-run effects on the physical and mental development of the children. Hans Singer described his reaction. The findings of this study hit him like "a bolt of lightning." Nutrition for children was amongst the most basic of human investments, with life-long effects on human productivity. Even more important, if the opportunity for these early investments in nutrition were missed, there would be no second chance. There would be lifelong damage. Investment in children is central to development.

As soon as Singer got back to New York, he went to see Maurice Pate to express his willingness to take on the project. Maurice Pate was pleased – but insisted on checking carefully that Hans saw the importance of children before agreeing that he should do the work.

Hans is best known in development for his work on what is known as the Prebisch-Singer thesis on the long-run terms of trade. In fact, Hans put aside his work on trade for several months, in order to prepare to produce his pioneering study for UNICEF on "The Role of Children in Economic Development" (Singer, 1947). Low productivity in human investment in developing countries was due in part to malnutrition in early childhood. As Singer later put it, "An invitation to the banquet of life is not very appealing when the menu consists of a forty per cent chance of surviving birth and childhood, followed by forty or forty five percent rachitic and mentally retarded years of near starvation."[15]

---

[15]This account draws on my own interview and discussions with Hans as well as on the excellent account in Shaw, D. J. (2002). *Sir Hans Singer: The Life and Work of a Development Economist.* London: Palgrave-Macmillan, pp. 144-147. Interestingly, there is no mention of this study in the otherwise excellent history of UNICEF - Black, M. (1986). *Children and the Nations.* UNICEF New York, printed in Adelaide.

UNICEF's next major encounter with economists came a decade or so later. By the late 1950s, UNICEF became convinced that children would never receive the priorities they deserved unless their needs were fully integrated into national economic planning. "[E]xperience in the poorer countries had shown that it was not only very difficult to compartmentalize children's needs, but positively counter-productive."[16]

From humanitarian welfare agency to development agency for children

In 1964, UNICEF invited a core of distinguished economists and planners to a round-table meeting in Bellagio, the Rockefeller Conference Centre by Lake Como in Italy. Jan Tinbergen, later to be the first winner of the Nobel Prize in economics, was present along with Alfred Sauvy, and Hans Singer. Professor V.K.R.V. Rao, chairman of the Indian Planning Commission and initiator of earlier UN work on Special United Nations Fund for Economic Development (SUNFED) chaired the conference. Ministers of economic planning from Tunisia and Tanzania, then Tanganyika, also participated along with observers from two of the UN economic commissions and from FAO, WHO, ILO and the Bureau of Social Affairs. Perhaps I might add that at the time I was in Addis Ababa, as a graduate student, collecting data for my thesis on African education. Hans told me of the conference and I sent along a brief paper.

The starting point for the Bellagio conference was questions set out in the background paper prepared by UNICEF:

- How can the needs of children and youth be integrated into the general objectives of development?
- Given that the long-run objectives of development will within fifteen years depend greatly on the present younger generation for their achievement, how can this generation be prepared for the tasks ahead?

---

[16]Black, M. (1986). *Children and the Nations*. UNICEF New York, printed in Adelaide, p. 201. Maggie Black provides an excellent account of the Bellagio conference and its long-run importance for UNICEF.

Both questions were recognized to be related to economic policies, going far beyond the traditional humanitarian approach to children and far beyond approaches focused mostly on under-privileged or handicapped children.

The Bellagio round-table was later described as the most important meeting in its seventeen-year history. It marked the change of UNICEF from being a humanitarian welfare agency for children to becoming a fully-fledged development agency - concerned with children in all aspects of life. It laid the foundations for UNICEF's subsequent "country programme approach," introduced in 1972. The country programme involved three steps: first, an analysis of the needs of children in the country, building on the comprehensive Bellagio perspectives; second, an assessment of what the country and other groups within the country needed to do in response to these needs; third, and only as a later and separate third stage, an analysis of what UNICEF could do to help get country action underway. In other words, UNICEF recognized that the main actions for children needed to be part of the country's whole effort for development to which its own resources and support could be catalytic but not more. Gradually over the years, the country programme approach was improved – and, much later, spread to other parts of the UN.

Commitment to policy change in the face of crisis

The 1980s were years of debt, recession and structural adjustment, with the most serious and severe repercussions on people – and children –especially in Africa and Latin America. The focus of economic concern within UNICEF had to shift from long-term to short-term, from development to protection. By that time, Jim Grant was Executive Director of UNICEF and I was his deputy responsible for programmes. We also had the great help of Andrea Cornia. In 1982 and 1983, Andrea and I organized a series of country assessments of how children were being affected by the triple economic onslaught – and we pulled the results together in a publication, *The Impact of World Recession on Children*. Hans Singer and K.N. Raj joined with us in the analysis. Hans insightfully analyzed how the impact on children arising from downturns of recession in the North were multiplied several fold in the repercussions affecting children in the South.

By this stage, structural adjustment was in full swing. At the periodic meetings of the then UN's Administrative Committee on Coordination (now UN's Chief Executives Board for Coordination, UN CEB), chaired by the Secretary General with the participation of all the UN agencies, usually including the heads of the World Bank and of the IMF, Jim Grant became the leading voice arguing the need for some change in policy – especially to respond to the immediate and urgent needs of children. Within a few months, we had worked out an agenda of specific actions – *Adjustment with a Human Face*. Again, this combined careful analysis with country case studies – with Ghana and Sri Lanka among the first of the case studies. Interestingly, it was M. deLarosiere, the then Managing Director of the IMF who initially showed more interest than the Bank – and brought some of our findings into one of his ECOSOC speeches. By 1988, UNICEF had published its two-volume study, *Adjustment with a Human Face*, with strong inputs from Frances Stewart as well as Andrea Cornia.

From *adjustment* with a human face to *development* with a human face

Soon, UNICEF started moving from *adjustment* with a human face to *development* with a human face. By this, we meant that the real problem was not so much to provide short term protection to offset the setbacks of structural adjustment but to get back to a positive path of development, with concerns for children fully incorporated into advancing human development, even if economic growth was still constrained by the international context and pressures. For UNICEF country programmes, this meant a strong focus on child survival and development – through priority actions in health, education and the provision of safe water and basic sanitation.

In the 1980s, there was a sharp focus on reaching 80% coverage of immunization and associated actions by 1990. In spite of the lost decade for economic development, the immunization goal was largely achieved on average in developing countries and specifically in some 70 individual countries. The IMF and perhaps the Bank too was impressed that UNICEF not only talked the talk of a different approach to adjustment but walked the talk, by showing that it was possible to achieve big expansions in immunization and other priority child-focused actions, even during a decade of severe economic setbacks. By 1990, child deaths worldwide had been reduced from 15 to 12 million, even at a time when the number of child births had risen considerably.

In 1990, UNICEF organized the World Summit for Children, which re-iterated a call for a new approach to adjustment and agreed a larger core of goals. By the year 2000, the goal-oriented approach had developed much further, into the Millennium Development Goals (MDGs) for 2015.

A broader development strategy

These developments in the 1980s and 1990s added three further links to broaden the development strategy, still important today. First, UNICEF developed the concept of *First Call for Children*, which stated that in bad times as in good, countries should ensure that children's priority needs have a first call on resources – a principle accepted by most families for their own children but still only rarely recognized in national economic policy.

Secondly, the concept of 20/20 was developed – created jointly with Mahbub ul Haq at the time of the World Summit for Children and then incorporated in the 1992 Human Development Report. Given the desperate squeeze on resources faced by most countries, the 20/20 principle recognized that additional resources needed for children would need to be found from restructuring existing spending rather than from new resources. We calculated that the additional resources needed to ensure basic services for all – primary health care, primary education, reproductive health and family planning and the provision of safe water and sanitation – could be found if each country allocated 20% of its national public expenditure to these basics and each donor country, in parallel, allocated 20% of its aid budget to the same priorities. Two or three conferences were held in the 1990s to generate support for the 20/20 commitments, and some 30 developing countries demonstrated their practical willingness. But the partnerships with donors and the donor commitments required for the package never came operationally together.

The third link was directly with economic growth. Analysis in the Human Development Report of 1996 showed that it was possible to sustain and even to advance human development in situations of stagnant or declining economic growth. But unless economic growth could be resumed within a decade or so, the advance in human development would begin to slow or even fall back. This is an important point to emphasize, especially in sub-Saharan Africa and some other least developed countries, where conventional remedies for restoring growth have failed for two and sometimes three decades.

Renewed commitment to economic policy work in the context of children's rights

In recent years, an Economic Policy Unit has been created in UNICEF, led by committed staff such as Jan Vandemoortele, Saad Houry and Richard Morgan. A strategic meeting was first held in Pratolino (Italy) in 2004, where the main areas of UNICEF economic policy work were identified to become part of UNICEF's Medium Term Strategic Framework, namely, multidimensional child poverty and inequalities, public budgets for children, social protection, among others, overall ensuring that national development strategies respond to children. These areas were approved by UNICEF Board, which fully supports UNICEF to strengthen the capacities of States and societies to design and implement social and economic policies, legislative measures and budgetary allocations that enable them to meet their obligations under the Convention on the Rights of the Child (CRC) and the Convention on the Elimination of All Forms of Discrimination against Women (CEDAW).

The pool of economists expanded in UNICEF. Apart from the policy team in headquarters, economists were recruited in country offices and regional centers. Building on its field experience and in alliance with other United Nations agencies, UNICEF has been collaborating with partners to stimulate dialogue around macroeconomic and sector policies that guide national frameworks, and advocating for actions, budgets and investments that contribute to fulfilling the best interest of the child. As of 2011, 111 UNICEF country offices are involved in social budgeting and child-friendly public finance; 55 UNICEF country offices are undertaking analysis of multidimensional child poverty and inequalities/disparities and advocating policies to reduce them; 88 UNICEF country offices are engaged in building social protection systems; and 44 UNICEF country offices are tackling issues of economic policy reform and children.

More recently, concerned with the implications of worsening inequity in many countries, UNICEF is intensifying its efforts to address bottlenecks to the realization of children's rights. A key area to ensure equitable outcomes for children is the lack of an enabling policy environment. Indeed, history shows that economic policy frameworks focusing on growth but not on redistribution have resulted in widening inequity, which in turn is bad for long-term growth, and that austere structural adjustments risk disrupting essential social services, which could have largely irreversible adverse impact on children's survival and development, as we demonstrated in 1987 with *Adjustment with a Human Face.*

This focus on equity cannot be more pertinent today, as an increasing number of developing countries are undertaking austerity adjustments with potentially adverse implications for equity and children. UNICEF's latest report, "Austerity Measures Threaten Children and Poor Households," finds that the scope of austerity is severe and widening quickly, with 70 countries reducing spending by nearly three percentage points of GDP during 2010, and 91 planning cuts in 2012. Moreover, nearly a quarter of developing countries are undergoing excessive fiscal contraction, defined as slashing public spending to below pre-crisis levels.

If history is any guide, planned austerity measures will risk removing essential support to the most vulnerable when their need for public assistance is urgent and great, thus further exacerbating existing inequalities. It is thus critical for UNICEF and its partners to engage in international advocacy to highlight these risks and show the possibilities for policies that are inclusive and equitable. Again, history may provide some guidance on how UNICEF can effectively engage in advocacy for equity.

Conclusion

In UNICEF's involvements with economists over the years, there are many lessons for today:

1. The many links between children and development are well deserving of more attention from economists, with concern for issues that go far beyond investment in human capital or social welfare.
2. Human development provides a better frame for this analysis than orthodox development economics or neo-classical theory. Strengthening human capabilities in the early stages of life as a step towards broadening choices and ensuring human rights are essential points for the analysis.
3. Though the MDGs are important priorities, concern for children even today must be set in a broader frame to reduce inequality and ensure fulfilment of children's rights. UNICEF's country programme approach provides a mechanism for exploring country-by-country what this should involve.

Hopes for children – one's own and children of one's community, country and the world - are a reminder that development needs to be seen as a broad process of human advance and discovery. Thinking about children means thinking about the future. Economists can help with this, but they need to be sensitive to a wide range of children's issues if they are to do so.

References

Black, M. (1986). *Children and the Nations.* UNICEF New York, printed in Adelaide.

Black, M. (1996). *Children First – The Story of UNICEF, Past and Present.* Oxford: Oxford University Press.

Cornia, G. A., Jolly, R. and F. Stewart (eds). (1987). *Adjustment with a Human Face, Protectingthe Vulnerable and Promoting Growth.* Volume I. Oxford: Oxford University Press.

Cornia, G. A., Jolly, R. and F. Stewart (eds). (1988). *Adjustment with a Human Face, Ten Country Case Studies.* Volume II. Oxford: Oxford University Press.

Jolly, R. and G. A. Cornia (eds.) (1984). "The Impact of World Recession on Children. Special Issue." World Development, 12, 169-391.

Ortiz, I., Chai, J. and M. Cummins (2011). "Austerity Measures Threaten Children and Poor Households." Social and Economic Policy Working Paper, UNICEF Policy and Practice. New York: UNICEF.

Shaw, D. J. (2002). *Sir Hans Singer: The Life and Work of a Development Economist.* London: Palgrave-Macmillan.

Stein, H. (1965). *Planning for the needs of children in developing countries.* New York: UNICEF.

UNDP (1994). *Human Development Report.* Oxford: Oxford University Press.

Child Poverty, Policy and Evidence: Mainstreaming Children in International Development
Nicola Jones and Andy Sumner[17]

Mainstreaming child poverty in development research and policy

This book is about child poverty, evidence, and policy. It is about how children's visibility, voice, and vision in ideas, networks, and political institutions can be mainstreamed in development research and policy. Children account for, on average, 37% of the population in developing countries and 49% in the least-developed countries. Not only are a large proportion of these children poor, but the impacts of poverty suffered during childhood are often enduring and irreversible. We use the lens of **3D wellbeing** to convey a holistic understanding of child poverty and wellbeing, whereby research and policy are approached from multiple angles, with multiple understandings of power and policy change.

There is, of course, already a wealth of literature on child poverty. An important development has been a child-centred approach based on children as active agents in terms of **voice** (in decision making in communities and societies), **vision** (of deprivation and wellbeing), and **visibility** (in terms of the local meaning ascribed to or social construction of childhood). We build on this literature and attempt to move the debate forward by exploring several pressing and interconnecting themes, including: how understandings and the realities of child poverty, well-being, and knowledge generation

---

[17]Nicola Jones is Research Fellow at the Overseas Development Institute (ODI), and coordinates the institute's gender theme

Andy Sumner is Research Fellow at the Institute of Development Studies (IDS), and Visiting Fellow at the Centre for Global Development (CGD)

processes vary across different country contexts; linkages between knowledge generation, policy, and power; and the use of evidence in catalysing change to support children's visibility, voice, and vision.

Another way of conceptualising child poverty and well-being

Child poverty and well-being are distinct from adult experiences of poverty and wellbeing. The long-term impacts of poverty experienced during childhood are well documented. It is therefore critical that policy design, implementation and evaluation processes are informed accordingly. Yet, important dimensions of children's experiences of poverty are often missed by many mainstream approaches to international development.

Child Poverty, Evidence and Policy

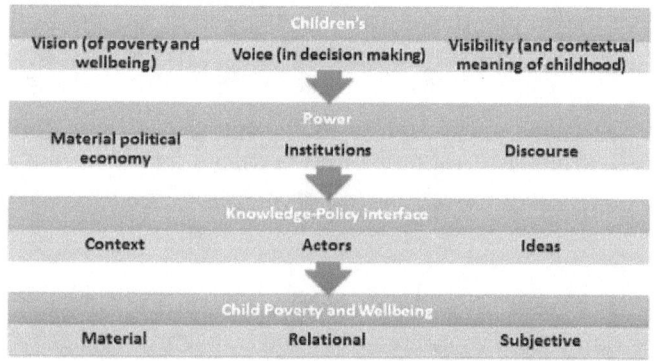

Rights-based approaches—based on the notion that poverty is a violation of human rights—have become dominant in international policy discourses and have emerged as the primary instrument for thinking about childhood poverty at UNICEF and amongst international NGOs. Similarly, the Human Development approach has also influenced much of the international debate. Yet, there is still a need for an approach that can more comprehensively account for the different experiences of children. A 3D child well-being approach examines what a child has, what a child can do with what he/she has, and how a child thinks about what he/she has and can do. This emerging 3D well-being approach can contribute to understanding child poverty in three ways. First, it puts children and their agency (what they *can* do and be) at the centre of analysis. It is thus a means in itself of achieving a child-centred analysis by bringing together understandings based on children as active agents. Second, it encourages a positive perspective on children in development by avoiding labelling certain children as 'poor' and thus applying the stigma that accompanies labels of inferiority. Third, it explicitly integrates relational and subjective perspectives into the material dimension of wellbeing and recognises that the material, relational, and subjective dimensions of children's lives are co-evolving, interdependent, and dynamically interactive.

Knowledge about the nature, extent and trends in child poverty and well-being in developing country contexts

There are now numerous sets of child indicators, such as the Bristol child deprivation indicators (used for UNICEF's Global Study on Child Poverty and Disparities), the Child Friendliness of Policy Indices, the Child and Youth Network Indicators, the Child Well-being Index, OECD's Social Institutions and Gender Index, among others (see Resources below). Indeed, 'child indicators' is a major area of research, with its own association, the International Society for Child Indicators.

Yet, it is important to understand the debates about the process of generating evidence or knowledge that underpins key policy and practice decisions, and how these play out with regard to childhood poverty and well-being in developing country contexts. Evidence is not a neutral concept, but is embedded within a set of power relations between knowledge producers and knowledge users, particularly in the case of evidence about childhood well-being, as children's perspectives are too often hidden or silenced in mainstream development debates.

While there has been growing recognition of the importance of including children's voices in knowledge generation initiatives, we argue that methodological improvements are needed to adequately reflect linkages between child well-being and intra-household dynamics, community-child relations and macro-micro policy linkages. If knowledge is to play a constructive role in policy processes about child well-being then it is important to adopt an iterative 'knowledge interaction' approach to policy change whereby there is an explicit recognition of the power dynamics which shape which types of knowledge are privileged or overlooked by different policy actors. Such awareness is especially important in the case of efforts to shape policies related to child well-being given the particular voicelessness of children in many contexts and their exclusion from conventional policy spaces.

3D Wellbeing evidence catalyzing change to support children's visibility, voice and vision

Given the complexities of power relations in the production of knowledge and its use within the policy process, our developing country case studies suggest that there is no single recipe for child-sensitive evidence-informed policy influencing processes, but that there are certain *key 'ingredients'* upon which we can agree. We identify three clusters of factors that support policy change: policy

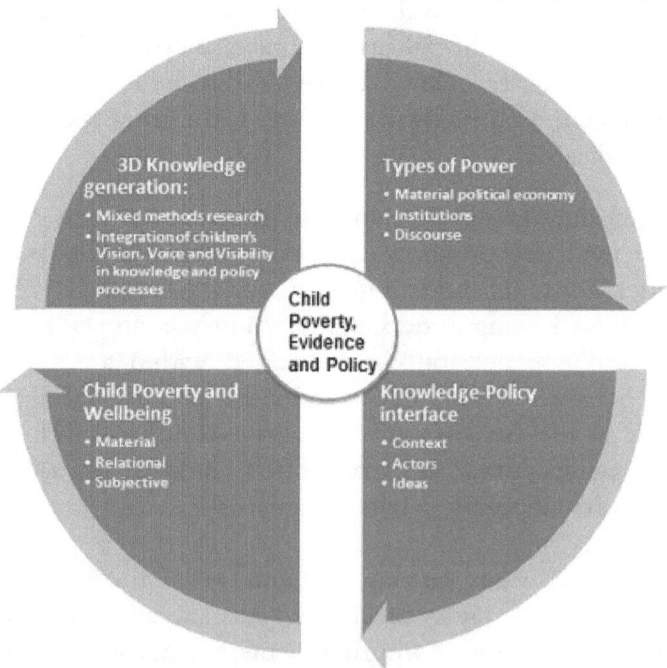

ideas and narratives (including the way in which knowledge is 'repackaged' for different policy, practitioner or lay audiences); policy actors and networks (including the forging of relationships with policy makers or research-policy 'intermediaries'); and policy contexts (including being able to identify specific 'windows of opportunity' for change).

Policy ideas and narratives: The role of knowledge in policy circles and the power that shapes the acceptability of some forms of knowledge but silences others is increasingly acknowledged. Accordingly, *the ways in which new and existing knowledge is synthesised and presented* to diverse policy, practitioner and lay audiences requires particular attention if investments in child-focused research are to have maximum value. We suggest that given limited awareness of children's rights issues by civil society and government actors alike, borrowing from framing techniques in other areas of development ('frame extension') may be effective in promoting quick buy-in in that the language and its policy implications are already relatively familiar (for instance, drawing on 'mainstreaming' or 'pro-poor budget monitoring' discourses). However, there is also the risk that such an approach may be perceived as 'yet another special interest lobby' so a *careful assessment of existing relations between civil society and the state* in a specific context would need to guide such choices.

Investing in *innovative strategies to dismantle dominant paradigms,* which assume that children will automatically benefit from broader and household-level poverty reduction interventions is also critical. Without an appreciation of the specific and multidimensional nature of childhood poverty, vulnerability and resilience, the fulfilment of children's rights will remain only partial. As such, there is a pressing need to better understand the power dynamics operating to privilege particular narratives about human well-being and the ways in which they serve to subtly obscure new knowledge.

In the same vein, it is also important to promote the triangulation of knowledge about children from a wide variety of sources, ranging from children's testimonies and participatory photo projects to survey data and budget monitoring efforts, from guidelines for journalists and key informant discussions to content analysis of African Union policy statements and international rights conventions.

Policy actors and networks: The relative marginalisation of child well-being issues on the development policy stage necessitates *forging alliances* among a broad array of governmental and non-governmental actors to ensure that new ideas have a chance of gaining adequate policy purchase. For instance, given the importance of macro-micro policy linkages in shaping children's experiences of poverty and vulnerability, establishing relationships with actors in government agencies charged with mainstream poverty reduction and economic development issues can be critical to promote child-sensitive policy change.

Different audiences are likely to subscribe explicitly or implicitly to different knowledge hierarchies. We argue that evidence that is expert-led (i.e. based on the work of technically trained persons) and evidence which is derived from citizens' experiences can both be child-sensitive under certain conditions. The choice of advocacy or knowledge interaction approach in part depends on the policy/sector/issue and available entry points for policy influence – some sectors require a high level of technical expertise (e.g. macro-economic and trade policies, budget processes) and are less amenable to participatory forms of knowledge. However, while it is valuable to frame research findings with this in mind, it is equally important to work with actors to begin to *break down conventional knowledge hierarchies* given the complexity and diversity of childhood poverty and vulnerability.

Children's participation in poverty policy processes is still in a fledgling state and the evidence to date suggests that its contribution to tangible policy changes has been limited. However, perhaps just as importantly, our analysis has highlighted ways in which children's participation can contribute to other change objectives. This includes introducing new ideas on to the policy agenda, bringing about procedural shifts (so that children become more routinely involved in citizen consultation processes for example), and gradually transforming the attitudes of those in power towards the potential contribution that children and young people can make to policy debates.

Policy contexts: In light of our growing knowledge base about the impact pathways between macro-level political and economic development shifts, meso-level policy and community responses, and micro-level impacts on children and their care-givers, there is a need for proponents of child-sensitive policy change to embed their policy engagement efforts within a strong understanding of broader policy process dynamics. This could include, for example, trade liberalisation processes, shifting aid modalities, the fallout of economic crises, budget processes or post-conflict reconciliation processes.

Our analysis also highlights that it is critical to invest more in understanding multiple policy levels – international, regional, national and sub-national levels. Indeed the latter appears to be especially important as our case study on Andhra Pradesh shows: not only because of the challenges involved in overcoming extant data constraints, but also because as decentralisation processes gather apace, this is increasingly where the implementation of social policies—which help to mediate the effects of macro-development policy changes on children and their families—take place. In the case of transitional or post-conflict political contexts where trust in political institutions has been eroded or is fragile as is the case with our Peruvian case study, employing a multi-media rather than a conventional research communication approach may be important in order to reach policymakers and citizens alike. In the same vein, as our analysis of efforts to mainstream children into Ethiopia's PRSP underscores, policy engagement strategies need to have in-built flexibility given that windows of opportunity within a specific context can open and close rapidly with little prior warning. Issues that are seemingly distant from children's lives such as national elections may have a profound impact on the contours of the policy process landscape.

Lastly, evidence-informed policy engagement initiatives need to be cognisant of the existing breadth and depth of communities of practice working on child-related issues, and to have an appreciation of the strengths and limitations of the existing evidence base on child well-being in a given region or country. Our analysis emphasises that child-focused communities of practice and knowledge producers are considerably more plentiful in Latin America, than in Africa or Asia, and that capacity-strengthening efforts could be usefully tailored accordingly.

References

African Child Policy Forum's Child Friendliness of Policy Indices: http://www.africanchildinfo.net/africanreport08/

Carden, S. (2009). *Knowledge to Policy: Making the Most of Development Research.* Sage/IDRC.

Foundation for Child Well-being's Child Well-being Index: http://www.soc.duke.edu/~cwi/

IDS Vulnerability and Poverty Reduction Team page: http://www.ids.ac.uk/go/research-teams/vulnerability-and-poverty-reduction-team

International Society for Child Indicators: http://www.childindicators.org/

Jones, N. and A. Sumner (2011). *Child poverty, evidence and policy: Mainstreaming children in international development.* Bristol: Policy Press.

Nutley, S., Walter, I. and Davies, H. (2007). *Using Evidence: How Research Can Inform Public Services.* Bristol: Policy Press.

ODI theme page on Childhood and youth: http://www.odi.org.uk/work/themes/details.asp?id=31&title=childhood-youth

OECD's Social Institutions and Gender Index: http://genderindex.org/

Save the Children's Child Development Index: http://www.savethechildren.org.uk/en/54_7201.htm

UNICEF's Global Study on Child Policy and Disparities: http://unicefglobalstudy.blogspot.com/

Just Give Money to the Poor – and Children Will Benefit

Armando Barrientos[18]

Direct transfer to households in poverty: essential component of poverty reduction

The main message from the book *Just Give Money to the Poor: The Development Revolution from the Global South* (Barrientos, Hanlon and Hulme, 2010) is that direct transfers to households in poverty are an essential component of poverty reduction and development strategies in the South. Growth generates economic opportunity and basic services support human development. Direct transfers to household in extreme poverty enable them to access services and link up to growth.

The book provides an accessible account and assessment of the rapid growth of social protection programmes in developing countries in the last decade. This is described as a 'quiet' revolution in development thinking. Large-scale programmes like *Bolsa Família* in Brazil, the Child Support Grant in South Africa, or the National Guarantee Scheme in India reflect Southern responses to poverty and deprivation. The book argues that the emergence of innovative antipoverty programmes in many developing countries demonstrates that knowledge on how to eradicate poverty is already freely available if only we care to learn from the South.

The impacts of social protection and cash transfers on children

Children are the majority of the world's poor, and any serious attempt to reduce poverty must consider the impact of policy on children. Moreover, permanent and sustainable exit from poverty requires that policymakers focus on children's development. Malnutrition, deficient health care and immunization, limited

---

[18]Armando Barrientos is Research Director of the Brooks World Poverty Institute, University of Manchester

schooling, and early entry into the labour market raise the likelihood of poverty, and contribute to ensuring poverty persist across generations. Innovative social protection programmes emerging in the South have incorporated these insights in setting programme objectives and design.

Figure 1. Simulated poverty impact of a child benefit for selected countries in Africa. Transfer is set at 30% of the poverty line

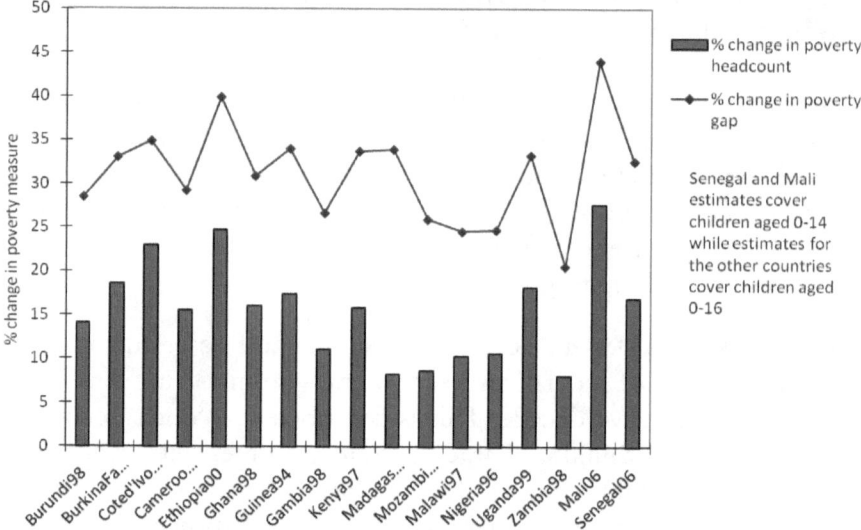

Source: Kakwani, N., Veras Soares, F., and Son, H. H. (2005).

Human development transfer programmes in Latin America (also known as conditional cash transfer programmes in the international policy discourse), Mexico's *Oportunidades* or Brazil's *Bolsa Família*, combine cash and in-kind transfers with schooling and health care utilization strongly focused on children, with the aim of breaking the intergenerational persistence of poverty. Impact evaluation of Mexico's *Oportunidades* has identified significant improvements in child nutrition, health status and schooling. Human development focused programmes are increasingly influential in Africa and Asia.

Income transfers to households in poverty will impact children's development even where programmes are not directly focused on children. Studies on the impact of social pensions, for example, also show impacts on child development.

Figure 2. Difference in height for age between *Oportunidades* treatment (joined 1998) and control (joined 2000) groups in 2003 for 2-6 year olds

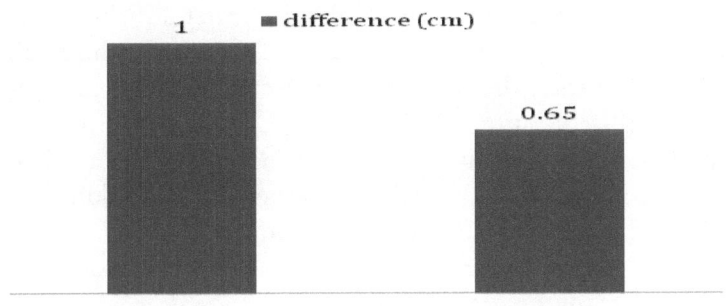

Source: Gertler, P. and Fernand, L.C. (2005).

Impacts of social protection on female infants, schoolchildren and adolescents

The gender impacts of social protection programmes vary depending on objectives and design. Programmes focused on children's development usually route the transfers through the mother, with the expectation that they will ensure the additional resources are used effectively. In some human development focused programs, improving girls' development is reflected in differential transfer amounts. Because women live, on average, longer than men, a majority of direct beneficiaries from social pensions are women. This has some implications for girls' outcomes. In South Africa, for example, girls show improved schooling and nutrition in households with female pensioners. The challenge is to further strengthen the gender dimension of programme objectives and design.

Social transfer programmes and effects on child labour

Few social protection programmes aim to reduce child labour explicitly, although programmes focused on raising school enrolment and attendance do so implicitly. The issue is that children's time can be spent at school, at work, and in other activities (play for example). In practice, it is hard to measure changes in time use of children accurately. Social protection programmes have demonstrated effectiveness in raising children's schooling, and overall show some reduction in child labour outside the home. But it is hard to observe changes in child labour, especially girls', inside the home. As a result, we must be cautious in answering this question. Perhaps the policy focus should be on ensuring that children complete the schooling cycle, as this will improve their prospects in the labour market, while working hard to eradicate child labour in hazardous occupations.

Children and transfer programmes

Studies on a variety of transfer programmes give some confidence in saying that all transfers focused on households in poverty will benefit children. At the same time, they show that transfer programmes which are specifically focused on children tend to have stronger impacts on their welfare. Studies on Mexico's *Oportunidades* show significant improvements in school enrolment outcomes for girls and boys, and particularly for girls of secondary school age.

It is also important to pay attention to the scope of child-focused transfer programmes. South Africa's Child Support Grant provides transfers to children in poor households, but relies on other programmes and policies to ensure children access health care, nutrition, etc. Mexico's *Oportunidades* packages these interventions within an integrated programme. Chile's *Chile Solidario* goes one step further in integrating interventions on seven dimensions of wellbeing: income, employment, health, education, housing, registration and intra-household relations. Integrated antipoverty programmes can address more effectively the multidimensional nature of poverty, especially extreme and persistent.

Conditional Cash Transfers in countries with low levels of or poor quality service delivery

Conditions in antipoverty programmes are not new. Public works and employment guarantees make transfers conditional on beneficiaries providing labour, as a means to encourage households in poverty to self-select into the programme. Human development focused programmes require beneficiary households to ensure their members access primary health care and children are at school. In this case, conditions are intended to ensure that programme objectives are achieved.

In low-income countries with significant deficits in health and schooling infrastructure, conditions cannot be implemented simply because beneficiary households could not comply with them. This is common sense, but misses the point about conditions. In Latin America, human development focused programmes aim to improve levels of human development as a means of breaking the intergenerational persistence of poverty. If this was also the main objective adopted in low-income countries with limited service infrastructure, unconditional transfers will not be successful. The point is to ensure that antipoverty programmes plan direct transfers to poor households in combination with improvements in service infrastructure.

Affordability of transfer programmes
Social protection programmes are affordable in most contexts. South Africa spends around 3.5% of GDP on social assistance grants and Lesotho spends 2.4% of GDP on its social pension, but they are the exception. Mexico's *Oportunidades* and Brazil's *Bolsa Família* absorb around 0.5 to 0.7% of GDP. In low-income countries, finance is a harder constraint on expanding social protection. There are many sources of financing for social protection: domestic taxes and revenues from the exploitation of natural resources; redirecting expenditure from underperforming programmes; revenues from debt cancellation; and international aid. Social transfer programmes have high set up costs and for this reason international assistance is important in low-income countries. Nonetheless, sustainability and legitimacy requires domestic political support and finance in the medium term.

References

Barrientos, A., and J. DeJong (2006). "Reducing child poverty with cash transfers: A sure thing?" Development Policy Review, 24(5), 537-552.

Barrientos, A., Hanlon, J. and D. Hulme (2010). *Just Give Money to the Poor: The Development Revolution from the Global South.* Kumarian Press.

Barrientos, A., Maitrot, M. and M.A. Niño-Zarazúa (2010). "Social Assistance in Developing Countries Database Version 5.0." Brooks World Institute Working Paper: Chronic Poverty Research Working Paper.

Gertler, P., and L. C. Fernald (2005). :Impacto de mediano plazo del Programa Oportunidades sobre el desarrollo infantil en áreas rurales." In B. Hernandez Prado and M. Hernández Avila (eds.), *Evaluación Externa de Impacto del Programa Oportunidades 2004: Alimentación* (Vol. 3, pp. 51-85). Cuernavaca: Instituto Nacional de Salud Pública.

Kakwani, N., Veras Soares, F., and H. H. Son (2005). "Conditional cash transfers in African countries." Working Paper 9. Brasilia: International Poverty Centre for Inclusive Growth (IPC-IG).

Social Protection: Accelerating the MDGs with Equity

Isabel Ortiz, Gaspar Fajth,
Jennifer Yablonski and Amjad Rabi[19]

The UN Secretary-General has highlighted the urgent need for social protection to achieve the MDGs in his report to the UN General Assembly: *Keeping the promise: a forward-looking review to promote an agreed action agenda to achieve the Millennium Development Goals by 2015.* To quote:

"Achieving the Millennium Development Goals will need accelerated interventions in key areas. These interventions should be framed within the broader development framework of national development strategies. The immediate priority would be to ensure the sustainability of economic recovery....Progress must be protected in an era of increased economic insecurity arising from global economic instability, volatile food prices, natural disasters and health epidemics. This requires universal social protection and measures to support the most vulnerable communities."

This paper illustrates how social protection programmes can help to accelerate progress to the MDGs by facilitating access to essential services and decent living standards; summarizes evidence on the breadth and effectiveness of social protection programmes in promoting development, enhancing equity and delivering results for vulnerable children, women and households; and highlights

[19]Isabel Ortiz is Associate Director, Policy and Practice, UNICEF
Gaspar Fajth is Regional Social Policy Advisor for UNICEF Eastern and Southern Africa
Jennifer Yablonski is Social Protection Specialist, Social Policy and Economic Analysis Unit, Division of Policy and Practice, UNICEF
Amjad Rabi is Social Policy Specialist with UNICEF Zimbabwe

opportunities for using these programmes more widely in the global context of a recovery for all.

Social Protection and the importance of MDGs with Equity

A significant amount of MDG progress has been achieved in recent years. However, the overall evidence suggests that improvements have often not reached those who most need them. Figure 1 shows how a country like Namibia has substantially reduced its under-five mortality rate, from 72 per thousand deaths in 1992, to 42 in 2008; however, disaggregating this reduction by income quintiles shows that most of this progress is due to a reduction of under-five mortality in the richer income groups. Many other countries that have made overall progress show a similar pattern when national data on child mortality are disaggregated (Garde 2010; Yablonski and O'Donnell 2009).

Figure 1. MDGs and Inequality – Beware of National Averages
Namibia: Reduction of Under-five Mortality Rate 1992-2008

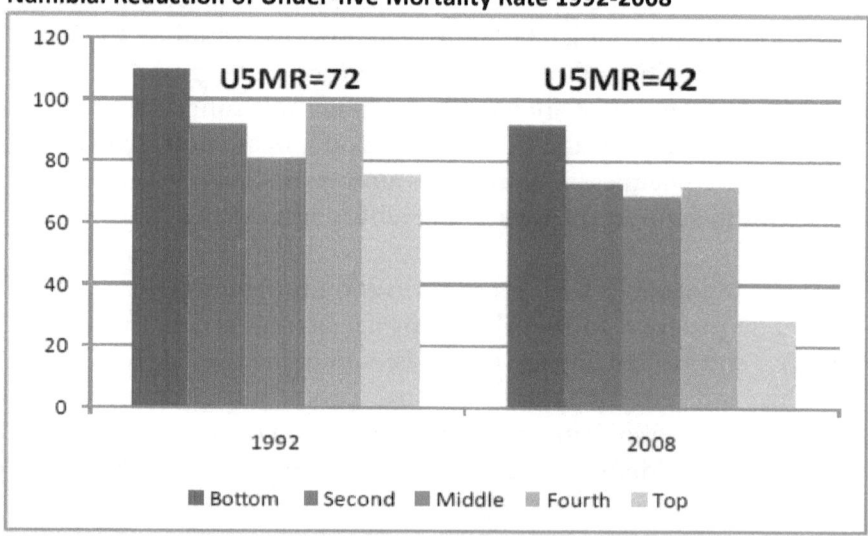

Source: Vandermoortele, J. (2010). Presentation on equity. UNICEF (June 2010).

It is widely recognized that pre-economic crisis progress on the MDGs was uneven across and within countries. Much of the progress in reducing income poverty has been concentrated in a few countries–notably China and India–where pre-crisis growth patterns also fuelled domestic inequalities. Across the developing world, evidence shows how progress has left behind large groups of disadvantaged children, women and families. Despite global reductions in under-five mortality, child death rates remained intolerably high in many countries. Only half of the developing world's population has access to improved sanitation, such as toilets or latrines. Although school enrollment has improved, girls in the poorest quintile of households are still 3-4 times more likely to be out of school than those from the richest households, and four times more likely than boys from this background. In some developing regions still less than half of the women benefit from maternal care by skilled health personnel when giving birth.

The Millennium Declaration, signed by all UN Member States in 2000, stresses the importance of equality, where no individual or nation is denied the chance to benefit from development. While tackling inequality requires structural change, social protection mechanisms and approaches have proven effective in advancing MDG results. Crucially, well-designed social protection can help to achieve greater equity by channeling resources to disadvantaged, poor areas and expanding access for vulnerable populations who are excluded from services.

Social protection accelerates MDG 1: poverty, employment and hunger

Poverty: Social protection is a crucial instrument to reduce income poverty. Cash transfer schemes have successfully combated poverty in Africa, Asia, Central and Eastern Europe and Latin America, and helped to accelerate progress. Although in practice benefits have tended to be lower than needed, a cash transfer at an adequate benefit level can bring a person or household above the income poverty line. Equally important, cash transfers have had even larger effects on reducing the depth of poverty and inequality.

- For example, the *Oportunidades* programme in Mexico reduced the poverty headcount ratio by ten percent, the poverty gap by 30%, and the poverty severity index by 45% (Skoufias and Parker 2001).
- Social pensions and transfers have reduced South Africa's poverty gap by 47% (Economic Policy Research Institute 2004).

In countries such as Senegal and Tanzania, the International Labour Organization (ILO) estimates that poverty could be reduced by 35% to 40% (Gassmann et al 2006).

- The Kyrgyz Republic's Social Protection Programme is estimated to have reduced extreme poverty headcount and poverty gap among beneficiaries by 24% and 42%, respectively. Overall, poverty ratios are estimated to have reduced by 10% and 22% for the extreme poverty headcount and poverty gap respectively (World Bank 2003).

- In Brazil the combination of the Continuous Cash Benefit (BPC) —a means-tested pension and disability grant— and the *Bolsa Família* contributed an estimated 28% of the fall in the Gini coefficient between 1995 and 2004 (Soares et al 2006).

- A WHO cross-country study showed how poor households can be protected from poverty resulting from catastrophic health expenditures by reducing the health system's reliance on out-of-pocket payments and providing more financial risk protection (Xu et al 2003).

- EUROSTAT data show how social protection reduces poverty in most European countries by 50%; for lower income countries, a basic social security system can make the difference between achieving or not achieving MDG 1 of halving poverty by 2015 (Ortiz and Yablonski, 2010).

Employment. Social protection has a major role in achieving full and productive employment and decent work for all, including women and young people, through cash transfers, active labour market, health insurance and family support policies. These have been shown to encourage labour market participation in low- and middle-income countries through guaranteeing public work opportunities, covering the costs of job-seeking and supporting family childcare responsibilities – with strong effects for women in particular.

- In South Africa, labour market participation among those receiving cash transfers increased by 13 - 17 per cent compared to similar non-recipient households with strongest effects for women (Economic Policy Research Institute 2004).

- The impact of vouchers which provided a wage subsidy to employers in Argentina increased the probability of employment for the workfare recipients, particularly for women and young workers (World Bank 2003).
- For young people who are structurally unemployed young people and at high social risk, the *Joven* programme in Chile combines work experience, training and apprenticeships, and this mode has been replicated in other South American countries (World Bank 2003).

Hunger. The evidence of nutritional impacts of cash transfers is also strong, including protection against shocks and their long-term effects for children's physical and cognitive development:

- There is strong evidence across programmes in Africa, Asia and Latin America that cash transfers improve quantity and diversity of food consumption, and protect food consumption during shocks or lean periods. Programmes in Mexico, Malawi, and Colombia all demonstrate reductions in stunting (Yablonski and O'Donnell 2009).
- The *Red de Protección* cash transfer programme in Nicaragua reduced stunting among children 6-59 months by 5.3 percentage points within a two year period (2000-2002) in an area with a malnutrition rate 1.7 times the national average, with stronger impacts among poorer families (Maluccio and Flores 2004). Moreover, following the coffee price shock between 2000 and 2001, beneficiaries of this programme were able to maintain and modestly increase per capita food consumption, while in other comparable households per capita consumption declined sharply (Maluccio 2005).
- Children in South African households receiving a pension have on average 5cm greater growth than those in households without a pension – this is the equivalent of approximately half a year's growth for Black and Coloured children (Case 2001).

Social protection accelerates MDGs 2 and 3: Better education and gender outcomes

Social protection programmes can lead to higher school enrolment rates, less school drop-outs and child labour by removing demand-side barriers to education, reducing the need for families to rely on harmful coping strategies, and addressing barriers to gender equality and empowerment of women (MDG 2, 3 and 5). Social protection policies can also support inclusive education by introducing changes in the supply side to address the specific needs of children who are marginalized or excluded (such as children with disabilities and learning difficulties or girls who may not go to school if families consider it unsafe for them) to ensure they can access and benefit from education.

Cash transfers, removal of user fees, and school feeding programmes have been shown to lead to higher enrolment and attendance, and lower incidence of child labour. In addition, there is some evidence of better cognitive and language skills and fewer behavioural problems. With few exceptions, the increases as a result of these programmes are as strong, or stronger, for girls.

- Transfer programmes in Ethiopia, South Africa, Malawi, Mexico, Nicaragua, Brazil, Ecuador, Cambodia, Pakistan and Turkey have all demonstrated significant percentage point increases in enrollment and/or attendance (Adato and Bassett 2008).
- Between 2002 and 2005, the gross enrollment rate in Kenya increased from 88% to 112%, linked to the abolition of school fees (World Bank and UNICEF 2009).
- Between 1996 and 2002/3, girls' net primary enrolment in Bangladesh increased from 48% to 86%. Many researchers attribute this increase in part to the stipend program for girls' education (Raynor 2006).
- In the Malawi cash transfer scheme, new enrollment was twice as high in participating households (8.3% *vs* 3.4%) within a one year period (Miller et al. 2008).
- *Oportunidades* in Mexico had little impact at primary level (where enrollment was already high), but at increased secondary school enrollment of girls increased by 11-14%, compared to 5-8% for boys. It also resulted in a reduction in probability of working for children aged 8-17 (Skoufias and Parker 2001).
- In Brazil, the Programme for the Eradication of Child Labour (PETI) reduced both the probability of children working and

their likelihood to be engaged in higher-risk activities (Yap et al 2002).

Social protection accelerates MDGs 4, 5 and 6: Improved health care and reduced illness

Social protection can contribute to better and more equal health outcomes (MDG 4, 5 and 6) through various pathways. Clearly progress on several MDG targets – including targets on child and maternal mortality – will require addressing inadequate supply of public or affordable health services. Poor health infrastructure, insufficient staff and unaffordable drugs, lack of sanitation tend to plague those countries and geographical areas where the burden of illness is also the heaviest.

However, evidence shows that progress can be accelerated when countries use social protection programmes and approaches to complement supply side interventions by increasing demand and access to services. Basic education and awareness raising campaigns have long been considered important in underpinning demand for health. More recently, cash transfers have emerged as particularly successful tools to generate effective demand with measurable results in anthropometric outcomes and accessing health services.

- In Peru, the *Juntos* conditional cash transfer programme reduced the number of women giving birth at home, in geographical areas with high levels of maternal mortality (Jones et al 2007)
- The *Oportunidades* programme combined cash transfers and free health services with improvements in supply of health services, leading to a 17 per cent decline in rural infant mortality (8 percentage points on average) in Mexico over a three-year period. Maternal mortality was also reduced (by 11%); and both impacts were stronger in more marginalized communities (Barham 2010, Adato and Bassett 2008).
- Newborns whose mothers participated in the Colombian *Familias en Acción* in urban areas increased in average weight by 0.58 kilograms in one year, which is attributed to improved maternal nutrition (LaGarde et al 2007).

- In all cash transfer programmes for which there is data, with the exception of the PATH programme in Jamaica, incidence of illness has decreased among children, particularly younger children (Yablonski and O'Donnell 2009)
- In Malawi, 80 per cent of households participating in the Mchinji District reported that their children received enough healthcare when they were ill, compared to 20 per cent of other households (Miller et al 2008).

The evidence of social protection impacts on service utilization and health expenditure is strong; and in cases where it has been possible to measure differences between groups, poorer and more marginalized participants often benefit more.

- In Ghana, user fee exemptions for pregnant women led to a reduction in their maternal mortality rate. In the Volta region the largest increase in facility utilization was amongst the poorest (Witter et al., 2007; Witter et al., 2009).
- In Niger, consultations for children under 5 quadrupled and antenatal care visits doubled after the removal of user fees in 2006 for children under 5 and pregnant women (Monde 2008).
- User fee removal was also associated with an increase in health service utilization by 40% for under-

Children Under 5
Cost in Percentage of GDP
Select Countries

Angola	0.66
Azerbaijan	2.26
Bangladesh	1.43
Benin	2.23
Bolivia	0.65
Botswana	0.15
Brazil	0.11
Burkina Faso	3.22
Cambodia	0.93
Cameroon	1.20
Central African Republic	5.10
Chad	2.50
China	0.25
Congo Rep	1.18
Cote d'Ivoire	1.44
Djibiuti	0.73
Egypt	0.23
Ethiopia	3.25
Gabon	0.12
Gambia	2.58
Ghana	1.89
Guinea	3.70
Guinea-Bissau	5.17
Haiti	3.45
India	0.54
Indonesia	0.31
Kenya	1.86
Laos	1.18
Lesotho	2.00
Madagascar	3.81
Malawi	5.41
Mali	3.52
Mauritania	1.39
Mexico	0.09
Morocco	0.32
Mozambique	5.13
Nepal	2.64
Nigeria	1.94
Pakistan	0.56
Papua New Guinea	1.09
Peru	0.16
Philippines	0.52
Rwanda	5.36
Senegal	1.75
Sierra Leone	5.65
South Africa	0.17
Swaziland	0.63
Tajikistan	0.00
Tanzania	3.60
Togo	2.75
Turkmenistan	0.40
Uganda	4.29
Yemen	1.03
Zambia	3.32

Source: Save the Children UK (2009)

Note: Cost calculations are based on a transfer amount per child equal to the national average poverty gap to reach the $1.25 PPP per day poverty line plus 15% administrative costs. For full methodology see Yablonski and O'Donnell (2009).

fives in Burundi (Médecins Sans Frontieres 2008).

More recently, there is also evidence on the usefulness of broader social protection interventions in HIV and AIDS prevention, treatment and care and support. Cash transfers, for example, were found effective in supporting families to care for those impacted by HIV/AIDS and in improving access to treatment and adherence. The evidence shows that social protection measures which are more broadly targeted, rather than AIDS-exclusively targeted, work better and with fewer negative consequences (e.g., stigma) for policies which aim to address the multiple vulnerabilities that underlie – or result from – HIV/AIDS (for certain interventions which address specific vulnerabilities of people living with HIV/AIDS, such as ARV distribution, specific targeting still makes sense).

In Malawi, cash transfers to adolescent girls increased school attendance, and led to a significant decline in early marriage, pregnancy, self-reported sexual activity and HIV prevalence among beneficiaries in a one year period (Baird et al. 2010). In Kenya, cash transfers were used by households to increase anti-retroviral treatment for children and adults (Adato and Bassett 2008).

A multi-country review of HIV workplace policies - anti-discrimination policies, access to workplace-based HIV related education and services - found improved attitudes towards people living with HIV and awareness of HIV-related services. The review also found increased condom use among participants, although there was no comparison group (ILO, 2008). Within six months of introducing Namibia's pilot basic income grant programme, women participants reported more control over their sexuality - an important factor in the gendered risks of HIV infection (Temin 2010).

Facing the challenges
The lack of adequate pre-existing social protection systems became a liability during the current global economic crisis. Maintaining 80 per cent of world population without basic social protection translated into continuing and exacerbated hardship for many households.

This low level of social protection coverage exists in part because building and expanding social protection systems is not without its difficulties. Some of these are not uncommon in developing and middle-income countries, such as human resources and administrative capacity. In addition, social protection faces some specific challenges:

- Financing. Affordability remains a concern for many governments, particularly where revenues are low or unpredictable. In light of the increasing numbers of developing countries adopting or expanding programmes, however, the equally important question is how these programmes are financed in different contexts. An increasing number of countries have used different options for financing social protection, and greater shared practice and understanding on how different countries have been able to sustainably finance social protection is needed.

- Integrated systems and collaboration across sectors. Particularly when viewed through the MDG lens, social protection requires an integrated approach -which combines different social protection interventions with investments in social services - in order to be most effective in achieving human and economic development outcomes. However, adopting this approach faces both political and practical challenges in terms of coordination, sequencing, and resources. These synergies are often under-utilized, and in some cases programme conflicts or inconsistencies arise.

- Context-specific design. The growing body of practice and evidence on social protection offers substantial lessons across countries. Nonetheless, work remains in understanding which programmes and modalities work best in different contexts.

- Participation and Accountability. In many developing countries, citizen participation in social protection design, implementation and monitoring is also weak. For long-term sustainability and effectiveness of social protection programmes however, transparency, participation, and accountability mechanisms are crucial.

Despite the challenges however, progress is both possible and necessary. In the face of the substantial evidence of the potential of social protection to help accelerate MDG progress, particularly for the most disadvantaged, there is an imperative to overcome these challenges. And there is evidence that countries are doing so.

A historic opportunity to expand social protection in the developing world

Crises often oblige policy-makers to rethink development models. The 1929 Financial Crash led to a New Deal in which forms of social protection were used as a powerful tool to raise living standards and domestic demand in many countries. Likewise, the current crisis is a historical opportunity to rethink development.

The crisis has triggered a shift in the way the international community sees the relationship between growth, public intervention and social protection. In the Asia-Pacific region, for example, policymakers are increasingly shifting away from export-led growth approaches alone towards more inclusive employment-intensive recovery strategies which emphasize the need to reduce high domestic savings rates and improve the region's underdeveloped social protection programmes (UNDP, 2010). In Africa and elsewhere, the food price crisis highlighted the limitations of family and community-based traditional support systems in responding to aggregate shocks and spurred efforts to strengthen local agriculture and livelihoods and to put more formal social protection mechanisms in place. At the global level, there is awareness now on the need to reduce poverty, expand internal markets, and be better prepared for future shocks by building up stronger systems during the current recovery period.

In response to the crisis, social protection has been a major component of fiscal stimulus plans; on average, an estimated 25 per cent of fiscal stimulus was invested in social protection measures in both middle and higher income countries (Figure 2). Also in response, the chiefs of the United Nations called in April 2009 for nine urgent UN Joint Initiatives to confront the crisis, ensure progress in development goals and build a more inclusive globalization. One of them is the Social Protection Floor Initiative, which brings together national governments, civil society partners and international organizations such as the ILO, WHO, UNICEF, UN, UNFPA, UNDP, FAO, UNDP and the World Bank in a forward-looking collaborative strategy to build a recovery for all.

Figure 2. Size of Social Protection Component of Stimulus Packages (in percent of total announced amount)

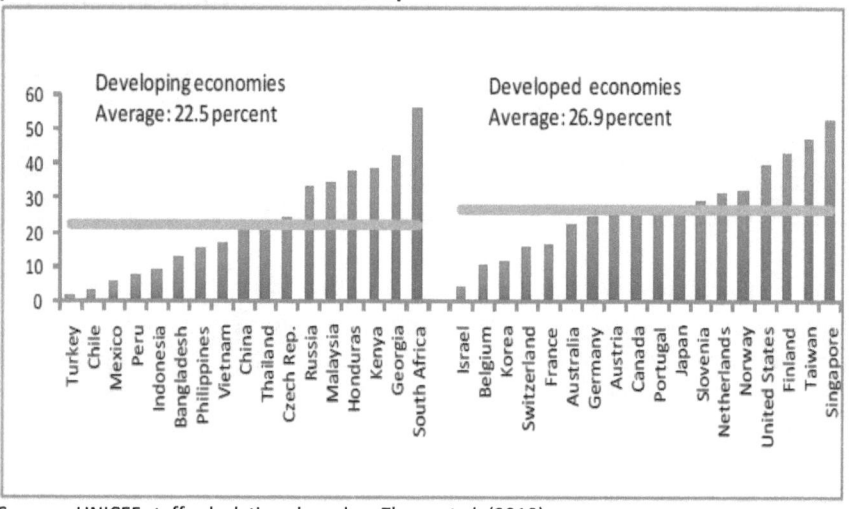

Sources: UNICEF staff calculations based on Zhang et al. (2010)

However, there is a need to keep up the momentum. Investments in social protection rose during the crisis: current calls for fiscal consolidation should not sacrifice progress. There remains potential fiscal space in the wake of the crisis. Economic growth is projected to be strong in the coming years in those countries and regions where social protection programmes are comparatively weak or absent. According to the World Bank, low and middle-income countries will grow at an annual rate of 6 per cent on average. Even excluding China and India, the developing world is expected to post 4-5 per cent growth annually over 2010-2012. According to IMF country reports, about half of governments in middle and low income countries continue to think they have other ways to maintain fiscally sustainable budgets than introducing belt-tightening measures.

Countries that succeed in building a stronger social protection system in the current recovery period will be able in a better position to achieve faster and more equitable results along the Millennium Development Agenda up to 2015 and beyond. In words of the UN Secretary General:

"We must act now. We must avoid reverting to the pre-crisis conditions that denied too many of our fellow human beings a fair chance at a decent living… We must work together to establish the basis for a more secure, prosperous and equitable world for all."

References

Adato, M., and L. Bassett (2008). "What is the Potential of Cash Transfers to Strengthen Families Affected by HIV and AIDS? A Review of the Evidence on Impacts and Key Policy Debates." Joint Learning Initiative on Children and HIV/AIDS.

Baird, S., Mcintosh, C., B. Ozler (2010). "Cash or condition? Evidence from a randomized cash transfer program." World Bank, Policy Research Working Paper No. 5259.

Barham, T. (2010). "A Healthier Start: The Effect of Conditional Cash Transfers on Neo-Natal and Infant Mortality." Boulder: Department of Economics and Institute of Behavioral Science, University of Colorado.

Case, A. (2001). "Does Money Protect Health Status? Evidence from South African pensions." NBER Working Paper 8495. Cambridge: National Bureau of Economic Research (NBER).

Economic Policy Research Institute (2004). "Final Report: The Social and Economic Impact of South Africa's Social Security System." EPRI Research Paper 37. Cape Town: EPRI, South Africa Department of Social Development

Fajth, G., and C. Vinay (2010). "Conditional Cash Transfers: A global perspective." MDG Insights No 1. New York: UNDG.

Garde, R. with N. Sabina (2010). "Inequalities in Child Survival: Looking at wealth and other socio-economic disparities in developing countries." London: Save the Children UK.

Gassmann, F. and C. Behrendt (2006). "Cash Benefits in Low-income Countries: Simulating the Effects on Poverty Reduction for Senegal and Tanzania." ILO Issues in Social Protection Discussion Paper 15. Geneva: ILO.

ILO (2008). "Saving lives, Protecting jobs: International HIV/AIDS Workplace Education Programme." SHARE: Strategic HIV/AIDS Responses in Enterprises, SECOND REPORT. Geneva: ILO.

ILO and WHO (2009). The Social Protection Floor Initiative. Geneva: ILO.

IMF country reports on Article IV consultations at http//www.imf.org.

Jones, N., Vargas, R., and E. Villar (2007). "Conditional Cash Transfers in Peru: Tackling the Multi-Dimensionality of Childhood Poverty and Vulnerability." New York: New School and UNICEF.

LaGarde, M. with Haines, A., Palmer N. (2007). "Conditional cash transfers for improving uptake of health interventions in low- and middle-incomes countries: a systematic review." JAMA, 298, pp. 1900-10.

Maluccio, J.A. (2005). "Coping with the 'Coffee Crisis' in Central America: The Role of the Nicaraguan Red de Proteccion Social." FCND Discussion Paper 188. Washington DC: International Food Policy Research Institute (IFPRI).

Maluccio, J., and R. Flores (2004). "Impact Evaluation of a Conditional Cash Transfer Program: The Nicaraguan Red de Protección Social." FCND Discussion Paper 184. Washington DC, International Food Policy Research Institute.

Médecins Sans Frontieres (2008). "No Cash, No Care: How 'user fees' endanger health."

Miller, C. with Tsoka, M. and K. Reichert (2008). "Impact Evaluation Report: External Evaluation of the Mchinji Social Cash Transfer Pilot." Boston: Boston University School of Public Health and the Centre for Social Research, University of Malawi.

Monde, M. D. (2008). "Improving financial free access to primary health care: a rewarding strategy."

Ortiz, I. and J. Yablonski (2010). "Investing in People: Social Protection for All." Manila: Asian Development Bank.

Raynor, J. (2006). "The Girls' Stipend Program in Bangladesh." Journal of Education for International Development.

Skoufias, E. and S. Parker (2001). "Conditional Cash Transfers and Their Impact on Child Work and Schooling: Evidence from PROGRESA Program in Mexico." Economia, 2: 45-96.

Soares, F., Soares, S., Medeiros, M. and R. Osório (2006). "Cash Transfer Programmes in Brazil: Impacts on Inequality and Poverty." International Poverty Center Working paper No 21. Brasilia: International Poverty Centre for Inclusive Growth (IPC-IG).

Temin, M. (2010). "HIV-Sensitive Social Protection: What does the evidence say?" Paper prepared for IDS, UNICEF and UNAIDS Meeting on the Evidence for HIV-Sensitive Social Protection. June 14-15, 2010, Brighton, UK.

United Nations (2010). "Keeping the Promise: A forward-looking review to promote an agreed action agenda to achieve the MDGs by 2015." New York: United Nations.

United Nations System Chief Executives Board for Coordination (2009). CEB Communiqué, 5 April 2009, Paris.

UNDP (2010). "Asia Rebounds But Lasting Recovery Needs New Paradigm: A Synthesis Study Incorporating Evidence from Country Case Studies." Colombo: UNDP Regional Centre for Asia and the Pacific.

UNICEF (2009). Child-Sensitive Social Protection. New York: UNICEF

UNICEF (2010). A Recovery for All. New York: UNICEF.

Vandermoorteele, J. (2010). Presentation on inequity to UNICEF staff June 2010.

Witter, S., Adjei, S., Armar-Klemesu, M. and W. Grah (2009). "Providing free maternal health care: ten lessons from an evaluation of the national delivery exemption policy in Ghana." Global Health Action , Vol 2.

Witter, S., Arhinful, D., Kusi, A. and S. Zakariah-Akoto (2007). "The experience of Ghana in implementing a user fee exemption policy to provide free delivery care." Reproductive Health Matters, 15, pp. 61-71.

World Bank. (2003). "The contribution of Social Protection to the Millennium Development Goals." Washington DC.

World Bank and UNICEF. (2009). "Abolishing User Fees in Africa: Lessons from Ethiopia, Ghana, Kenya, Malawi, and Mozambique." Washington DC: World Bank.

World Bank and IMF. (2010). Global Monitoring Report 2010: The MDGs after the Crisis. Washington DC.

Xu, K., Evans, D., and K. Kawabata (2003). "Household Catastrophic Health Expenditure: a Multi-Country Analysis." The Lancet, 362, pp. 111-117.

Yablonski, J. and M. O'Donnell (2009). "Lasting Benefits: The role of Cash Transfers in Tackling Child Mortality." London: Save the Children UK.

Yap, Y.-T., Sedlacek, G., and P. Orazem (2002). "Limiting Child Labor through Behavior-Based Income Transfers: An Experimental Evaluation of the PETI Program in Rural Brazil." Washington DC: InterAmerican Development Bank.

Zhang, Y., Thelen, N., and A. Rao (2010). "Social Protection in Fiscal Stimulus Packages: Some Evidence." Working Paper. New York: Office of Development Studies, UNDP.

Social Protection for All – An Agenda for Pro Child Growth and Child Rights

Timo Voipio[20]

Social Protection: High priority on all development agendas

The single most remarkable shift in the global poverty reduction agenda of the new millennium is indeed the emergence of Social Protection as a top priority for most international organizations and development agencies. Ten years ago, when world leaders agreed on the UN Millennium Declaration and in the UN MDG-Roadmap of 2001, social protection was not even once mentioned. Now in 2010, at the UN MDG Review Summit, world leaders agreed that promoting national social protection *systems* that reduce inequality and social exclusion is essential for MDG-progress. They recognized the need to start by providing social protection *floors* for all, as a human right, and to continue towards progressive realization of comprehensive national systems of social protection that provide universal access to essential social services and income/livelihood security for all.

World leaders also reaffirmed the need to create full and productive employment and decent work for all. The G20 Leaders Declaration (Nov-2010) recognized the importance of addressing the concerns of the most vulnerable by providing social protection and decent work in low-income countries. The African and European Heads of State, representing more than 1.5 billion citizens at the AU-EU Summit in Tripoli 29-30 Nov, 2010, committed themselves to the promotion of "the Global Decent Work Agenda, with a special focus on more, more productive and better jobs, and the link to social protection." The European Report on Development 2010,

---

[20]Timo Voipio is Chair of the Poverty Reduction Network (POVNET), OECD-DAC Paris, and Senior Adviser for Global Social Policy, Ministry of Foreign Affairs for Finland

the new 'Flagship Report' of the European development cooperation is entitled *"Social Protection for Inclusive Development: A new perspective of EU cooperation with Africa."*

Another forthcoming EU-Guideline on *"Social Transfers in the Fight against Hunger"* emphasizes that global food security can never be achieved only by increasing agricultural production: Too many people in the world are food insecure because they do not have enough incomes to buy food. Therefore, social protection must always be recognized as an essential instrument in the fight against hunger.

Furthermore, the African Ministers of Labour and of Social Development in their recent meetings in Yaounde and Khartoum, respectively, emphasized social protection. The Yaounde Tripartite Declaration of governments, employers' organizations and trade unions "recognized the urgent need for all African Member States and Social Partners to start the effective and rapid implementation of a Social Protection floor to all Africans." The African Social Ministers emphasized social protection as one of the four key functions of the African Social Policy Framework Implementation Strategy – the other three functions being production, reproduction and redistribution.

Finally, it's also worth noting that the African Development Bank (AfDB) is now developing an AfDB Social Protection Strategy in order to use social protection instruments for: (a) income poverty and risk vulnerability reduction in Africa; (b) national capacity building; and (c) enhanced food security.

Social Protection as a key element of Pro-Poor Growth
OECD Development Assistance Committee (DAC) is the donor governments' joint think-tank. POVNET is DAC's *Poverty Reduction Network - a tool for policy discourse and interaction.* The first POVNET Guidelines on Poverty Reduction (2001) were instrumental in creating a consensus among development partners about the *multi-dimensionality* and *context-specificity* of the poverty challenge. That was a remarkable vote-of-no-confidence to the overly economistic and 'one-size-fits-all' doctrine that the World Bank and IMF had been

imposing on poor countries – and on bilateral donors – through the Structural Adjustment Programmes of the 1980s and 1990s. The POVNET Poverty Reduction Guideline showed that poverty has multiple and interlinked causes and dimensions: economic, human, political, socio-cultural and protective, and hence needs a broad range of proactive and interlocking policies to tackle it.

Between 2003 and 2006, the POVNET focused its work on the most controversial of the poverty dimensions: the economic. That was regarded as an area where much re-thinking would be required if the poverty reducing impacts of development in 'productive' sectors, e.g. agriculture, infrastructure and private sector development, was to be increased. POVNET concluded that 'just any' GDP-growth would *not* reduce poverty: There were – and are – too many examples of countries that have achieved rapid rates of GDP-growth, yet failed to reduce poverty and inequality and to provide decent work and social protection to the majority of women and men, children and the elderly. If we are serious about reducing poverty, POVNET concluded, we have to achieve a *pro-poor pattern* of growth, i.e. an inclusive, equality-enhancing and employment-intensive pattern of growth, where poor people can participate in, contribute to and benefit from growth.

Livelihood insecurity and lack of reliable social protection make it difficult, however, for poor people to participate in and contribute to growth. They know that by moving from low-productivity crops to higher yielding crops, or from un-profitable to more profitable micro-businesses they could increase their productivity and incomes. But they often decide not do so, i.e. not to improve their businesses and move forward in life, due to the high risks of falling into destitution if the new crop or the new micro-business fails.

A reliable 'social protection floor' for all citizens can transform such a vicious circle into a virtuous one. It can secure access to health services as well as to social assistance in the case of accident, sickness, or old age and thereby promote socio-economic security and predictability. Moreover, it can 'unlock' the human capabilities and entrepreneurship of millions of poor people. Mothers and fathers will dare to take initiative and risks in their income-generating activities today, knowing that if the venture fails, reliable last resort support will be available from social protection to make sure that the family will not go hungry next week and the children need not drop out of school. The POVNET Guideline on Social Protection provides also other good arguments that can be used to show to Ministers of Finance why social protection is not only a human right, and morally right, but also good economics and good for the economy.

Social Protection, Child Rights and Child Protection

We care for children not because it is "good economics" (although it is!), but because it is the right thing to do. The rights of the child are spelt out in a systemic fashion in the Convention on the Rights of the Child. UNICEF takes a *human rights based approach* to development. So do we at the Government of Finland.

The human right to social security is confirmed in Article 22 of the UN Universal Declaration of Human Rights – the right to decent work, adequate standard of living and education are confirmed in Articles 23, 25 and 26, respectively. In the Convention on the Rights of the Child the right to social security is stated in Article 26. Dr. Magdalena Sepulveda, the UN Human Rights Council's Independent Expert on Extreme Poverty, has produced an impressive series of reports that provide all the arguments for those who need to convince lawyers and politicians about the human right to social protection.

Child welfare and protection concerns are often at the heart of social protection efforts, since children are the most vulnerable members of society, and the impact of violations of their rights - to food and nutrition, health, education, and to recreation can be irreversible in terms of stunting their prospects in every domain.

There is a growing body of evidence from a range of developing countries that social protection programmes can effectively increase the nutritional, health and educational status of children and reduce their risk of abuse and exploitation, ensuring their rights, and offering long-term developmental benefits. Social protection is also, in a more instrumental mode, increasingly viewed as a key investment in human capital and in breaking inter-generational poverty traps. So there are two intertwined rationales for child rights champions to engage actively in the national social protection planning processes and make sure that children's interests are taken into consideration from the outset.

Implications for UNICEF

UNICEF plays a key role in informing policy, practice and advocacy in the area of children's rights, welfare and protection. Long considered a privilege of developed countries, social protection is now recognized for the role it can play in addressing poverty and vulnerability in developing countries as part of the essential package of basic social services and transfers ('social protection floor') that the state ought to provide to its citizens.

Together with its international development partners, UNICEF has published *a Joint Statement on Child Sensitive Social Protection*. According to this highly useful Guide, the best way to promote child-sensitive social protection is not necessarily one that focuses only on children. The best results for children are achieved through an *integrated* approach to social protection, or comprehensive social policy. This means that instead of temporary, narrowly focused projects we should build permanent, sustainable, and transparent national social protection *systems,* with strong mandates, professionalized staff and sufficient budget resources to promote the realization of social protection for children as well as their families and communities.

Concretely, child-sensitive social protection should focus on aspects of well-being that include: providing adequate child and maternal nutrition; access to quality basic services for all, complemented by social inclusion polices and affirmative action to ensure that the poorest and most marginalized have equal quality access as all other groups in society; supporting families and caregivers in their childcare role, including increasing the time available within the household; addressing gender inequality; preventing discrimination and child abuse in and outside the home; eliminating child labour; increasing caregivers' access to incomes for care services, or employment in the labour market; and preparing adolescents for their own livelihoods, taking account of their role as current and future workers and parents.

Role of UNICEF partners in social protection

Social cash transfers have received the most attention in discussions about social protection. Much less has been written and said about the *professionals of care* who will be needed to meet poor, vulnerable and disadvantaged families, understand their diverse life situations in their real contexts, and be inclusive and offer high quality services. Their important work should be recognized and respected.

Cash transfers alone will never solve the problems of poverty. But regular and predictable pensions for the aged and the disabled, as well as child/family allowances can empower the poor if the transfer schemes are well facilitated, predictable, do not stigmatize and are accompanied by accessible and high quality care services.

With the rapid development of ICT-based cash transfer delivery mechanisms (smart cards, biometric identity recognition and cell-phone/SMS-transfers) the social workers/community development officers or other care professionals will be less and less occupied with the physical distribution of cash transfers to recipients. This is wonderful for two reasons: 1) the fiduciary risks of corruption or dependencies and clientelism in the delivery of social transfers will be minimized; 2) this will liberate these professionals to do what they are meant and motivated to do: provide quality and inclusive care services for children, elderly, sick, disabled, substance abusers, immigrants, and other vulnerable individuals and households.

Care work in most societies falls on women and girl children, as un-paid care work within households and communities. Formalization of care work would be good for both those women who would receive regular incomes (and in due course accrue social security entitlements) from the local government or NGOs, as well as for those women who could engage more actively in other productive work if liberated from their care responsibilities. The new UNRISD Flagship Report on Poverty and Inequality discusses the important aspects of care economy and care work much more widely. I recommend it to all.

References

EU/AU Tripoli Declaration Nov 2010:
    http://europafrica.net/2010/12/01/tripoli-declaration/
European Report on Development (ERD) 2010: http://erd.eui.eu/erd-
    2010/final-report/
G20 Leaders' Declaration Nov 2010:
    http://www.g20.utoronto.ca/2010/g20seoul.html
Independent Expert on human rights and extreme poverty:
    http://www.ohchr.org/EN/Issues/Poverty/Pages/PovertyExpertIndex.asp
    x
OECD-POVNET Guidelines: http://www.oecd.org/dac/poverty
The Universal Declaration of Human Rights:
    http://www.un.org/en/documents/udhr/
UN Convention on the Rights of the Child:
    http://www2.ohchr.org/english/law/pdf/crc.pdf
UN MDG Review Summit Outcome Document 2010:
    http://www.un.org/en/mdg/summit2010/pdf/mdg%20outcome%20docu
    ment.pdf
UN MDG Road Map 2001:
    http://www.un.org/documents/ga/docs/56/a56326.pdf
UN Millennium Declaration 2000:
    http://www.un.org/millennium/declaration/ares552e.pdf
Yaounde Tripartite Declaration on the implementation of the Social Protection
    Floor:
    http://www.ilo.org/gimi/gess/RessShowRessource.do?ressourceId=19140

Rising Food Prices and Children's Welfare
Nora Lustig[21]

After three consecutive decades of decline, world prices of food commodities have risen over the past few years at an alarming pace. Rising food prices are a cause of major concern because high food prices bring significant and immediate setbacks for poverty reduction, nutrition, social stability, inflation and a rules-based trading system. Food prices are unique since food is unlike any other good. Food is essential for survival; it is the most basic of basic needs. Access to basic nutrition permits humans to live, work, reproduce and fend off disease. It should come as no surprise that the poor themselves list hunger and food insecurity as their core concerns. Food is special from the production point of view as well. It is the key ingredient in generating human energy, and human energy is essential to any, and all, economic activity. Food is also special because there are both net buyers and net sellers of food commodities among the poor.

In country after country, the poor distinguish themselves from the non-poor because there is hunger in their households. The poor forego meals on a regular basis and eat nutritionally inadequate diets. For the poor lack of access to food means distress at being unable to feed their children, anxiety from not knowing where the next meal will come from, and insecurity from not being able to work at full potential because of weakness and disease. Rising food prices, however, not only cause poverty to go up. They may also reduce poverty for millions of poor farmers if the higher market prices actually reach them too. However, this should not be a source of comfort. While it is important to point out that some of the poor gain from higher food prices, netting the impact is not the

---

[21]Nora Lustig is Samuel Z. Stone Professor of Latin American Economics at Tulane University and non-resident fellow at the Center for Global Development (CGD)

right approach: one of the worst types of redistribution is one in which some of the poor benefit at the expense of others who are also poor. Food insecurity is very painful to the poor who are hurt by higher food prices.

Until recently, analysts and policymakers used to be concerned that world food commodity prices were kept artificially low by agricultural support policies in advanced countries, thereby hurting millions of poor farmers in the developing world. Now, the concern is the opposite. With food prices sharply up, multilateral organizations and governments fear that the livelihoods of millions of poor consumers throughout the world have been put at risk. The risk is particularly high for poor children because malnutrition can cause illness and death. And it can cause irreversible damage to cognitive abilities. Unfortunately, governments' responses to deal with the consequences of rising food prices are inadequate. They are inadequate because: they reach only a fraction of the children that are affected; even for those who are reached, the compensatory mechanisms fall short of what is needed; and, existing social protection measures are not designed to deal with rising (and volatile) food prices.

Rising food prices and the poor

How can higher food prices be potentially good and harmful to the poor at the same time? The answer is simple: the poor include both net buyers and net sellers of food in significant proportions. Small poor farmers benefit from higher food prices. However, the poor in urban areas and those in rural areas with little or no access to land are hurt, and hurt badly, when food prices increase. This contradictory impact of food prices on the poor has been called the "food price dilemma." This dilemma has been the source of a futile debate regarding when the poor are better off: when food prices go up or when they go down? Rather than trying to measure and base the policy response on the net impact of higher (lower) food prices on poverty, policymakers should simply accept the unavoidable fact that if food prices rise (fall) poor net buyers (net sellers) will need help and rejoice in the fact that poor net sellers (net buyers) will be better off. In either case, existent social protection programs will have to be expanded in coverage and size to compensate the group of the poor who get hurt. In addition, when food commodities prices increase, there is an opportunity to help poor net sellers translate this windfall into a more long-term improvement in living standards.

As a general proposition, the impact on poverty generated by an increase in the price of food will depend on: i. the relative importance of different food commodities in the production set and consumption basket of different households and the difference between the two; ii. the magnitude of the relative price change; and, iii. the degree to which households are compensated for the price shocks by changes in their income (i.e., by the indirect effect on wages and employment originated by the price change). Evidence suggests that: the poor spend between 60% and 80% of their income on food on average; the increase in domestic food price has been significant, and the positive effects on wages take time.

Overall, existing empirical evidence shows that an increase in food prices will make many of the already poor worse off and make some of the near poor (households with incomes just above the poverty line) poor. This, however, does not always translate into an increase in aggregate poverty (in, for example, the headcount ratio) because higher food prices also make part of the poor better off. But, there is a consensus that—at least in the short-run-- high food prices are bad for the poor because most of the poorest of the poor are net food buyers, even in rural areas and even where agriculture is the dominant activity. That is, in the majority of countries, the net effect will be a higher poverty rate. However, as argued above, the net effect may not be the relevant indicator when deciding on the policy response. Even in countries where the net effect is a reduction in poverty, poor net buyers should have access to a broadened social protection system.

Even if in the short-run higher food prices hurt more poor households than benefit them, could it be that in the medium-term higher incomes to net sellers induce higher incomes for net buyers through multiplier effects between agricultural and non-farm incomes in rural areas? There is a large body of evidence that correlates higher agricultural incomes with higher nonfarm activity and incomes; in general, studies show that the virtuous circle might take considerable time to manifest itself. In the short-run, the negative impact on the majority of poor households' welfare is inevitable. In the case of the poor, the short-run effect is particularly important because the damage to health, nutrition and cognitive development might be irreversible.

Recent studies on the poverty impacts of increases in food prices use different methods, poverty lines and assumptions about price increases, pass-through to domestic prices, substitution effects, and wage (and other indirect income) effects. Also, some include net sellers while others don't. However, in spite of all these differences, on average, the evidence finds that in the majority of countries, higher food commodities prices increase poverty for practically all the food commodities. The orders of magnitude of the estimated short-term impact of higher food prices on poverty are significant. Ivanic and Martin (2008) show that about 105 million people in the least developed countries have been added to the world's poor since 2005 because of rising food prices. This is equivalent to about ten percent of the people living with less than a dollar a day and, according to the authors, and "close to seven lost years of progress in poverty reduction" (p.17). Even middle-income Latin America has not remained impervious: Robles et al. (2008) estimate that the increase in world food prices between January 2006 and March 2008 resulted in an increase of 4.3 percentage points in the headcount ratio or 21 million additional poor individuals. CEPAL (2008)—the UN Economic Commission for Latin America and the Caribbean-- estimates that the ranks of the extremely poor and the moderately poor increased by 10 million each. The Asian Development Bank (2008) suggests that a 20% increase in food prices would raise the number of poor individuals by 5.65 and 14.67 million in Philippines and Pakistan, respectively.

Rising food prices and social protection
Are developing countries ready to compensate the poor and vulnerable groups for their loss in purchasing power? In particular, do social protection programs exist and can they be easily expanded to incorporate the "new" poor? Do governments have the fiscal space to accommodate the additional resources needed to fund the

social protection programs? Unfortunately, 19 (out of 49) low-income and 49 (out of 95) middle-income countries do not have safety net programs. Although cash transfers programs (conditional and unconditional) are increasingly more common (16 (out of 49) low-income and 37 (out of 95) middle-income countries that have cash transfers programs), they are still not pervasive. School feeding programs are a bit more common in low-income countries that cash transfers programs but still only 24 of low-income countries have such programs. While they will not compensate the poor for the loss of purchasing power associated with higher food prices, school-feeding programs can insulate (at least in part) the children of poor households from suffering a cut in their food intake as a result of higher food prices.

In addition to the fact that there are many low- and middle-income countries which do not have social protection programs to help the poor who get hurt by higher food prices, those which do may have very limited coverage. In the case of Latin America and the Caribbean, for example, the coverage of cash transfer programs exceeds 25% of the population living in poverty only in 8 out of 26 countries: Brazil, Colombia, Chile, Ecuador, Honduras, Jamaica, Mexico and Panama. The poorest countries in the region either do not have programs or have them in a very limited scale.

Furthermore, most of these programs do not have a mechanism to incorporate the "new" poor or increase the size of the benefit in the face of adverse shocks as part of their design. Some governments (Brazil and Mexico, for example) have increased the amount of the transfer to compensate for the loss in its purchasing power. However, the programs have not incorporated as beneficiaries those who became poor as a result of the food price increase. So far it is not clear how many of the countries that have cash transfers programs increased the amount of the transfer and incorporated the "new" poor into the program (or implemented a complementary program).

In sum, the existing social protection programs and policies in developing countries leave much to be desired, especially to cope with rising food prices. In too many countries it is either inexistent or small; and, even in the countries in which cash transfers programs are large and effective in addressing chronic poverty, they are not designed to respond to shocks. This means that the majority of the poor who have been hurt or those who have become poor as a result of higher food prices are not being protected from the impact of higher food prices on their living standards.

In the cases in which these programs have been expanded, this was done as an ad hoc measure implemented many months (or even years) after food price increases appeared in the scene. Low-income countries for whom higher commodity prices represent a negative terms of trade shock may not have the fiscal space to finance an expansion let alone launch new social protection programs. These countries are candidates for receiving multilateral support in the form of grants or concessional loans whose destination should be to fund social protection programs to cope with rising food prices.

Are there other measures that can be implemented to help poor consumers cope with rising food prices? De Janvry and Sadoulet (2008) suggest that measures geared to increase access to land and improve the productivity of subsistence and below-subsistence farmers can be a more appropriate intervention particularly in the case of poor countries. In low-income countries between 80% and 90% of the poor live in rural areas and between two thirds and three fourths of them have access to a plot of land. However, even if they home produce some of the food they consume, most of them are net buyers of food and are hurt by higher food prices. If this group could have more access to land and/or increase the productivity of the land they already have, one could achieve two goals simultaneously. First, one could reduce the impact of higher food prices on the rural poor by lowering the amount that must be purchased by them in the market and converting those with sufficient assets into self-sufficient farmers or even marginal net sellers. Second, one could begin to address the supply-side constraints on food commodity production mentioned in Section 1 at the lower end of the spectrum. De Janvry and Sadoulet recommend that policy measures should increase the access to:

improved seeds and fertilizers for crops, and to small animals; credit to purchase inputs; more land; and, technical assistance.

World food commodities prices have risen substantially in the past few years. The impact of rising food prices on poverty has been the subject of some debate. When food prices rise (fall) poor net consumers (poor net sellers) of food get hurt and poor net sellers (poor net consumers) are better off. Available evidence suggests that in the majority of countries, an increase in food prices is likely to result in an increase in overall poverty. The appropriate policy response is to have a package of social protection programs to help those who get hurt.

Social protection programs and policies in many developing countries are lacking or inadequate. If they are to be used in future episodes of rising food prices, they need to be put in place now (Lustig, 2009). It is essential that the new or existing programs are designed in such a way so that they can increase (decrease) the size of the transfer and the number of beneficiaries when the shock occurs (unwinds). That is, they should include an "insurance" component; this is not a feature that most current programs have. In addition, governments should have mechanisms in place to ensure than when cash or in-kind transfers need to be expanded, they will have the required fiscal space.

Multilateral organizations can help countries design, implement and finance an adequate social protection system to mitigate the impact of higher food prices on poor net consumers.

References

FAO (2009). "Country Responses to the food security crisis: nature and preliminary implications of the policies pursued." Initiative on soaring food prices. Rome: FAO.

ILO, WHO (2009). "Social Protection Floor Initiative. Manual and strategic framework for joint UN country operations." Developed by the Group of Co-operating agencies and development partners, Geneva

Lustig, N. (2008) "Thought for Food: the Challenges of Coping with Soaring Food Prices." Working Paper No. 155. Center for Global Development, Washington, DC.

Lustig, N. (2009) "Coping with Rising Food Prices: Policy Dilemmas in the Developing World." Working Paper No. 164. Center for Global Development. March 2009 and Tulane Economics Department Working Paper 0907.

World Bank (2008). "Rising food prices: policy options and World Bank response." Background note for the Development Committee, Washington, D.C.

The Plundered Planet and The Bottom Billion: Why the mismanagement of nature matters for the world's most vulnerable
Paul Collier[22]

The world's most vulnerable

For over forty years the development challenge has been a rich world of one billion people facing a poor world of five billion people. This way of conceptualizing development, however, has become outdated, as about 80% of the five billion live in countries that are indeed developing, often at amazing speed. The real challenge of development is that there is a group of 58 countries, mostly in Africa and Central Asia that amount to a population of about one billion people that is falling behind. Most people in these countries are extremely vulnerable: average life expectancy is fifty years, whereas in other developing countries it is sixty-seven years; infant mortality is 14%, whereas in the other developing countries it is four percent; the proportion of children with symptoms of long-term malnutrition is 36%, against 20% for other developing countries.

Causes of vulnerability

All societies used to be poor. Although most are now lifting out of poverty, this group of countries has experienced either no or negative economic growth, even during the 1990s, the golden age between the end of the Cold War and 9/11. They have fallen into development traps that have caused them to be stuck. Poverty itself is not intrinsically a trap, otherwise we would all still be poor. The

---

[22]Paul Collier is Professor of Economics, Director for the Centre for the Study of African Economies at the University of Oxford and fellow of St. Antony's College

distinctive feature of the bottom billion countries is that they are caught in one or another of the following traps:

- **The conflict trap**: Although all societies have conflict, the form of conflict in the bottom billion societies is much more violent and pervasive (civil wars, coups d'état). Three economic characteristics make a country prone to conflict, namely low income, slow growth and dependence upon primary commodity exports. The risk that a country in the bottom billion falls into civil war in any five-year period is nearly one in six. In fact, 73% of people in these societies have recently been through a civil war or are still in one;

- **The natural resources trap**: Three main reasons explain why natural resource abundance is a trap, namely the "Dutch disease" phenomenon, volatility in commodity prices, and the fact that resources rents are likely to induce autocracy. A low-income, resource-rich society that is either an ethnically diverse autocracy or acquires the instant lopsided democracy of electoral competition without checks and balances is likely to misuse its opportunities in ways that make it fail to grow. About 29% of the people in the bottom billion live in countries in which resource wealth dominates the economy. The resource trap is not unique to the bottom billion, but it is important to them;

- **The trap of being landlocked with bad neighbours**: Geography matters, and so do your neighbours. If you are landlocked with poor transport links to the coast that are beyond your control, it is very difficult to integrate into global markets for any product. Transport costs for a landlocked country depend upon how much its coastal neighbour has spent on transport infrastructure. Furthermore, landlocked countries also depend upon their neighbours as direct markets. If the neighbouring markets are stagnant or caught in a trap themselves, the situation is aggravated. However, whether being landlocked matters at all depends upon what other opportunities are open to the country (e.g., resource wealth). 38% of the people in the bottom billion societies are in countries that are landlocked, but this is overwhelmingly an

African problem, where about 30% of the population live in landlocked, resource-scarce countries;

- **The trap of bad governance in a small country**: Bad governance and policies can destroy an economy with alarming speed, and ruin the most promising prospects. Yet, qualifiers are necessary: in the short term, if the external shocks such as export prices are sufficiently favourable, a society can get away with them; and because governance and policies are multidimensional, not all dimensions matter in all circumstances (e.g., corruption may not matter if the development strategy adopted in the country can succeed with a "minimal state" model). Thus, governance and policies matter, conditional upon opportunities.

As the bottom billion diverges from an increasingly sophisticated world economy, integration will become harder.

The significance of nature for moving out of poverty and vulnerability

Nature matters enormously for the poorest countries. Unlike the richer societies, their natural assets, such as minerals, fish and timber, are more valuable than their invested assets. But too often, these assets are being plundered. Plunder takes two forms: the few expropriate assets that should belong to the many, and the present generation burns up assets that should belong equally to the future. The issue is how to prevent such plunder.

Nature misunderstood

Nature has been moralized before it has been analyzed. It has aroused strong passions, indeed the environment is virtually our new religion. But like all religious belief, in the absence of understanding it can be dangerous. To date, the high moral ground has been occupied by romantic environmentalists whose priority is to *preserve* nature. I have no truck with the ostriches who carelessly ignore our destructive practices, but often in poor societies preservation is not the ethical imperative. Natural assets are valuable, and the best strategy will often be to harness them for development, converting them into other assets such as schools, factories and ports, that are more productive. Properly used, they are the best shot that many of the countries of the bottom billion have at prosperity. Ethical behaviour is that as natural assets are depleted, at least their equivalent value should be passed on to the future. This is a more pragmatic environmentalism that is not intrinsically at loggerheads with development.

Harnessing natural assets for prosperity

The history of exploitation of natural assets in the poorest societies is evident. Rather than let natural assets be plundered, it would be better to leave nature undisturbed. But history need not repeat itself. In order to harness natural assets a chain of economic decisions must hold. The chain starts with the discovery process: to date, contrary to popular perception, far fewer natural assets have been discovered in low-income societies than in rich societies, because the search process has been mismanaged. The next link is to ensure that the local inhabitants in the area of extraction are properly protected and compensated. To date this usually does not happen. But the rights of local communities should not usually extend to ownership. The Niger Delta should not own the oil beneath it: the revenues from oil should benefit all the children of Nigeria rather than privileging only those who happen to live closest to it.

The next link in the chain is to tax revenues from resource extraction so that the benefits accrue to society as a whole rather than to the few. In many countries at present this is going spectacularly wrong, but tax systems could be much better designed and enforced. The fourth link is to save and invest a high proportion of these revenues. This is the ethical responsibility to the future. To date, in most poor societies natural assets have been depleted for consumption rather than investment. But the investment should be domestic: the Norwegian model of a future generations fund held in foreign financial assets is usually inappropriate for poor societies. Unlike Norway, they are short of capital and need to invest at home. Unfortunately, many poor societies are now setting up Norway-style funds: fifty governments have asked Norway for advice. The final link in the decision chain is to improve the process of domestic investment. Currently, although these societies are short of capital, their investment processes are so inefficient that the return on investment can be modest. The IMF refers to this as 'limits on absorptive capacity'. While this is correct, the inference that savings should therefore be held abroad is not: the right inference is that the capacity to invest must be built. I term this link in the decision chain 'investing-in-investing' and it is likely to prove the most difficult.

The decision chain is a weakest link problem – if any link fails the result is plunder in one form or the other. What is more, the entire link has to hold again and again for at least a generation, which is what it will take to lift an impoverished society to prosperity.

The need for a critical mass of informed opinion

There is no substitute for a critical mass of informed opinion, society-by-society. The issues are sometimes about transparency and accountability. Here, the *Extractive Industries Transparency Initiative* is helping to achieve change, insisting that citizens have a right to know what revenues are flowing in, and how extraction contracts are designed. The EITI was the right place in the decision chain to start, and there are still important battles to be won. But it would be the wrong place to stop. All along the decision chain coalitions of appropriate stakeholders need to be built to help support decisions that promote the ethical exploitation of natural assets. Currently, the least energy is in the downstream issues – how money is spent – yet these are the links in the chain where typically most goes wrong.

In order to build a critical mass of informed opinion, the costs of information must be lowered and citizens must be able to assets the decisions taken in their own society against realistic benchmarks.

A new effort to provide societies with information on the decision chain is the website *http://www.naturalresourcecharter.org/*. The Natural Resource Charter is a civil society initiative completely independent of any official institution. It is overseen by Ernesto Zedillo and Mo Ibrahim, and has technical support from a team including the Nobel Laureate Michael Spence. Pitched for several different levels – citizens, journalists, and practitioners – the Charter aims to lay out in clear terms the entire decision chain. It is endorsed by the African Development Bank and promoted on the EITI website. Bringing it to the attention of citizens in resource-rich poor countries is a simple and practical way in which anyone can help to lower the costs of knowledge for these societies.

There is, of course, a vast specialist literature on the management and mismanagement of natural assets. In *The Plundered Planet* I try to make the key ideas accessible to a wide audience. Like *The Bottom Billion*, it is my attempt to build a more informed society. *The Plundered Planet* focuses on the most important opportunity that most low-income societies will face over the next decade. These societies are the last frontier for resource discoveries and, with high global commodity prices, they will be discovered. The new scramble for Africa is on: the challenge is to prevent a repeat performance.

References

Centre for the Study of African Economies at Oxford University: http://www.csae.ox.ac.uk/

Collier, P. (2007). *The Bottom Billion: Why the poorest countries are falling and what can be done about it.* Oxford: Oxford University Press.

Collier, P. (2010). *The Plundered Planet: How to reconcile prosperity with nature.* Oxford: Oxford University Press.

Extractive Industries Transparency Initiative - sets a global standard for transparency in oil, gas and mining: http://eiti.org/

Natural Resource Charter - sets out the entire decision chain and provides extensive references: http://www.naturalresourcecharter.org/

TED Talk – Paul Collier on the "bottom billion" (video): http://www.ted.com/talks/paul_collier_shares_4_ways_to_help_the_bottom_billion.html

Children in Urban Poverty: Can They Get More than Small Change?

Sheridan Bartlett[23]

It's widely recognized now that the world is more than half urban – it has been three years since we reached that turning point. Less widely acknowledged is the catastrophic extent of urban poverty or its implications for hundreds of millions of children. We are used to thinking of urban children as being better off than rural children in every way – better fed, better educated, with better access to health care and a better chance of succeeding in life. For many children, this is true. But for growing numbers, the so-called "urban advantage" is a myth.

Urban poverty widespread

How widespread urban poverty is considered depends on how you measure it. Poverty is usually defined in monetary terms. If a poverty line is set too low, only a small proportion of people appear to be poor. Most national poverty lines are misleading, because the cost of living in different places is not taken into account. It can, of course, cost a lot more to live in an urban area (especially a successful city) and in a cash-based economy. Housing and water cost more, food has to be purchased, for many getting to and from work is expensive, in short, everything has its price. Even where urban poverty lines are set a little higher than rural poverty lines, as in India, they generally fail to take into account the high cost of non-food essentials, and especially of housing. Many urban families that are earning enough to place them well above the official income poverty line may in fact be struggling to get by. Yet they are not counted among the country's poor.

[23]Sheridan Bartlett is Senior Research Associate in the Human Settlements Program at the International Institute for Environment and Development (IIED) in England. She is the managing editor of IIED's journal, Environments and Urbanization

And it's not just about money. Keetie Roelen and Geranda Notten, in the UNICEF's *Child Poverty Insights* August 2011 issue, point out that, in fact, the overlap between monetary poverty and other forms of deprivation may be quite limited. There has been growing recognition over recent decades of the multi-dimensional quality of poverty, and it is the cumulative effect of a range of deprivations that is most troubling. Neighborhood problems and access to basic services, for instance, have significant impacts even for those children whose parents have work. Poverty is not just about the capacity to afford a basic food basket; it is a matter of lack of access and exclusion in a range of areas, including basic civil and political rights, and this may be especially evident in cities.

Many urban dwellers remain effectively cut off from the benefits of citizenship. Because land ownership or renting formal housing are out of reach for so many households, they often live in unauthorized informal settlements, under bridges, along railway lines, on whatever land that is not already occupied, even though it may be hazardous or unfit for habitation. These settlements and their residents are often not recognized by the city or included in the country's census or other surveys. Children growing up here remain essentially invisible, not only uncounted but frequently unreached by any basic services. In Bishkek, Kyrgyzstan, the official population of the city was 800,000 last year. However, it is widely acknowledged that if all the people living in the settlements on the edges of the city are counted, the figure would be closer to 1.5 million. The residents of these peripheral neighborhoods, mostly migrants from rural parts of the country, live in wretched housing. There are no proper roads, no provision for water or sanitation, no schools, no health services. Children who might have had access to health services back in the village might never even see the inside of a clinic in Bishkek.

When these invisible citizens are counted and when the true cost of living and the multi-dimensional nature of poverty are factored into the equation, the numbers of people in urban poverty begin to go way up. UN Habitat estimates, for example, that one in six people in the world live in deprivation in urban slums and squatter settlements. Given the demographics of poor countries and communities, with their relatively high numbers of children, it is not unrealistic to estimate that one out of every four children in the world is living in urban poverty.

Urban poverty receives less prominence than rural poverty

Most figures show that three quarters of poverty is concentrated in rural areas. This is in part related to the unrealistically low poverty line issue and to the invisibility of many urban residents. But the tendency to rely on urban and rural averages is also very deceptive. Wealth tends to be concentrated in cities, along with many higher-level services. In most countries, the most affluent, well-educated, healthy people are urban. So average figures, whether for income or mortality or malnutrition or school attendance, look better in urban areas. But this can mask the *extent of disparities within those same urban areas and the depth of the deprivation there*. Equity is an especially poignant concern in cities, where people as deprived as those in any rural area may live side by side with the most privileged, in many cases helping to make their privilege possible.

Even urban averages in some cases are beginning to show a different story as more and more of the world's deprived people take up residence in towns and cities. In many nations, the urban advantage in health and quality of life is increasingly becoming an urban penalty. As far back as the 1990s, the gap between urban and rural infant mortality rates began to disappear in Latin America. The same thing is happening now in sub-Saharan Africa, as rural rates improve and urban rates stagnate. The gap in school enrollment rates, traditionally much higher in urban areas, is also narrowing as rural rates climb, and in a handful of countries—Bangladesh, for instance—enrollment is now higher in rural than in urban areas.

This is by no means to minimize the scale or the depth of rural poverty. There is no question that this must remain a development priority. But it's not just a question of numbers. It shouldn't matter to us whether there are *more* deprived children in rural or in urban areas. They don't cancel each other out. The concern is to understand what poverty means in their lives, and to find the most effective ways of addressing it. The intent is not to downplay the realities of rural poverty but to stress that *urban deprivation and exclusion present some different and particular challenges.* The same standards used when analyzing rural poverty cannot always be applied in identifying those at risk in urban settings, nor are the same responses always appropriate.

Particular challenges of urban poverty for girls and boys

It depends of course on a number of factors, and perhaps the most significant is the quality of local governance. Where this is inclusive and accountable, children even in low income countries may enjoy the benefits that by rights should accompany urban living – the economies of scale and proximity that can make it far more affordable to provide a decent quality of life, the levels of investment and opportunity that can help to ensure that these benefits are available to all. But in the absence of good governance, children may grow up in the grimmest conditions, which may entrench and perpetuate their poverty.

To start with, between 30% and 60% of urban dwellers in low-income countries *live without the secure tenure* that can protect them from eviction. Although this does not necessarily mean they will be evicted, people in their millions are in fact evicted every year in cities around the world, even in such democratic countries as South Africa and India. This can create terrible upheaval and distress for children and their families; social networks are destroyed, jobs lost, possessions damaged or destroyed. Many children who are in school cannot finish the year and end up dropping out. Even just the threat of eviction can mean chronic anxiety and an unwillingness to make the kinds of investments in housing and neighborhood that can provide a better environment for children and help a family over time to work its way out of poverty. Insecure tenure permeates every aspect of life. Having no formal address often means no right to vote, no access to credit or insurance, no police protection. As in Bishkek, it can mean no schools or clinics, no provision for basic amenities like sanitation, running water, waste removal or emergency services.

The sheer *concentration* of people in urban areas changes the way that many of these deprivations are experienced. Toilets, ventilation, drainage, waste collection, open space for play, the availability of recreational facilities, for instance, all become more critical in the context of high density. There may be a latrine no more than 100 metres away for instance, but this does not take into account the long time spent waiting in line or the strain that is put on these facilities. Proximity does not mean access. There may be drains, but when they end up clogged by plastic bags filled with excrement, they do little good. Global figures for "improved" water and sanitation show that urban areas are comparatively well provided. But the same standards are applied everywhere, and do not come close to meeting the minimal requirements for health in a dense settlement and with shared toilets. There is copious documentation of the implications of overcrowding and a lack of provision for rates of diarrhoeal disease, other water and food borne illnesses, respiratory illness, worms, skin and eye conditions and malnutrition, and the burdens are by far highest for young children.

Urban children can be heavily exposed to *toxics and pollutants*, living in areas contaminated by industrial waste or close to heavy traffic. There is also the rapidly growing problem of *road traffic injuries*, with urban child pedestrians facing the highest risk. This is especially the case in poor settlements without sidewalks or safe crossing lights. Urban dwellers living in poor-quality housing and in settlements without proper infrastructure are also among the groups most at risk from *disasters and the direct and indirect impacts of climate change*. Here again, children are most vulnerable – to flooding, heat stroke, water-borne illness, injury and death.

Even the simple matter of play, so essential to children's development, can be a problem in crowded urban settlements. Poor neighborhoods **can** be rich, stimulating environments for play, learning and social growth, and children in these communities may actually be better off in some ways than their more isolated peers in wealthier areas. But safety concerns and the lack of appropriate space can also mean that children are confined to small, overcrowded homes with little opportunity for *exploration or physical activity*. When small children are constantly underfoot, tempers can fray easily and the potential for harsh treatment goes up. Difficult living conditions also inevitably mean some level of neglect for young children. A lack of sanitation, long distances to water points, unsafe cooking equipment and lighting in crowded rooms, dilapidated housing, an absence of safe play space often occur in clusters; overburdened, exhausted caregivers can be forced to leave children unsupervised, to cut corners and make compromises.

Many poor urban communities are characterized by a strong social fabric, an essential support for children's well-being. But the degree of transience, crowding, insecurity and poor conditions in many settings can mean high levels of stress, undermining social capital and resulting in lower levels of reciprocity and higher rates of *crime and violence.* This is seen by many as an equity issue – clear connections have been drawn between deprivation and exclusion and the frustrations and anger that can contribute to violence. The impacts for children are powerful. Insecurity at neighborhood level restricts their mobility and can erode their right to associate with others and take part in the lives of their communities. It can lead to depression and anxiety. It also spawns violence. The most powerful predictor of violent behavior is exposure to violence, whether as an observer or a victim. Children and young people in violent communities are more likely to have problems with aggression and self-control along with lower levels of achievement in school and higher dropout rates.

People continue to migrate to cities

It's true that many migrants may just exchange one set of problems for another and still end up having trouble feeding their children. But still, the world is becoming urban at a rapid rate. By 2030 it is anticipated that 60% of the global population will live in towns and cities. To take a larger view – although urban migration is often viewed as a problem, and many countries have policies to restrict it, the fact is that the scale of economic growth in any country is closely tied to the rate of increase in the level of urbanization. Urbanization is a response to the fact that most new jobs and investments are in industries and services concentrated in urban areas. Migration plays a critical role in the strategies of individuals and households to adapt to changing realities – they go where the opportunities are.

The rate of movement is especially high for children and young people, who often move to urban areas on their own. In sub-Saharan Africa, for instance, there is *a much higher proportion of adolescents in urban areas than in rural areas*. A survey of 10 sub-Saharan countries found that a quarter of urban girls between 10 and 14 lived without either parent. Research has demonstrated that the great majority of these young migrants are not trafficked or running away. They are purposeful migrants, seeking the economic opportunities and social mobility that only towns and cities can offer. They don't want to spend their lives bent over a hoe, subject to the scrutiny of their elders.

Cities exercise enormous appeal, despite the risks – and there are many. The economic gains, after all, can be hard won. Most urban dwellers work in the informal sector with no job security; work can be irregular and poorly paid, and informal workers can be vulnerable to harassment by the police. Many individuals find it necessary to hold down two or three jobs to get by. They have to be resourceful, determined, willing to accept exploitation in many cases. This can be especially true for girls, who may be extremely vulnerable. Working as domestic servants, for example, can leave them at high risk of mistreatment. Transactional sex can in some cases be a critical survival strategy, and it is no accident that HIV rates for girls are much higher than for boys in many countries, and that these are mostly urban girls. The cost of mobility can be high indeed. But in the estimation of the millions who make this move, the gamble is worth taking.

Improving the situation for urban children in poverty
It is crucial that policymakers understand that poverty reduction approaches developed to tackle rural poverty will not necessarily work in urban settings, as the nature of urban poverty is different from that of rural poverty. In order to address child urban poverty in an effective manner, policymakers need to have a good understanding of the scale and nature of the issue. For that, accurate data and analyses of the dynamics, trends and conditions of children in urban poverty are critical. It is thus imperative to address the gaps in data collection, research, and monitoring. Governments and national and international organizations involved

in data collection should *add missing questions to their surveys* (Censuses, Demographic and Health Surveys-DHS, Multiple Indicator Cluster Surveys-MICS, etc.) and build on existing mechanisms to encourage intra-urban disaggregation of data. Community-led "enumerations" and monitoring should be supported to expand the information base while also expanding learning and organization and to increase accountability.

Understanding also what poverty means in urban children's lives, governments can more easily find ways to help their households and communities to protect their health, support their right to development, and ensure that they have the tools to cope productively with the world they live in. There are numerous effective measures to improve the health, well-being and life-opportunities of urban girls and boys in poverty, targeted at the specific deprivations they experience. Birth registration drives, improved maternal and child health care, non-formal alternatives to education, reproductive health services, vocational training, can all be extremely effective.

But it is unlikely that any intervention targeted at children and young people will have as great an impact as a focus on building the *relationship between local government and the urban poor*. Creating the decent living environments, supportive social fabric and responsive services that underpin the rights of urban children and adolescents means a concern with *policy and advocacy* at the highest level, of course, but these have to be translated into local realities. In most urban settings, local government controls most of the realities that define poverty. Local power structures, land owning patterns, political interests, bureaucratic decisions and regulations can all stand in the way of poverty reduction. Decisions about land tenure, building regulations, roads, open space, police protection, voter rolls, access to schools and health care systems – these are all controlled by local government departments and agencies. The levels of provision that are fundamental to health – decent water and sanitation, drainage and waste removal, depend on the decisions of local government. Infrastructure and services in areas where the urban poor live and work have a direct impact in their income-earning opportunities and their productivity. A lack of tenure and inadequate living conditions underpin and exacerbate the violation of many other basic rights for children, but for changes to go to scale, coordination with effective, accountable local structures is essential.

Community-driven responses, in partnership with local government, appear to have the greatest chance of effecting lasting change. There are many examples of constructive local actions by urban poor organizations and federations; inevitably, these become more effective and better able to go to scale as local governments begin to see these groups as part of the solution rather than the problem, recognizing them and building on their work. The Asian Coalition for Community Action Program is an excellent example and has managed to initiate a process of city-wide upgrading in 150 cities in Asia, in partnership with government. The concerns of children and young people clearly need to be a conscious focus within such efforts, which should draw on the experience and input of both caregivers and boys and girls of different ages.

References

Bartlett, S. (2005). "Good governance: making age part of the equation- an introduction." Children, Youth and Environments, 15, pp. 1-17.

Bhapat, M. (2009). "Poverty lines and the lives of the poor: Underestimation of urban poverty – the case of India." Poverty Reduction in Urban Areas Series, Working Paper 20.

Montgomery, M. (2009.) "Urban poverty and health in developing countries." Population Bulletin, 64(2), Population Reference Bureau.

Moser, C. (2004). "Urban violence and insecurity: an introductory roadmap." Environment and Urbanization, 16(2), pp. 3-17.

Roelen, K. and G. Notten (2011). "Child poverty in the EU: The breadth of poverty and cumulative deprivation." UNICEF Child Poverty Insights 16, Available at http://www.unicef.org/socialpolicy/files/August2011_ChildPovertyInsights_EN(1).pdf

Satterthwaite, D. (2010). *Citizen Action for Urban Poverty Reduction in Low- and Middle- income Nations.* San Francisco: Jossey Bass.

Stephens, C. (2011). "Revisiting urban health and social inequalities: the devil is in the detail and the solution is in all of us." Environment and Urbanization, 23, pp. 29-40.

Tacoli, C. and R. Mabala (2010). "Exploring mobility and migration in the context of rural—urban linkages: why gender and generation matter." Environment and Urbanization, 22, pp. 389-395.

Van den Poel, E., O'Donnell, O. and E van Doorslaer (2007). "Are urban children really healthier? Evidence from 47 developing countries." Social Science and Medicine, 65, pp. 1986-2003.

Global Inequality: Beyond the Bottom Billion
A Rapid Review of Income Distribution
in 141 Countries
Isabel Ortiz and Matthew Cummins[24]

Viewed as an "unwelcomed" and "politically sensitive" topic, world income inequality received little attention in international fora for decades. In 2004, however, the International Labour Organization (ILO) published its pioneering report on the social dimension of globalization, *A Fair Globalization*. Soon after, major development institutions began to focus flagship publications on inequality, including the United Nations 2005 Report on the World Social Situation, *The Inequality Predicament*, the United Nations Development Programme's (UNDP) 2005 Human Development Report, *Aid, Trade and Security in an Unequal World*, the World Bank's 2006 World Development Report, *Equity and Development*, and the International Monetary Fund's (IMF) 2007 World Economic Outlook, *Globalization and Inequality*. UNICEF also initiated its Global Study on Child Poverty and Disparities in 2007, and the United Nations University's World Institute for Development Economics Research (UNU-WIDER) released a comprehensive study, The World Distribution of Household Wealth, in 2008 based on its World Income Inequality Database. More recently, the World Bank opened a research line fully devoted to global inequality: Poverty and Inequality. The unanimous drive of international institutions to understand and focus attention on income disparities shows that inequality can no longer be avoided in development policy discussions.

This paper focuses exclusively on income inequality. While income is just one measure of inequality, it is often closely associated with social inequalities in terms of coverage and outcomes. There are

[24]Isabel Ortiz is Associate Director, Policy and Practice, UNICEF
Matthew Cummins is Social and Economic Policy Specialist, Division of Policy and Practice, UNICEF

other inequalities; precisely, UNICEF supports a multidimensional approach to poverty, based not only on income poverty, but on other deprivations like access to food, water, health, education, shelter, information and others.[25]

This paper: (i) provides an overview of global, regional and national income inequalities based on the latest distribution data from the World Bank, UNU-WIDER and Eurostat; (ii) discusses the negative implications of rising income inequality for development; (iii) calls for placing equity at the center of development in the context of the United Nations development agenda; (iv) describes the likelihood of inequalities being exacerbated during the global economic crisis; and (v) advocates for urgent policy changes at national and international levels to ensure a "Recovery for All." To serve as a general reference source, Annex 2 provides a summary of the most up-do-date income distribution and inequality data for 141 countries.

1. Income Inequality at the Global Level

How unequal is our world in terms of income distribution? Our analysis of global inequality trends builds on earlier work by UNDP (1992, 1999 and 2005), Bourguignon and Morrisson (2002), Sutcliffe (2004) and Milanovic (2005). There are two common approaches for estimating global income distribution—the global and inter-country accounting models—and we estimate the results using both typologies. We first present the results in terms of market exchange rates and then discuss them under purchasing power parity (PPP) exchange rates (see Box 1 for discussion on income estimates and different exchange rates).

The purpose of this section is to provide a general picture as to how global income inequality has likely evolved between 1990 and 2007 and not to enter into the theoretical debate that underpins the art and science of distribution estimates, which involves, *inter alia*, accounting models, income metrics and exchange rates. As a result,

---

[25]UNICEF has produced an array of publications on different inequalities/deprivations facing women, children and poor families. See http://www.unicef.org/socialpolicy/index_43137.html.

we provide a detailed summary of the methodology used, along with the main challenges and caveats regarding our estimations at the end of the paper.

1.A.   Market exchange rates

We first look at global income distribution using market exchange rates, where all national income estimates are compared in constant 2000 U.S. dollars. Figure 1 and Table 1 show the distribution of world income from 1990 to 2007 according to the *global* accounting model, which decomposes national income by population quintiles and compares those across countries. This includes all individuals for which data is available, from the poorest quintile in the Democratic Republic of Congo to the richest quintile in Luxembourg (see Table 2). Annex 2 provides quintile information for all countries. The distribution data reveal an incredibly unequal planet. As of 2007, the wealthiest 20% of mankind enjoyed nearly 83% of total global income compared to the poorest 20%, which had exactly a single percentage point under the global accounting model. Perhaps more shocking, the poorest 40% of the global population increased its share of total income by less than one percent between 1990 and 2007.

Figure 1. Global Income Distribution by Population Quintiles, 1990-2007 (or latest available) in constant 2000 U.S. dollars

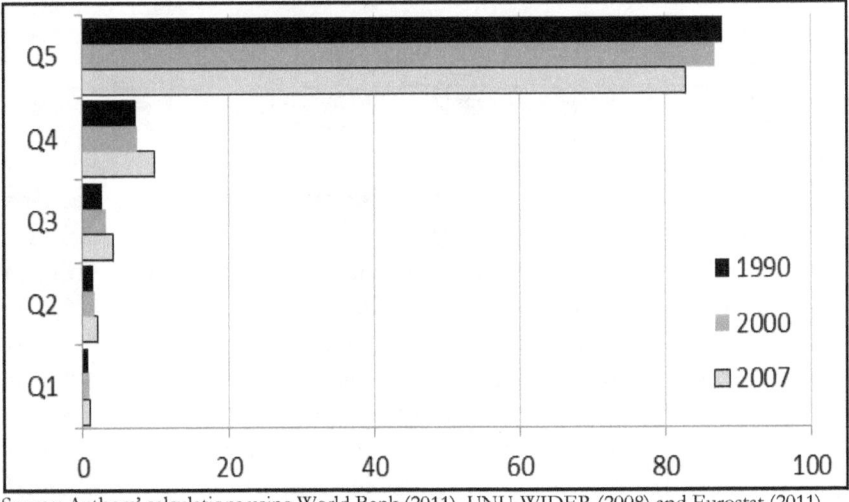

Source: Authors' calculations using World Bank (2011), UNU-WIDER (2008) and Eurostat (2011)

Table 1. Summary Results of Global Income Distribution by Population Quintiles, 1990-2007 (or latest available) in constant 2000 U.S. dollars

	Global Distribution (%)		
	1990	2000	2007
Q5	87.0	86.8	82.8
Q4	8.1	7.5	9.9
Q3	2.8	3.2	4.2
Q2	1.4	1.6	2.1
Q1	0.8	0.8	1.0
# of observations	100	126	135
% of global	86.3	91.1	92.4
% of global GDP	79.0	81.4	82.6

Source: Authors' calculations using World Bank (2011), UNU-WIDER (2008) and Eurostat (2011)

Table 2. Poorest and Richest Population Quintiles in the World, 2007 (or latest available) in constant 2000 U.S. dollars

Poorest				Richest			
Country	Q	GDP per capita	Population	Country	Q	GDP per capita	Population
Congo, DRC	1	26	12,504,557	Luxemb.	5	104,189	95,999
Congo, DRC	2	43	12,504,557	US	5	96,946	60,316,000
Liberia	1	47	725,457	Singapore	5	76,189	917,720
Haiti	1	49	1,944,017	Switzerland	5	73,404	1,510,223
Burundi	1	49	1,567,596	Norway	5	70,184	941,831
Niger	1	50	2,827,937	Luxemb.	4	63,986	95,999
Guinea-Bissau	1	51	308,208	Ireland	5	63,507	871,386
Malawi	1	52	2,887,899	UK	5	58,408	12,196,061
Cen. Afr. Rep.	1	60	851,481	Denmark	5	56,421	1,092,288
Congo, DRC	3	65	12,504,557	Sweden	5	55,543	1,829,618

Source: Authors' calculations using World Bank (2011), UNU-WIDER (2008) and Eurostat (2011)
Q = income quintile

The severity of inequality in global income distribution is perhaps best depicted by a distinctive three-dimensional figure based on country population quintiles. In Figure 2, each vertical column represents the income of one quintile of one country. Here, the tallest block in the back corner reflects the income of the richest quintile of the population of Luxembourg, while the column that is barely discernible in the nearest corner represents the income of the poorest quintile of the population of the Democratic Republic of Congo. Overall, this figure captures data for 135 countries as of 2007 using constant 2000 U.S. dollars.

Figure 2. A Visualization of Global Income Distribution, 2007
(or latest available) in constant 2000 U.S. dollars

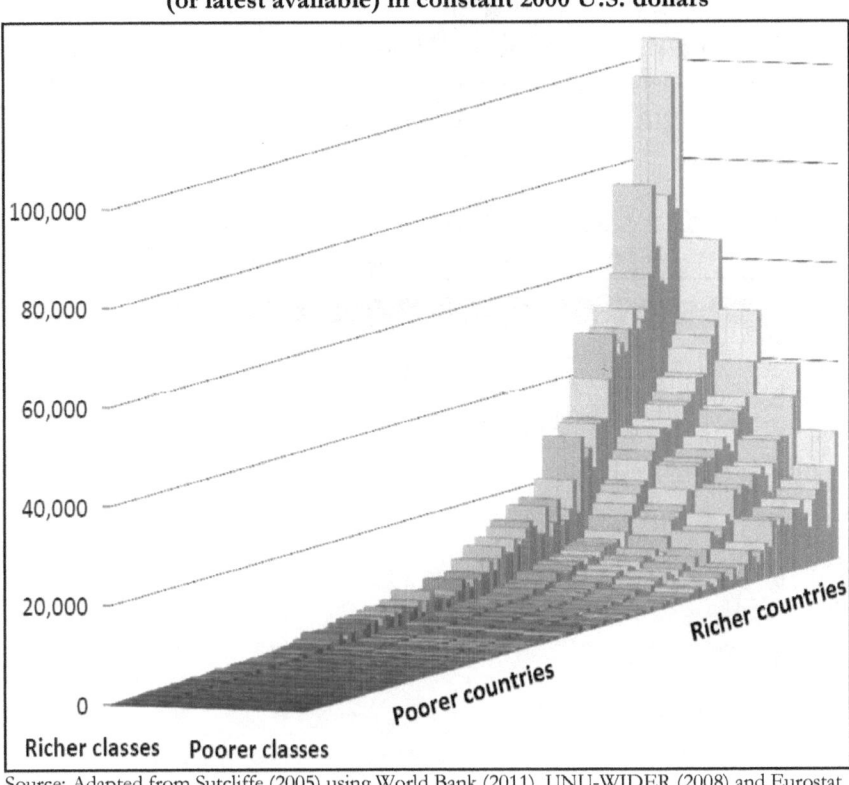

Source: Adapted from Sutcliffe (2005) using World Bank (2011), UNU-WIDER (2008) and Eurostat (2011)

However, not all countries have distribution data. As Table 1 shows, we have data for 100 countries in 1990, 126 countries in 2000 and 135 countries in 2007 (Annex 2). Still under market exchange rates, we now turn to a second approach to measuring global income distribution, which is known as the *inter-country* accounting model. This method looks at the average income differences between large groupings of countries by treating all members of a country as if they have the same income and then dividing the world into population quintiles. This method is less precise, but allows us to estimate global income distribution for most of the world, a total of 182 countries in 2007. Figure 3 and Table 3 present the income distribution results from 1990 to 2007. Here, the wealthiest 20% of the population enjoyed more than 81% of the world's income as of 2007, with the poorest 20% holding on to just over one percent. Similar to the global accounting model, the rate of change for the poorest 40% of the world population remains dismal at one percent between 1990 and 2007. The poorest and richest countries in the world as of 2007 are listed in Table 4 according to the inter-country accounting model under market exchange rates.

Figure 3. Global Income Distribution by Countries, 1990-2007 (or latest available) in constant 2000 U.S. dollars

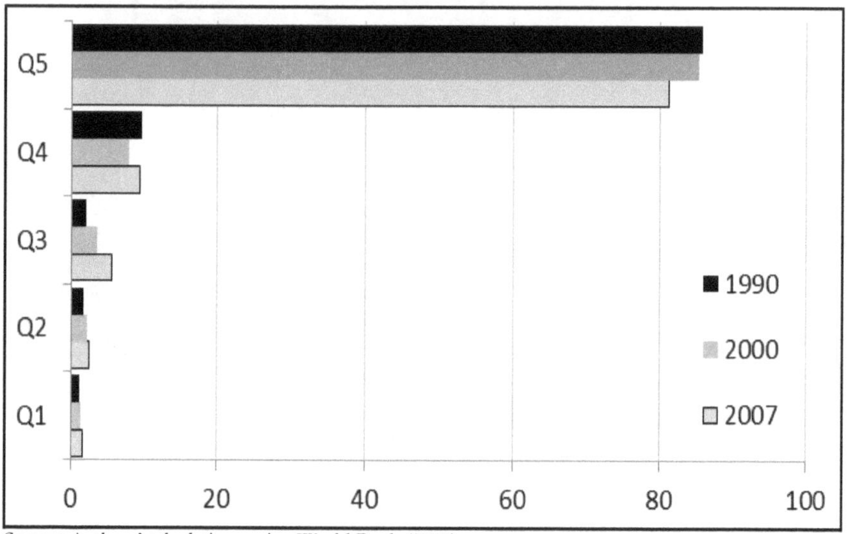

Source: Authors' calculations using World Bank (2011)

Table 3. Summary Results of Global Income Distribution by Countries, 1990- 2007

| | Inter-country Distribution (%) | | |
	1990	2000	2007
Q5	85.7	85.2	81.2
Q4	9.6	7.9	9.4
Q3	2.0	3.5	5.6
Q2	1.6	2.1	2.4
Q1	1.2	1.3	1.4
# of observations	173	180	182
% of global	97.0	97.6	97.6
% of global GDP	98.3	98.3	98.1

Source: Authors' calculations using World Bank (2011)

Table 4. Poorest and Richest Countries in the World, 2007
(or latest available) in constant 2000 U.S. dollars

Poorest 10 percent			Richest 10 percent		
Country	GDP per capita	Population	Country	GDP per capita	Population
Congo, DRC	94	62,522,787	Monaco	106,466	32,620
Burundi	110	7,837,981	Bermuda	72,296	64,000
Guinea-Bissau	140	1,541,040	Luxembourg	56,625	479,993
Liberia	144	3,627,285	Norway	41,901	4,709,153
Malawi	148	14,439,496	Japan	40,707	127,770,75
Eritrea	151	4,781,169	United States	38,701	301,580,00
Niger	171	14,139,684	Iceland	38,166	311,566
Ethiopia	176	78,646,128	Switzerland	37,935	7,551,117
Tajikistan	231	6,727,377	Qatar	34,960	1,137,553
Cen. Afr. Rep.	231	4,257,403	Hong Kong	34,041	6,925,900

Source: Authors' calculations using World Bank (2011)

1.B.   PPP exchange rates

The earlier set of findings for the global accounting model was based on market exchange rates. But what happens if we compare national income estimates using PPP-adjusted exchange rates?

Box 1. Two Different Benchmarks for Measuring GDP or Income

There are two main methods of comparing national income estimates across countries. The first uses the market exchange rate, which is the actual rate in the foreign exchange market. And the second uses the PPP exchange rate—the rate at which the currency of one country would have to be converted into that of another country to buy the same amount of goods and services in each country. The pros and cons of using PPP-adjusted exchange rates to estimate national income are briefly summarized below.

Drawbacks of PPP: The biggest downside to using PPP rates is that they are much harder to measure than market-based rates. The International Comparisons Program (ICP) was established by the United Nations and the University of Pennsylvania in 1968 to generate PPPs, which involves gathering national average prices for 1,000 closely specified products in participating countries (the previous round was held from 2003-06 and covered 146 countries). Apart from the vast amount of work, there are methodological questions regarding price surveys, meaning that PPP rates are unlikely to be consistent over time or between different estimates (Callen 2007).

The so-called "substitution bias" is another weakness of PPP exchange rates. This refers to the practice of assigning U.S. prices to services consumed by people in developing countries. In reality, however, U.S. prices for services tend to be much higher than those in developing countries, and PPP-derived income estimates are likely to be inconsistent with actual consumption structures and result in artificial substitution (Dowrick and Akmal 2005). Similar to this is the fact that it is unrealistic to compare countries with very different consumption patterns.

A further drawback to using PPPs is contrasting results. While there are three available series of PPP-adjusted GDP data—Maddison, Penn World Table and World Bank—all of which are based on the PPP rates produced by the ICP, comparing these different sources produces significant variations across countries. This means that PPP income estimates will vary according to the data source selected (Sutcliffe 2003).

Advantages of PPP: Many argue that PPP rates are better than market rates when comparing GDP across countries because PPP attempts to measure this value at a common set of prices. In particular, the exchange rate measure implies that all national output is sold on world markets and that all national consumption is imported—a very unrealistic assumption often referred to as the "traded sector bias." Since non-traded goods and services tend to be cheaper in low-income countries when compared to higher-income countries, any analysis that fails to take these price differences into account will underestimate the purchasing power of consumers in developing countries and, consequently, their overall welfare or income share. PPP exchange rates further have the advantage of being relatively stable over time whereas market rates are more volatile.

Does it make a difference? The per capita income gap between the richest and poorest global population quintiles—as well as individual countries—is reduced under PPP exchange rates according to our estimates, a finding that reflects the well-known fact that PPP exchange rates are higher than market ones. Some countries also move up or down the income scale depending on the metric used. Irrespective of method, however, income disparities remain exceptionally high.

Figure 4 and Table 5 show the distribution of world income from 1990 to 2007 using a PPP dataset in constant 2005 international dollars. While the overall picture of global inequality improves under the PPP measure, the data still confirm grave income disparities. As of 2007, the top 20% of the world controlled about 70% of total income compared to just two percent for the bottom 20%. Regarding change, the poorest 40% of the global population increased its share of total income by a meager 1.7% between 1990 and 2007. Table 6 lists the ten highest and lowest income quintiles for the world in 2007 using PPP exchange rates, and Figure 5 presents the three-dimensional illustration of income distribution also under PPP-adjusted exchange rates.

Figure 4. Global Income Distribution by Population Quintiles, 1990-2007 (or latest available) in PPP constant 2005 international dollars

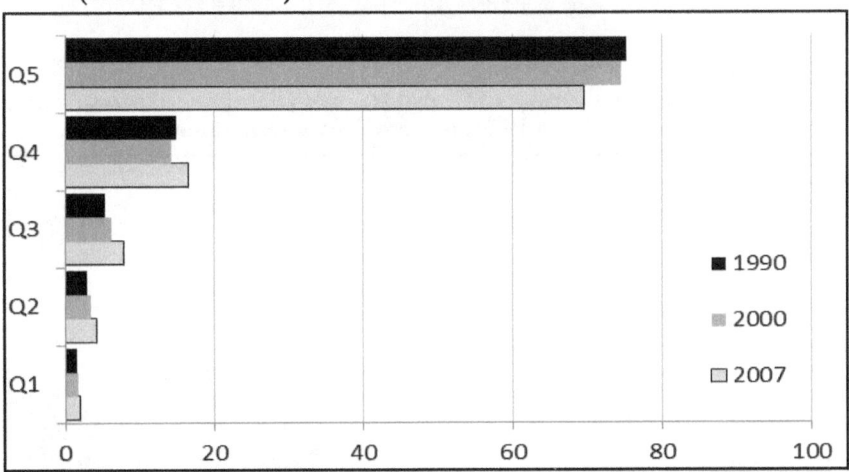

Source: Authors' calculations using World Bank (2011), UNU-WIDER (2008) and Eurostat (2011)

Table 5. Summary Results of Global Income Distribution by Population Quintiles, 1990-2007 (or latest available) in PPP constant 2005 intl. $

| | Global Distribution (%) | | |
	1990	2000	2007
Q5	75.3	74.4	69.5
Q4	14.9	14.2	16.5
Q3	5.4	6.3	7.8
Q2	3.0	3.4	4.2
Q1	1.5	1.7	2.0
# of observations	99	127	136
% of global	86.1	91.1	92.4
% of global GDP	85.3	87.4	88.6

Source: Authors' calculations using World Bank (2011) and UNU-WIDER (2008)

**Table 6. Poorest and Richest Population Quintiles in the World, 2007
(or latest available) in PPP constant 2005 international dollars**

Poorest				Richest			
Country	Q	GDP per capita	Population	Country	Q	GDP per capita	Population
Congo, DRC	1	77	12,504,557	Luxembourg	5	136,936	95,999
Liberia	1	113	725,457	Singapore	5	121,781	917,720
Congo, DRC	2	129	12,504,557	United	5	109,373	60,316,000
Haiti	1	132	1,944,017	Luxembourg	4	84,096	95,999
Burundi	1	156	1,567,596	Norway	5	81,739	941,831
Niger	1	175	2,827,937	Ireland	5	80,832	871,386
Cen. Afr. Rep.	1	178	851,481	Switzerland	5	73,248	1,510,223
Lesotho	1	191	406,335	Canada	5	72,032	6,595,200
Congo, DRC	3	193	12,504,557	Seychelles	5	70,113	17,006
Liberia	2	199	725,457	Netherlands	5	69,311	3,276,339

Source: Authors' calculations using World Bank (2011), UNU-WIDER (2008) and Eurostat (2011)
Q = income quintile

**Figure 5. A Visualization of Global Income Distribution in 2007
(or latest available) in PPP constant 2005 international dollars**

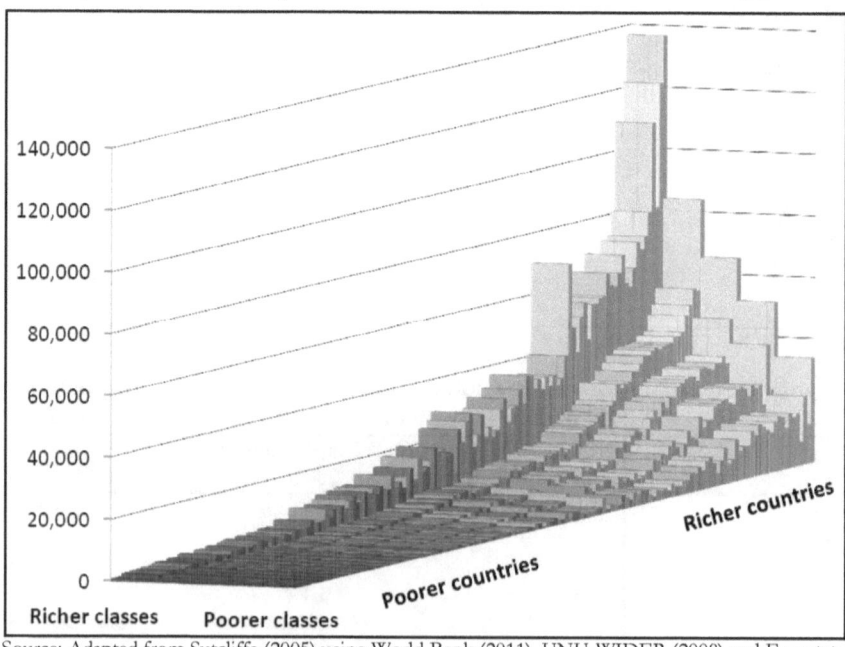

Source: Adapted from Sutcliffe (2005) using World Bank (2011), UNU-WIDER (2008) and Eurostat
(2011)

We also present the inter-country accounting model using PPP estimates in order to allow us to see the picture for almost the entire world countries instead of a smaller set of countries (Figure 6 and Table 7). As in the PPP-adjusted global accounting model, inequality marginally improves under this method, but world income disparities are still severe. Whereas the top 20% of the global population controlled about 64% of total income as of 2007, the bottom 20% had just over three percent. Similarly, in terms of change, the poorest 40% of the global population increased its share of total income by only three percentage points over nearly two decades. Table 8 lists the ten highest and lowest income quintiles for the world in 2007 under PPP exchange rates.

Figure 6. Global Income Distribution by Countries, 1990-2007 (or latest available) in PPP constant 2005 international dollars

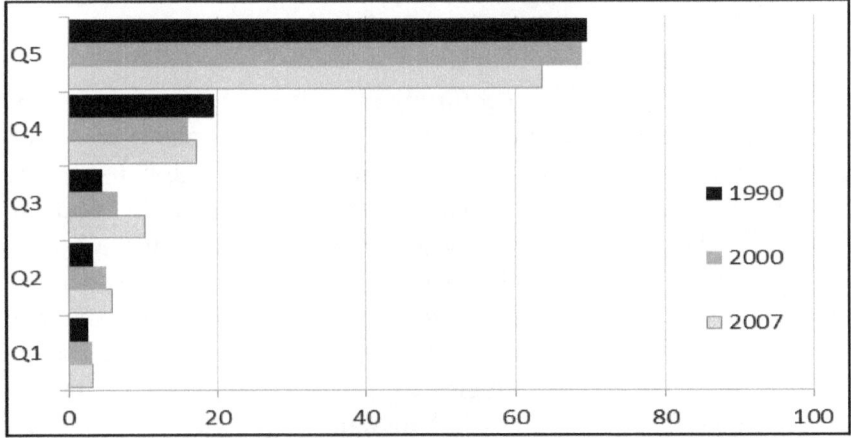

Source: Authors' calculations using World Bank (2011)

Table 7. Summary Results of Global Income Distribution by Countries, 1990-2007 (or latest available) in PPP constant 2005 international $

	Inter-country Distribution (%)		
	1990	2000	2007
Q5	69.7	69.0	63.6
Q4	19.7	16.1	17.2
Q3	4.6	6.7	10.2
Q2	3.4	5.1	5.8
Q1	2.7	3.1	3.2
# of observations	168	174	174
% of global	96.9	97.4	97.4
% of global GDP	98.2	98.3	98.2

Source: Authors' calculations using World Bank (2011)

Table 8. Poorest and Richest Countries in the World, 2007
(or latest available) in PPP constant 2005 intl. dollars

Poorest 10			Richest 10		
Country	GDP per capita	Population	Country	GDP per capita	Population
Congo, DRC	281	62,522,787	Qatar	75,415	1,137,553
Burundi	349	7,837,981	Luxembourg	74,422	479,993
Liberia	350	3,627,285	UAE	52,944	4,363,913
Eritrea	599	4,781,169	Singapore	49,739	4,588,600
Niger	599	14,139,684	Norway	48,800	4,709,153
Timor-Leste	675	1,064,141	United States	43,662	301,580,000
Cen. Afr. Rep.	683	4,257,403	Ireland	41,136	4,356,931
Malawi	697	14,439,496	Hong Kong	39,958	6,925,900
Sierra Leone	702	5,420,400	Switzerland	37,854	7,551,117
Mozambique	741	21,869,362	Netherlands	37,466	16,381,696

Source: Authors' calculations using World Bank (2011)

1.C.   The takeaway

Both income distribution accounting models offer strikingly similar results. Under market exchange rates, we inhabit a planet in which the top quintile controls more than 80% of global income contrasted by a paltry percentage point for those at the bottom. While the disparity improves under PPP exchange rates (67% to 2.6%), both models reveal a world that is deeply corroded by income disparities. Each of the accounting methods and exchange rate scenarios also suggest that some progress is taking place for the poorest; however, the sluggish pace of change is clearly unacceptable. Using the rate of change under the global accounting model with market exchange rates, it took 17 years for the bottom billion to improve their share of world income by 0.18 percentage points, from 0.77% in 1990 to 0.95% in 2007 (see Q1 in Table 1). At this speed, it would take more than eight centuries (855 years to be exact) for the bottom billion to have ten percent of global income.[26]

---

[26]Under PPP-adjusted exchange rates, it would take about three centuries (272 years) (see Q1 in Table 5).

2. Global Income Inequality Trends and the Poor, Children and Women

While the previous section showed the vast income inequalities that characterize our world, this section sets out to answer some of the more pressing questions regarding the overlying trends and impacts of this reality. In particular, what do we know about global inequality trends over a longer-term horizon? What do the extreme distortions in income distribution at the global level mean for different groups, such as the poor, children, women or the middle classes? And are there alternative measures of wealth that could shed further light on the overall state of global inequality at present?

2.A. Income inequality in historical perspective

What do we know about world income inequalities over the past centuries? Studies using longer time series conclude that income inequality has been constantly increasing since the early 19th century. Milanovic (2009), for example, calculates Gini indices[27] over time and finds that global income inequality rose steadily from 1820 to 2002, with a significant increase from 1980 onwards (Table 9).[28] To further inform the more recent trajectory, Cornia (2003) concludes that inequality increased globally between the early 1980s and 1990s following a review of different studies. While our analysis shows some reversal of this trend, there is a significant likelihood that income inequality is being exacerbated in the ongoing global economic crisis (Section 8).

Table 9. Estimated Global Gini Indices, 1820-2002	
Year	Gini
1820	43.0
1850	53.2
1870	56.0
1913	61.0
1929	61.6
1950	64.0
1960	63.5
1980	65.7
2002	70.7

Source: Milanovic (2009)

---

[27]The Gini index is the most commonly used measure of income inequality, where 0 is perfect equality (e.g. each person has exactly the same income) and 1 is perfect inequality (e.g. one person has all income). See Box 2 for a more detailed discussion on Gini indices.

[28]See Annex 2 for Gini index values for most countries in recent years.

2.B.   The poor

What does global inequality mean for the poor? An illustration of global income disparities adapted from UNDP (1992 and 2005) helps to contextualize the extremity of inequality that faces an incredibly large number of poor persons. In Figure 7, global income distribution resembles a "champagne glass" in which a large concentration of income at the top trickles down to a thin stem at the bottom. Overall, this provides a powerful graphic in terms of the scant amount of income that is available to the poor on a global scale. In particular, approximately 1.2 billion were living on less than $1.25 per day in 2007 (22% of the world population) and about 2.2 billion on less than $2 per day (or about 40% of the world population).[29] An alternative way of viewing the "champagne glass" is to compare the top percent of world income earners versus the bottom. In doing so, we find that the wealthiest 61 million individuals (or one percent of the global population) had the same amount of income as the poorest 3.5 billion (or 56%) as of 2007.

Figure 7. Global Income Distributed by Percentiles of the Population in 2007 (or latest available) in PPP constant 2005 international dollars*

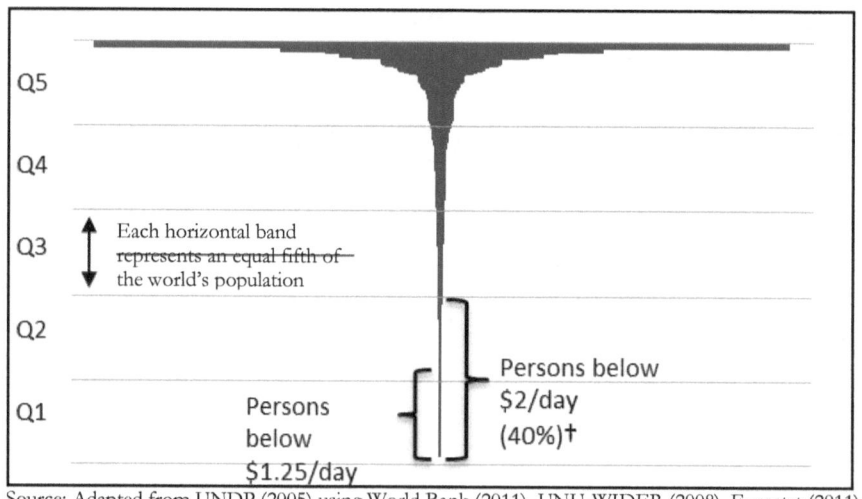

Source: Adapted from UNDP (2005) using World Bank (2011), UNU-WIDER (2008), Eurostat (2011)
* According to the global accounting model
† Based on Chen and Ravallion (2008)

---

[29]Based on PPP estimates in constant 2005 international dollars from Chen and Ravallion (2008).

2.C. Children and youth

How does the global distribution of income affect children and youth? At the global level, most children live in the poorest income quintiles (Figure 8). When comparing the concentration of youth populations across global income distribution quintiles, we find that about half (48.5%) of the world's young persons are confined to the bottom two income quintiles. This means that out of the three billion persons under the age of 24 in the world as of 2007, approximately 1.5 billion were living in situations in which they and their families had access to just nine percent of global income. Such findings are not shocking given that poorer families tend to have higher fertility rates. Moving up the distribution pyramid, children and youth do not fare much better: more than two-thirds of the world's youth have access to less than 20% of global wealth, with 86% of all young people living on about one-third of world income. For the just over 400 million youth who are fortunate enough to rank among families or situations atop the distribution pyramid, however, opportunities abound with more than 60% of global income within their reach.

Figure 8. Global Income Distribution and Children/Youth in 2007 in PPP constant 2005 international dollars*

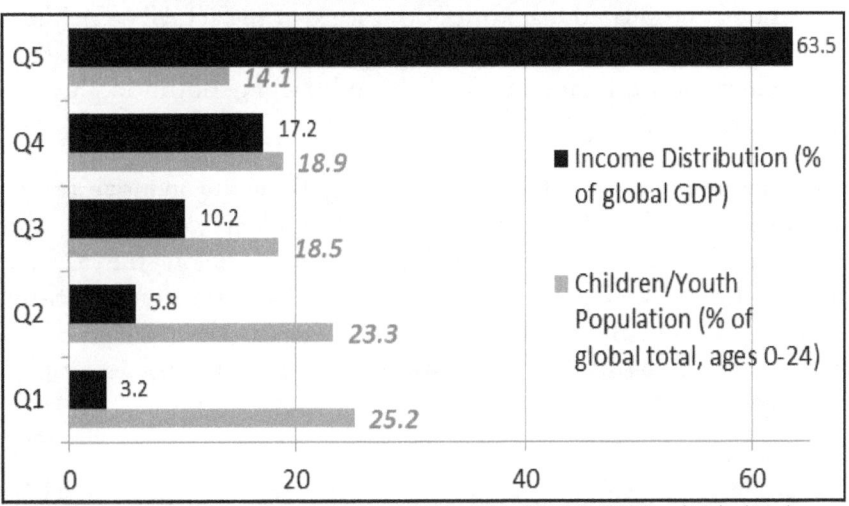

Source: Authors' calculations using World Bank (2011), UNU-WIDER (2008) and United Nations (2009)

* According to the inter-country accounting model

2.D. Women

Unlike children and youth, using the same data and methodology, the distribution of income at the global level does not appear to have a disproportionate, negative impact on women (Figure 9). When examining the percentage of females across global income distribution quintiles, we find that the dispersion is, in fact, nearly equal, with each income quintile containing about 20% of the global female population. Given that the female-to-male ratio was about 1:1 as of 2007,[30] this comes as little surprise. This finding remains unchanged even when further restricting the global female population to girls and young women: about half of women 24 years old or younger are situated in the bottom two income quintiles, which mirrors the proportion of children and youth as presented in Figure 8.[31]

In sum, using this methodology, the global distribution of income has a much stronger impact on age than gender, largely reflecting higher fertility rates among poorer women. This is not to say that intra-household income disparities don't exist; however, based on the available aggregate income data at the global level, it is not possible to identify the dispersion of income among household members. It should be noted that this does not imply that other gender and age-related disparities do not exist. In fact, UNICEF has long advocated for a multidimensional approach to addressing inequalities beyond income, such as education, nutrition, health, information, etc.[32]

Still, the numbers of adult women and girls living in poverty are alarming. As of 2007, roughly 20% of women were below the $1.25/day international poverty line, and 40% below the $2/day mark. Girls and younger women also suffer disproportionately from poverty, as more than one-quarter of females under the age of 25 were below the $1.25/day international poverty line, and about half on less than $2/day.

---

[30]According to United Nations (2009), females slighted outnumbered males globally in 2007—51.1% to 48.9%.
[31]These findings apply to both the inter-country and global accounting models.
[32]Please visit the following website for more information:
http://www.unicef.org/gender/index.html.

**Figure 9. Global Income Distribution and Gender in 2007
in PPP constant 2005 international dollars***

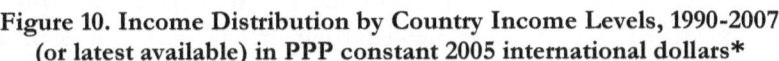

Q5
63.5
21.1
13.8

Q4
17.2
20.0
18.4

Q3
10.2
19.4
19.2

Q2
5.8
19.7
22.5

Q1
3.2
19.8
26.1

■ Income Distribution (%
of global GDP)

▨ Female Population (% of
global)

▢ Girls/Young Female
Population (% of global,
ages 0-24)

0   20   40   60

Source: Authors' calculations using World Bank (2011), UNU-WIDER (2008), United Nations (2009)
* According to the inter-country accounting model

2.E.   Middle classes

Looking at distribution information across country income groupings (e.g. low-, middle- and high-income) adds further insight into the evolution of income inequality in the world (Figure 10 and Table 10). Viewed from this perspective, there are two striking observations. One is the extremely high level of inequality that characterizes middle-income countries. The second is the relative loss of income—or absence of change—of the middle and lower classes in favor of the wealthier, upper-income groups in both low- and high-income countries over time.

**Figure 10. Income Distribution by Country Income Levels, 1990-2007
(or latest available) in PPP constant 2005 international dollars***

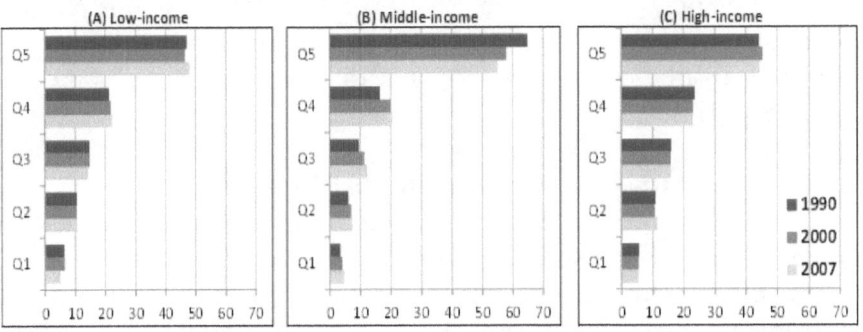

Source: Authors' calculations using World Bank (2011), UNU-WIDER (2008) and Eurostat (2011)
* According to the global accounting model

Table 10. Summary Results of Income Distribution by Income Levels, 1990-2007 (or latest available) in PPP constant 2005 international dollars*

	Low-income			Middle-income			High-income		
	1990	2000	2007	1990	2000	2007	1990	2000	2007
Q5	47.1	46.5	48.1	64.9	58.0	55.2	44.2	45.4	44.4
Q4	21.3	21.9	22.4	16.4	19.9	20.6	23.5	23.0	22.9
Q3	14.7	14.8	14.1	9.4	11.2	12.2	16.0	15.7	16.0
Q2	10.5	10.4	10.5	5.9	7.0	7.4	10.8	10.5	11.2
Q1	6.3	6.4	4.9	3.4	4.0	4.7	5.5	5.3	5.4
# of observations	31	26	17	49	70	74	33	31	31
% of global pop.	4.8	7.9	9.9	66.1	69.3	69.0	15.2	14.0	13.5
% of global GDP	0.6	0.8	1.0	29.7	32.0	38.5	55.0	54.5	49.1
% of sample	5.6	8.6	10.7	76.8	76.0	74.7	17.7	15.4	14.6
% of sample GDP	0.7	1.0	1.2	34.8	36.7	43.4	64.5	62.4	55.4

Source: Authors' calculations using World Bank (2011), UNU-WIDER (2008) and Eurostat (2011)
* According to the global accounting model

While most of middle-income countries increased inequality in recent years, it is important to note that middle classes and—to a lesser extent—poorer-income groups seem to be getting an increasing share of income in recent years. This advance is still vulnerable and needs to be quickly accelerated in the 21st century (Ravallion 2009).

Middle classes and poorer-income groups appear to be doing worse in both low- and high- income countries—for the benefit of the richest quintile. This has generated debate on how states need to meet the welfare needs of all of their citizens, including the middle classes who are critical for nation building (Birdsall 2010). From an equity point of view, what is clear is that growth and development should not only be "pro-rich," as it tends to be now, but ensure equitable outcomes for all. For lower-income countries, this implies evolving from "poverty reduction" to "inclusive development" (Deacon 2010).

2.F. Alternative metrics: Wealth distribution

It is important to note that income inequality measures, which are often based on household consumption, do not capture other household wealth, such as financial assets, real estate and savings instruments that high-income groups commonly possess. Some recent studies do include metrics for wealth, and they offer an even more unequal depiction of our world (Table 11). For instance, ILO (2008:44) estimates that the global Gini index based on wealth was 89.2 in 2000, a number which is significantly higher than most measures of global income inequality. And according to UNU-WIDER, the top ten percent of adults own 85% of global household wealth; the average member of the top decile has nearly 3,000 times the mean wealth of the bottom decile (Davies et al. 2008:7).

Table 11. Wealth Inequality in Selected Countries

Country	Wealth Gini (2000)	Income Gini	Year
Argentina	74.0	50.1	2005
Australia	62.2	31.2	2003
Bangladesh	65.8	33.5	1996
Brazil	78.3	56.6	2004
Canada	66.3	31.5	2000
China	55.0	44.9	2003
France	73.0	27.8	2000
Germany	67.1	31.1	2004
India	66.9	36.5	1997
Indonesia	76.3	39.6	1996
Italy	60.9	33.3	2000
Japan	54.7	31.9	1998
South Korea	57.9	37.2	1998
Mexico	74.8	49.9	2004
Nigeria	73.5	52.2	1996
Pakistan	69.7	39.8	1996
Spain	56.5	33.6	2000
Taiwan	65.4	33.9	2003
Thailand	70.9	42.7	2001
United States	80.1	46.4	2004
Viet Nam	68.0	37.3	1998

Source: Davies et al. (2008:9)

Having teased out some of the broader trends and implications of income and other inequalities at the global level, the following sections turn to income inequality at the regional and country levels.

3. Income Inequality across Regions

The recent publication of the Standardized World Income Inequality Database (SWIID) (Solt 2009) allows us to compare the evolution of income inequality in a sample of 141 countries from 1990-2008 using Gini indices (see Box 2 for a discussion on Gini indices).

Box 2. Gini Indices and Caveats

The Gini index is the most commonly used measure of income inequality. It is derived from the Gini coefficient, which is based on the Lorenz curve whereby 0 is perfect equality (e.g. each person has exactly the same income) and 1 is perfect inequality (e.g. one person has all income).

Selecting Gini indices to gauge national income inequality can be just as controversial as selecting distribution estimates, especially when comparing across countries (See Annex 1). In fact, most of the contention revolves around the same issues: differing household survey methodologies within and across countries—which are the basis for estimating Gini coefficients—and large data gaps over time. It is also important to note that Gini indices cannot be compared globally due to the different assumptions behind their calculations.

The SWIID (Solt 2009) is the most comprehensive attempt at developing a cross-nationally comparable database of Gini indices across time. The SWIID standardizes Gini estimates from all major existing resources of inequality data, including UNU-WIDER (2008), the World Bank's PovcalNet, the Socio-Economic Database for Latin America, Branko Milanovic's World Income Distribution data, and the ILO's Household Income and Expenditure Statistics, as well as a host of national statistical offices and other sources. Overall, the SWIID includes Gini estimates for gross and net income inequality for 171 countries from 1960 to 2009 and allows us to examine changes in *net income inequality* for 132 countries between 1990 and 2008. While this is, of course, far from the ideal set of Gini indices—all methodology caveats remain fully valid—it is the best database currently available.

The development of Gini indices across regions over the past two decades reveals mixed trends regarding income inequality (Table

12). According to 2008 Gini index estimates based on Solt (2009), Latin America and the Caribbean is the region with the highest levels of income inequality, and Sub-Saharan Africa is not far behind. On the other side of the spectrum, high-income countries emerge as the most equal group of countries—by a wide margin—with Eastern Europe and Central Asia ranking as the second most equal region.

**Table 12. Gini Index Values by Region, 1990-2008
(or latest available)* (unweighted average values)**

Region	1990	2000	2008	1990-2008 Change	2000-2008 Change
Asia	36.4	40.0	40.4	4.0	0.6
Eastern Europe/Central Asia	26.7	33.2	35.4	8.7	2.2
Latin America and Caribbean	46.9	49.2	48.3	1.5	-1.3
Middle East and North Africa	39.2	39.2	39.2	0.0	0.0
Sub-Saharan Africa	49.1	46.1	44.2	-4.8	-1.8
High-income Countries	27.4	30.8	30.9	3.5	0.0
Number of Observations	137	140	141	132	132

Source: Authors' calculations using Solt (2009)
* Gini index values based on net income

In terms of change, Eastern Europe and Central Asia along with Asia appear as the worst performers on average, having increased their Gini indices by nearly nine and four points, respectively, between 1990 and 2008. These regions also emerge as the worst performers over the nearer term, with 2.2 and 0.6 point increases, respectively, in their Gini indices since 2000. Sub-Saharan Africa, on the other hand, achieved the biggest gains towards increasingly equality by reducing its Gini index by about five points, on average, between 1990 and 2008. Sub-Saharan Africa also ranks as the best performer over the nearer term, as its regional Gini index decreased by about two points from 2000 to 2008, although Latin America and the Caribbean is close behind having reduced by about 1.3 points, on average, according to Solt (2009). Table 13 lists countries by region that achieved the biggest improvements in terms of income inequality since 2000.

Table 13. Top Performers in Reducing Inequality, 2000-8 (or latest available) [based on change in Gini index according to Solt (2009)]	
Asia	
Thailand	-4.0
Malaysia	-3.0
Philippines	-2.6
Mongolia	-2.0
Eastern Europe and Central Asia	
Azerbaijan	-14.7
Moldova	-4.9
Latin America	
Brazil	-4.6
Peru	-3.4
Argentina	-3.4
Chile	-3.2
Paraguay	-2.9
El Salvador	-2.4
Bolivia	-2.2
Mexico	-2.2
Panama	-2.1
Nicaragua	-2.0
Venezuela	-2.0
Middle East and North Africa	
Egypt	-2.9
Iran	-2.4
Sub-Saharan Africa	
Lesotho	-7.9
Malawi	-6.4
Ethiopia	-4.8
Burundi	-4.6
Mali	-4.6
Sierra Leone	-4.2
Burkina Faso	-4.0
Uganda	-3.5
Nigeria	-3.4
Gabon	-3.2
Swaziland	-2.9
Guinea	-2.6
Cameroon	-2.5
Senegal	-2.5
Niger	-2.3
High-income Countries	
Estonia	-4.1
New Zealand	-3.3
South Korea	-2.8
Spain	-2.3
Belgium	-2.2
Sweden	-2.2
Croatia	-2.1

Further examination reveals diverse inequality patterns within each of the regional groupings (see Figures 11-16). Asia offers an interesting mix (Figure 11). On the one hand, China and India—the most populous countries in the world—stand as examples of high growth (average annual GDP per capita growth rates of 10.1% and 6.3%, respectively, between 1990 and 2008, based on World Bank, 2011) and increasing income inequality (their respective Gini indices jumped by 12.2 and 3.8 points over the same time period). While income inequality permeates most Asian countries, there are exceptions such as Malaysia and Thailand, who are visibly reducing inequality through universal social policies, including basic education and health (Jomo and Baudot 2007).

As an aggregate, transition economies of Eastern Europe and the former Soviet Union, including the Russian Federation, have experienced the highest spikes in income inequality (Figure 12). The transition from centrally planned to more liberal regimes appears to have led to detrimental outcomes in terms of equity, due to the social impacts of privatization, changes in tax/transfer systems, financial and labour market liberalization, reliance on commodity exports, and migrant remittances, among others (Cornia 2010, Simai 2006).

Data for Latin America and the Caribbean suggest a varied, yet gravely unequal, region (Figure 13). Much of this appears to be rooted in historically unequal patterns in land tenure, ethnic discrimination and limited taxation coupled with the more recent effects of privatization and liberalization beginning in the early 1990s. Since 2000, however, the region has demonstrated significant signs of progress on the equality front, as 16 of the 21 countries with data experienced a decline in their Gini index between 2000 and 2008. Much of this reflects the combination of macroeconomic and social protection policies, which have been adopted widely throughout the region (Cornia and Martorano 2010, Lopez-Calva and Lustig 2010). According to Solt (2009), some of the Latin American countries that have recorded the largest improvements in inequality since 2000 include Argentina, Bolivia, Brazil, Chile, El Salvador, Mexico, Panama, Paraguay and Peru, all of which reduced their Gini indices by more than two points.

Compared to other regions, the Middle East and North Africa presents a more challenging assessment (Figure 14). This largely reflects the limited availability of data. For the observations that are afforded, however, two major trends appear. The first is that there appears to be general parity across the region in terms of income equality. Second, it seems that there has been very little change over time in either direction, whether improving or worsening equality. The exception here appears to be Yemen, which increased its Gini index by five points from 2000-08 according to Solt (2009). Yet such findings should be taken with caution. In particular, the wave of social unrest that swept across the Middle East and North Africa in early 2011 suggests that, perhaps, levels of inequality are more severe than official estimates indicate.[33]

Although Sub-Saharan Africa, on the aggregate, has some of the highest income inequalities in the world, there is a trend toward improvement (Figure 15). Since the 1990s, the biggest reductions have been reported in Cameroon, Gabon, Guinea-Bissau, Lesotho, Malawi, Senegal and Sierra Leone, all of which reduced their Gini

---

[33]This paper does not question the reliability of income distribution information reported in the main sources used for this analysis (e.g. Egypt and Pakistan appear as equal as France). See Annex 1 for description of caveats.

indices by ten or more points. Much of the major improvements in inequality, however, appear to have taken place during the 1990s. While the average reduction in a country's Gini index value was 7.3 points, on average, between 1990 and 2000, this fell to 3.3 points between 2000 and 2008. In any case, the best performers over the near period include Burundi, Ethiopia, Lesotho, Malawi, Mali and Sierra Leone, all of which reduced their Gini index values by two or more points since 2000.

Despite the positive signs of progress, the region still hosts some of the world's most unequal countries, including Namibia and South Africa. For high-income countries in our sample, which cover a broad mix of countries from North America, Eastern and Western Europe, and the Pacific Rim, among others, a wide range of trends are evident (Figure 16). On the one hand, Estonia, Hong Kong, Israel, Japan, Latvia, Slovakia and Slovenia are cases of significant increases in income inequality when looking at the 1990-2008 time period, all of which increased their Gini indices by six or more points. On the flip side, Denmark, Ireland, South Korea, and Trinidad and Tobago are successful examples of reducing income disparities over the last decades. In the more recent period, Belgium, Croatia, Estonia, New Zealand, Spain, South Korea and Sweden stand out as having reduced income inequality, each of which lowered its Gini index value by two or more points since 2000. Also interesting is the fact that many of the larger high-income countries achieved negligible change in inequality since 2000, as the Gini indices in Austria, Canada, France, Italy, Poland and the United States increased or decreased by less than one point.

Figures 11-16. Gini Indices and Changes by Region, 1990-2008
(or latest available)

Figure 11. Asia

Figure 12. Eastern Europe and Central Asia

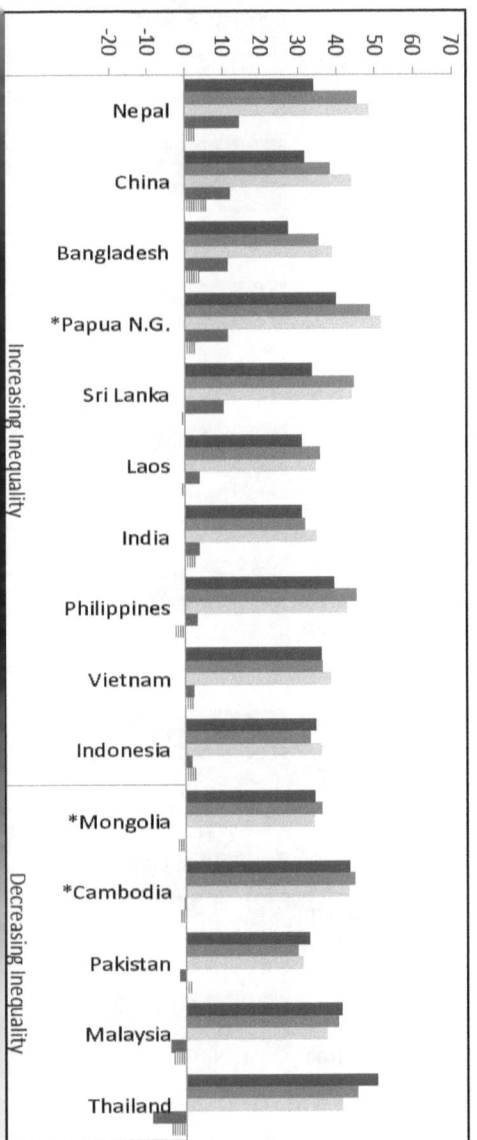

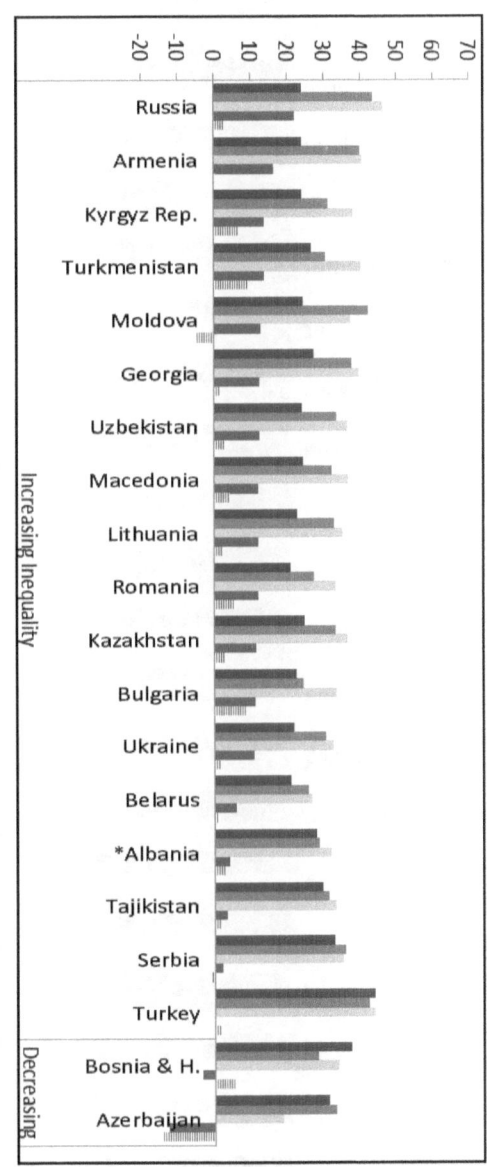

Source: Solt (2009)
* 1990 value reflects circa 1995

■ 1990
■ 2000
▨ 2008 (or latest available)
■ Change (2008-1990)
▨ Change (2008-2000)

Figure 13. Latin America and the Caribbean

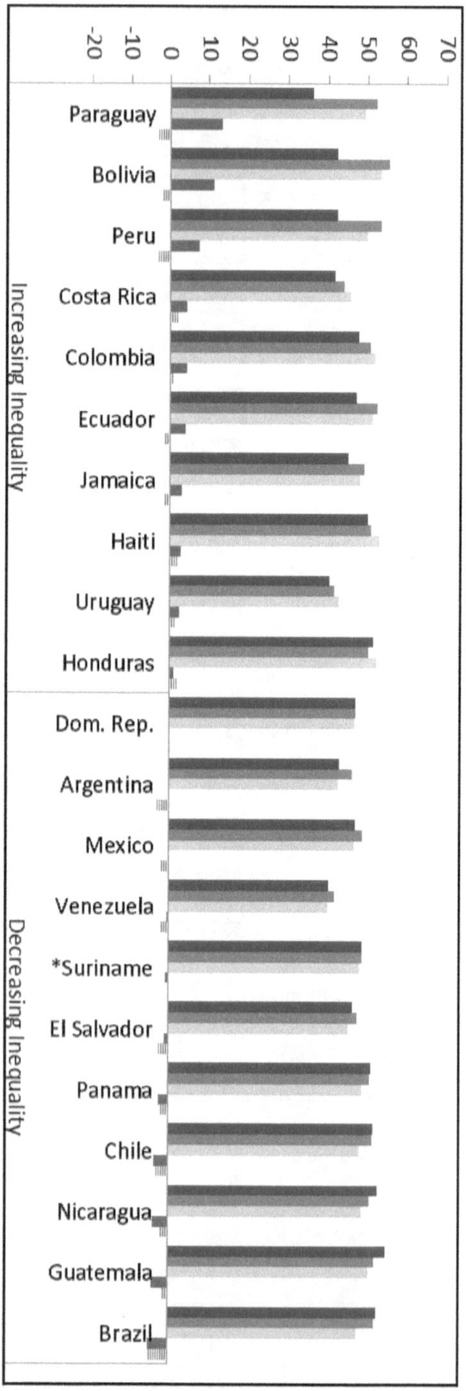

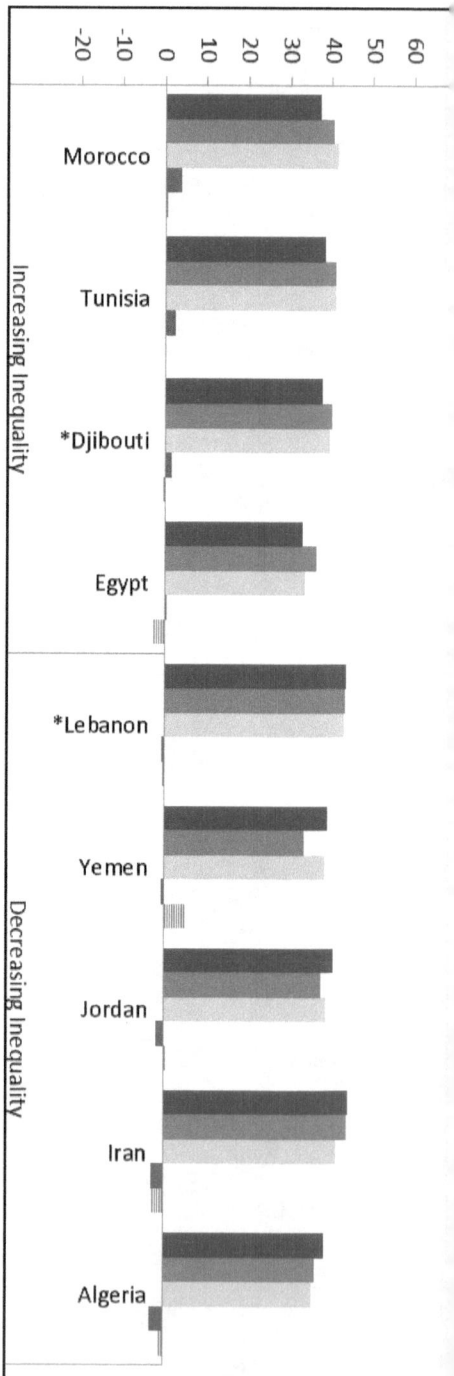

Figure 14. Middle East and North Africa

Figure 15. Sub-Saharan Africa

Figure 15. Sub-Saharan Africa

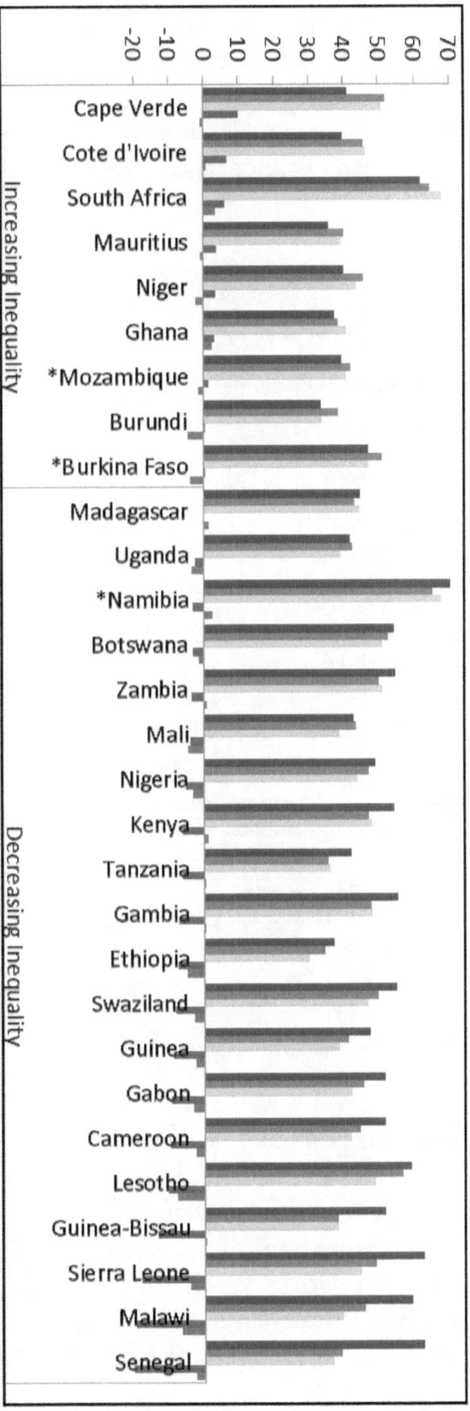

Figure 16. High-income Countries

Figure 16. High-income Countries

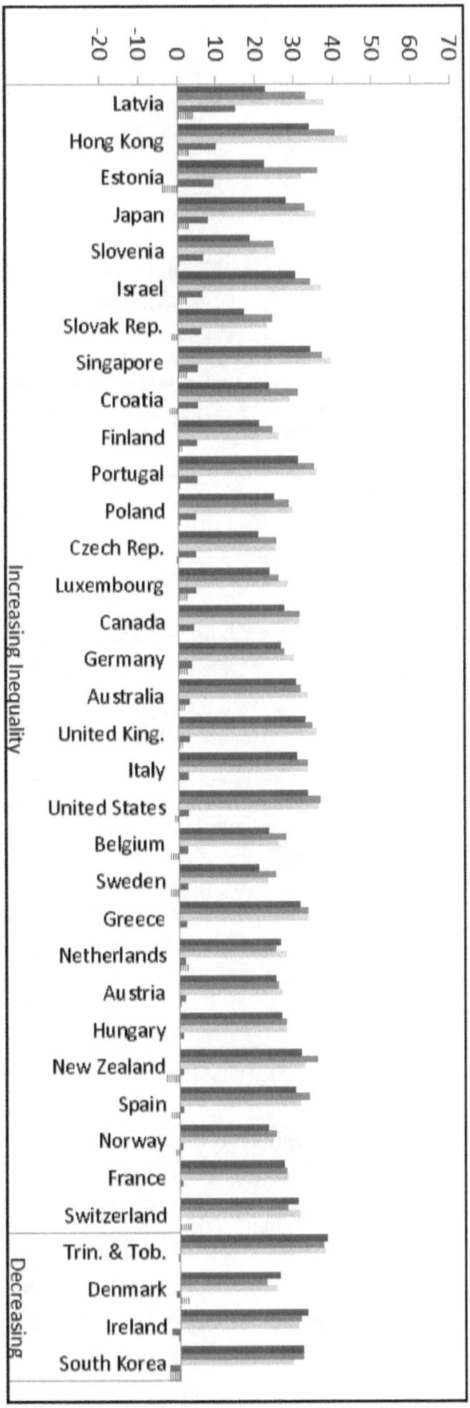

4. Income Inequality at the National Level

Looking at income distribution quintile estimates using recent data, some of the highest national disparities are found in countries like Colombia, Nepal, Russia and Zambia, despite recent governments' efforts to address it, while some of the most equal societies are found in countries like Australia, Azerbaijan, France and Sweden (Figure 17).

Figure 17. Snapshot of High and Low Inequality in Selected Countries, 2007 (or latest available)

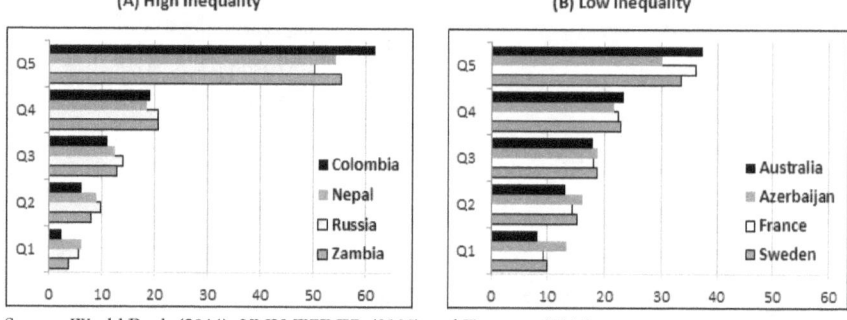

Source: World Bank (2011), UNU-WIDER (2008) and Eurostat (2011)

Figure 18. GDP Growth and High Inequality in Selected Countries, 1990-2005

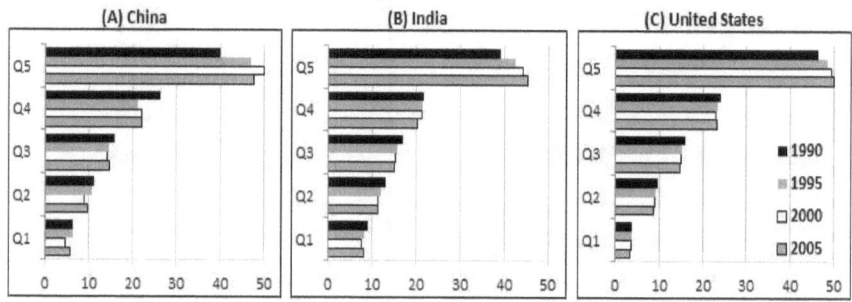

Source: World Bank (2011) and UNU-WIDER (2008)

Such differences could lead us to think that equality is a result of fast or sustained GDP growth over long periods of time. However, this is not necessarily the case. Income distribution data in China, India and the United States, which have ranked among the largest and strongest growing economies in the world over the past decades, suggest otherwise (Figure 18). In all three cases, significant and sustained economic growth (annual GDP per capita growth of

9.8%, 6.0% and 3.1%, respectively, between 1990 and 2005) has not led to more equal societies, but rather made the rich relatively richer and the poor relatively poorer (see top and bottom quintiles).

Perhaps most interestingly income inequality is significantly decreasing in countries like Brazil, Malawi and Malaysia, which have also experienced strong and consistent economic growth in recent years (they all experienced an average annual GDP per capita growth of roughly three percent between 1990 and 2005, which increases to 2.1%, 4.4% and 7.9%, respectively, if controlling for the impacts of the late-1990s Asian financial crisis) (Figure 19).

Figure 19. GDP Growth and Decreasing Inequality in Selected Countries, 1990-2005

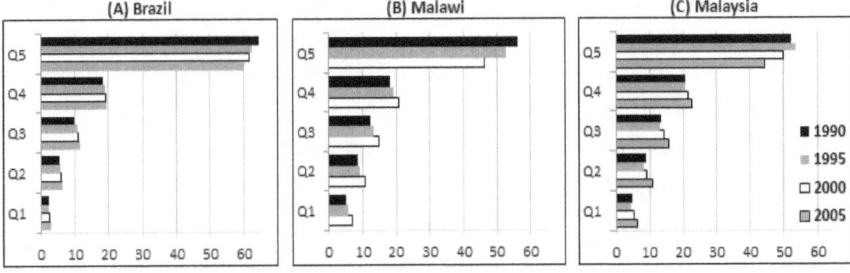

Source: World Bank (2011), UNU-WIDER (2008) and Eurostat (2011)

This suggests that, ultimately, addressing inequality depends on a society's willingness to reduce social disparities by financing equitable policies through taxes and investments. Addressing equity is at the center of the social contract between governments and citizens: how much a society is willing to redistribute and how to do so. But what happens if a society is unwilling or unable to address inequality?

5. Why Income Inequality is Dysfunctional

There is a vast literature documenting the effects of income inequality across a broad spectrum of economic and social indicators. It is not our purpose to offer a detailed review or to debate the merits of some of the more controversial topics, especially in terms of causality. Rather, the aim of this section is simply to highlight some of the key perils that are associated with high levels of income inequality both across countries—in terms of economic growth, health and social well-being, and political stability—as well as within countries—in terms of social inequalities, especially among children. Building on existing research, we also present updated empirical analyses where possible.

5.A. Slows economic growth

Some argue that income inequality is necessary for economic growth, following initial analysis by Simon Kuznets in the 1950s. Supporters of this position advise governments to invest in growth as a first priority, believing that the benefits will eventually "trickle down" to the poor. The argument is based on the following: (i) since the rich save more, higher inequality means higher rates of savings, investment and future growth; (ii) poverty and a flexible labour market keep wage levels cheap and encourage investment; and (iii) taxation on higher income groups should be limited to maximize the retained income available for investment. Such views are still influential in development debates, mostly via vague "trickle down plus" approaches that focus on growth first with some basic education, health and other limited social interventions.

Evidence, however, suggests otherwise. Alesina and Rodrick (1994), Bourguignon (2004) and Birdsall (2005), among others, have shown that developing countries with high inequality tend to grow more slowly. We build on Birdsall's analysis using more recent data and an expanded sample of countries, and we also look at changes in inequality over time alongside economic growth rates. For the 131 countries that allow us to estimate the change in Gini index values between 1990 and 2008, we find that, on the aggregate, those countries that increased levels of inequality experienced slower annual per capita GDP growth over the same time period ($\varrho=$ -0.20). Moreover, the strong negative correlation between high inequality and high growth remains virtually unchanged when restricting the sample to developing countries only (94 countries) ($\varrho=$ -0.19) (Figure 20).

Figure 20. Growth and Inequality: Per Capita Growth and
Change in Income Inequality in 94 Developing Countries,
1990-2008 (or latest available)

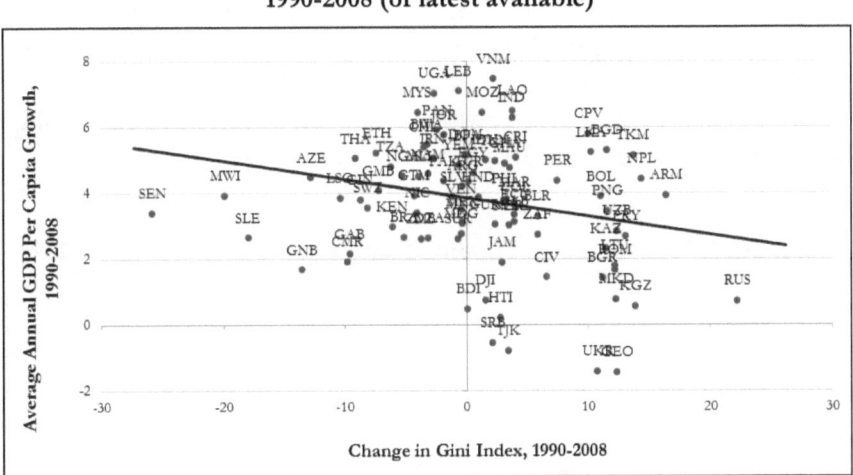

Source: Authors' calculations using World Bank (2011) and Solt (2009)

5.B.   Results in health and social problems

Wilkinson and Pickett (2010) examine the relationship between
income inequality and eleven unique health and social problems.
They carry out empirical tests across a group of OECD countries as
well as the 50 states in the United States. Among both settings, the
results clearly show that health and social outcomes are substantially
worse in more unequal societies. In particular, individuals in more
equal societies, *inter alia*, enjoy better health, live longer, are less
likely to experience mental illness, perform better in school, use less
illegal drugs, engage in less criminal behaviour, have better social
mobility, are more trusting, experience less violence and are less
likely to be teenage mothers when compared to those living in more
unequal societies.

One of Wilkinson and Pickett's most significant contributions was
the development of the International Index of Health and Social
Problems (IHSP). The composite index covers 23 OECD countries
and includes the following indicators: homicides, imprisonment,
infant mortality, life expectancy, maths and literacy score, mental
illness, obesity, social mobility, teenage births and trust. To date, the
IHSP offers perhaps the most comprehensive cross-national

snapshot of social outcomes without including an income parameter, which makes it an ideal source for income inequality analysis. We present Wilkinson and Pickett's compelling graphic, which captures the overall findings of their research, by placing the IHSP alongside the most up-to-date inequality data (Figure 21).[34] This unique dataset demonstrates a very strong relationship between increasing levels of inequality and greater health and social problems ($\varrho = 0.54$).

Figure 21. Income Inequality and Health and Social Problems, 2008

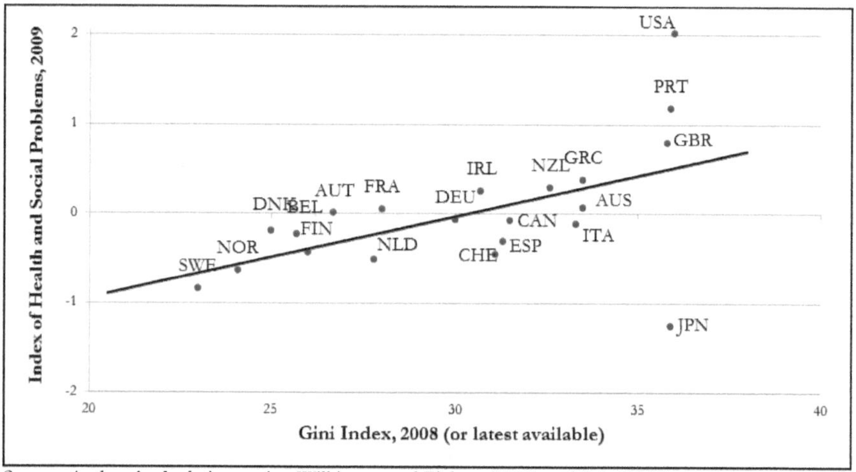

Source: Authors' calculations using Wilkinson and Pickett (2010) and Solt (2009)
Note: Lower index values represent better health and social outcomes.

While data limitations preclude us from testing the IHSP over a wider range of countries, we are able to examine income inequality and one particularly pressing social problem, violence (Figure 22). Looking at homicide rates and Gini indices across a sample of 138 countries, we find that countries characterized by high levels of inequality tend to be much more violent ($\varrho = 0.57$)

[34]Most of their data sources span the early 2000s, and the authors' also use inequality measures from UNDP that are dated (circa 2005). Figure 22, therefore, provides a more recent picture of the relationship between the IHSP and income inequality, especially in terms of Gini indices.

Figure 22. Income Inequality and Homicides in 138 Countries, 2008

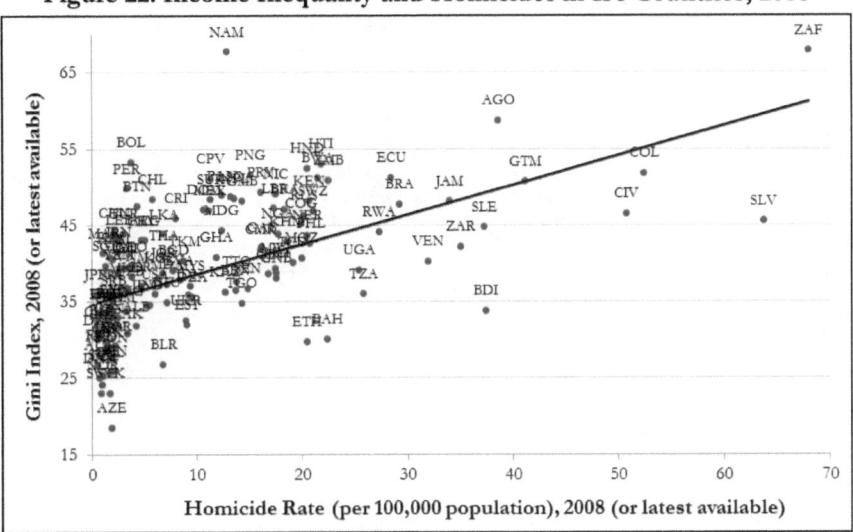

Sources: Authors' calculations using Solt (2009) and United Nations Office on Drugs and Crime (2008)

5.C.   Generates political instability

Given the predominance of health and social ills across more
unequal societies, there is little surprise that inequality is also
strongly associated with political instability. While the sources of
political conflict vary from country to country, conflict generally
originates from severe social grievances, including class conflict and
the perception of inequality among ethnic, religious or other
groups. Using one of the six dimensions included in the Worldwide
Governance Indicators (WGI) project (Kaufmann et al. 2010), we
find that unequal societies, in general, are much more prone to
political instability, or, in other words, to be destabilized or
overthrown by unconstitutional or forceful means, which includes
politically-motivated violence and terrorism ($\varrho = -0.33$) (Figure 23).

Figure 23. Income Inequality and Political Stability in 141 Countries, 2008

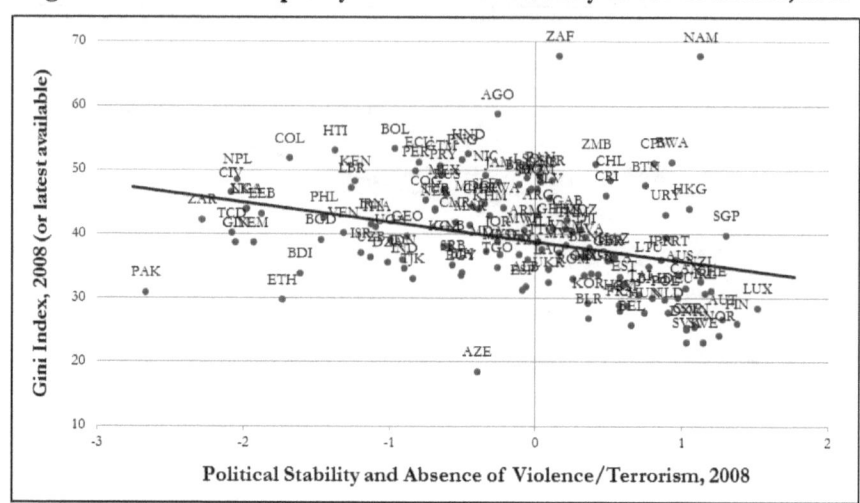

Sources: Authors' calculations using Solt (2009) and Kaufmann et al. (2009)
Note: -2.5 is high political instability and politically-motivated violence/terrorism and 2.5 is absence of.

5.D.   Leads to more severe social inequalities, especially among children

In addition to poorer growth, more health and social problems, and greater political instability, income inequality is also associated with graver social inequalities, among children in particular. UNICEF's 2010 Report Card 9 (UNICEF 2010a)[35] offers a compelling analysis of social inequalities in terms of child well-being by assessing three dimensions of inequality—including material, education and health—among a sample of rich countries. Given our interest in understanding the relationship between income and different social disparities, we adjust the overall child equality score by removing the material indicator and re-calculating country scores based on education and health scores alone.[36] This gives us a good estimate for levels of basic education and health inequality among 24 OECD

---

[35]The Report Card series is founded on the premise that a country's real economic and social progress is gauged by how well it cares for its children— their health and safety, material security, education and socialization, and inclusion in society, among others

[36]National education scores are based on literacy in reading, math and science, and national health scores reflect self-reported health complaints, healthy eating and physical activity.

countries, which we then compare to income inequality as measured by Gini index values (Figure 24). The data reveal a strong negative relationship between greater income inequality and lower levels of education and health inequalities as experienced by children ($\varrho = -0.28$).

Figure 24. Income and Education/Health Inequalities, 2010
(or latest available)

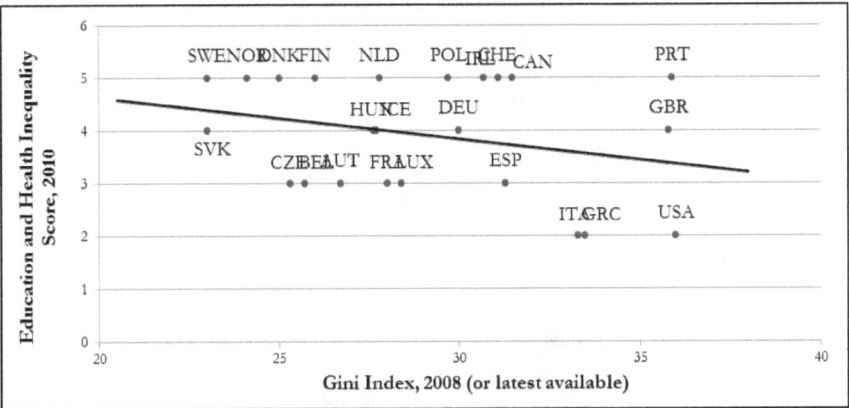

Source: Authors' calculations using UNICEF (2010) and Solt (2009).
Note: Higher scores equal greater education and health equality among children

As in earlier analyses, data limitations prevent us from examining a larger cohort of countries, but the strong relationship between income inequality and other social inequalities most certainly applies to developing countries. UNICEF (2010b) offers very conclusive evidence in its analysis of household survey data from across the developing world. In particular, children from developing country households in the poorest income quintile are:

- Less than half as likely to have benefited from antenatal care while in the womb
- Three times less likely to have been delivered by a skilled health professional at birth
- Less than half as likely to be registered after birth
- Nearly three times as likely to be underweight
- Twice as likely to be stunted
- Less than half as likely to sleep under insecticide-treated bed nets

- Nearly twice as likely to not receive measles immunizations
- Twice as likely to die before their fifth birthday
- Significantly less likely to have access to improved drinking water sources
- Less likely to attend primary school
- Much less likely to benefit from malaria interventions
- Three times as likely to get married before the age of 18 (for girls)

than those children from households in the richest income quintile of the same country.

In sum, there is overwhelming evidence that those at the bottom of the income chain are those most likely to be excluded from essential health care services, improved water and sanitation facilities, and primary and secondary education, among others. Moreover, in many instances trends in social inequalities can be exacerbated over time. In India, for example, 166 million people gained access to improved sanitation between 1995 and 2008, but little progress was made in the poorest households, which furthered social inequalities (UNICEF 2010b:43). In West and Central Africa, measles immunization coverage increased by ten percent in the wealthiest quintile of the population but only three percent in the poorest quintile, thus widening the gap in social inequalities (UNICEF 2010b:25).

6. Beyond the Bottom Billion: Bringing Equity to the Development Agenda

Given that the bottom billion requires urgent attention to alleviate their enduring hardships, social progress in the 21st century requires much greater efforts. To start with, attention needs to focus on the fact that the world's policy-making is accruing mostly to the top billion.

The extreme inequality in the distribution of income globally, regionally and nationally, coupled with the resounding negative effects associated with higher levels of income disparities, should make us question the current development approach (development for whom?) and the need to place equity at the center of the development agenda.

6.A.   Striking the right balance between equity and growth

From an historical perspective, Maddison (2006) shows that the rise of global GDP per capita over the past two centuries was largely driven by the industrial revolution in Western Europe and the United States along with a few countries that managed to position themselves as strategic exporters (Table 14). The extraordinary increase in GDP among these countries enabled them to become hegemonic and influence global policy in their own interest (Gilpin 1987, Chang 2003, Reinert 2007). Many developing countries did not grow as they could have in recent decades (Reddy and Minoui 2006). For developing countries to emerge, a similar employment-intensive productive development push is needed, as well as an international setting favorable to it.

Table 14. Per Capita GDP in Selected Countries and Regions, 1-2000*

Country / Region		1	1000	1500	1600	1700	1820	1900	1950	2000
Main Dri-vers	W. Europe	599	425	798	907	1,032	1,243	3,076	5,018	20,090
	United States	400	400	400	400	527	1,257	4,091	9,561	28,403
	Australia	400	400	400	400	400	518	4,013	7,412	21,549
	New Zealand	...	400	400	400	400	400	4,298	8,456	16,178
	Argentina	...	...	...	...	...	...	2,756	4,987	8,544
	Chile	...	...	...	...	...	694	2,194	3,670	10,311
Other Reg-ions	East Europe	412	400	496	548	606	683	1,438	2,111	5,901
	Former USSR	400	400	499	552	610	688	1,237	2,841	4,454
	Latin America	400	400	416	438	527	691	1,113	2,503	5,893
	Asia	456	470	568	574	572	581	638	717	3,807
	Africa	472	425	414	422	421	420	601	890	1,474
World Average		467	453	566	596	615	667	1,262	2,113	6,055

Source: Maddison (2006)
* In 1990 international Geary-Khamis dollars

An inclusive development agenda promoting employment and universal social policies was a key ingredient to legitimizing governments and nation building in the past. The late industrializers (Box 3) followed this pattern: they implemented universal social policies that ensured the buy-in of the middle classes and simultaneously focused on reducing poverty (Mkandawire 2006, Deacon 2010). This differs radically from today's standard development formula based on growth that benefits the highest income quintiles accompanied by a few targeted safety nets for the poorest.

Box 3. Lessons from the Late Industrializers

The development trajectory of most of the "late industrializers" was predicated on a strong integration of economic and social policies. Social policies tended towards universalism, benefiting all citizens and financed by tax contributions (providing public services only to the poor undermines the middle class commitment to pay taxes). Some of the late industrializers opted for universal services and social security from the outset, such as Holland and the Nordic countries. Others introduced universalism gradually, like Germany and Japan, where welfare was first directed to groups whose cooperation in economic modernization and nation-building was deemed indispensable by the government—the "productive" working and middle classes—and, over time, new beneficiaries were added by specifying new eligibility criteria.

Sources: Mkandawire (2006) and UNRISD (2010)

Former World Bank Chief Economist F. Bourguignon stresses that income distribution matters as much as growth for poverty reduction and that redistribution is a legitimate goal of public policy for balancing the tendency of the market to concentrate resources (Bourguignon 2004). Viewed in this light, sustained poverty reduction is a twin function of the rate of growth and of changes in income distribution, whereby more equal distribution tends to have faster impacts on reducing poverty than growth, but economic growth is also necessary to sustain the process over time. It is important to note that more equal distribution is not antagonistic to growth; in fact, it tends to stimulate consumption, raise productivity and help sustain growth itself (World Bank 2006).

Finding the right combination of instruments and policies to deliver both growth and equity remains the key to 21st century development (Kanbur and Lustig 1999, van der Hoeven et al. 2001). While exclusively focusing on distribution can lead to stagnation and leave populations worse-off, which has been the fate of countries under some "populist" governments, exclusively focusing on growth can lead to large inequalities, as many countries have experienced in recent decades (Cornia and Court 2001, Cornia 2005, United Nations 2005, Jomo and Baudot 2007).

6.B.   Mainstreaming equity in the development agenda
Achieving the equity/growth balance requires a major overhaul of current decision-making. Economic choices at both international and national levels have often been taken without adequate consideration of their distributional impacts; if there are negative social impacts, these may be mitigated, but equity and social progress cannot be achieved by this approach alone. As an alternative, the United Nations development agenda has been proposing the combination of social and economic policies in a complementary and mutually reinforcing manner.

The United Nations development agenda consists of a comprehensive set of goals agreed by global consensus in different United Nations conferences and summits over the last two decades. The agenda encompasses issues ranging from social inclusion and decent employment to sustainable development and finance. The UN agenda focuses on country ownership of national development strategies, integrating social, economic and environmental policy, and enabling frameworks for peace/conflict prevention, good governance and human rights, as well as addresses systemic issues, such as the differential impact of globalization and inequalities among and within countries. The United Nations development agenda has been shaped by a fundamental concern for equity and for equality of all persons, as human beings and as citizens (United Nations 2007 and 2008). United Nations agencies and other organizations have operationalized this agenda in recent years. An indicative summary of selected sector interventions is presented below in Table 15.

Table 15. Mainstreaming Equity in the Development Agenda

Area	Typical Interventions with Equitable Outcomes for Children and Households	Typical Interventions with Inequitable/ Regressive Outcomes	Good Guidance Sources
Education	Universal free education; scholarships and programmes to retain students	User fees; commercialization of education; cost-saving in teacher's salaries	UNICEF, UNESCO, UNRISD, World Bank's PRSP Sourcebook
Energy and Mining	Rural electrification; life-line tariffs (subsidized basic consumption for low-income households); windfall social funds; contract laws ensuring local benefits from natural resources	Untaxed oil/mineral extraction	UN Policy Notes, World Bank's PRSP Sourcebook, DFID
Finance	Regional rural banks; branching out to local areas; managing finance (regulating financial and commodity markets, capital controls); fighting illicit financial flows (IFFs)	Financial liberalization; rescue of banking system (transfers to large banks); subsidies to large private enterprises	UN Policy Notes, UNCTAD, CGAP
Health	Universal primary and secondary health services; nutrition programmes; free reproductive health services	User fees; commercialization of health; tertiary highly specialized clinics that benefit a few (e.g. cardiology centers)	UNICEF, WHO, UNRISD, UNFPA, UN Policy Notes
Housing	Subsidized housing for lower income groups; upgrading of sub-standard housing	Public housing finance for upper income groups	UN Habitat, IDS
Industry	Technology policy to support competitive, employment-generating domestic industries, SMEs	Deregulation; general trade liberalization	UNCTAD, UN Policy Notes, ILO
Labour	Active and passive labour programmes; employment-generating policies	Labour flexibilization	ILO, UN Policy Notes
Macro-economic Policies	Employment-sensitive monetary and fiscal policies; countercyclical policies; taxes on corporations, personal income, financial sector etc	An excessive focus on inflation control; cyclical policies; indirect taxation (VAT)	UN Policy Notes, ILO, UNDP, UNCTAD

Area	Typical Interventions with Equitable Outcomes for Children and Households	Typical Interventions with Inequitable/ Regressive Outcomes	Good Guidance Sources
Public Expenditures	Pro-poor expenditures; fiscal decentralization	Military spending; subsidies to activities benefiting upper income groups	World Bank's PRSP Sourcebook, UNICEF, IDS
Rural Development	Food security; land redistribution; access to water, markets; livestock, credit for smallholders, rural extension services;	Large investments that may benefit major landowners (e.g. irrigation systems)	FAO, WFP, World Bank's PRSP Sourcebook
Social Protection	A Social Protection Floor, comprising cash transfers and social services	Private funded pension systems	ILO, WHO, UNICEF, UN, UNRISD, Development banks
Tourism	Small-scale local companies; financing basic infrastructure; international marketing campaigns	Poorly taxed luxury hotel chains	DFID, Overseas Development Institute
Trade	Linking employment-generating local companies with export markets; taxing exporting sectors for domestic development	Most bilateral free trade agreements; current intellectual property agreements	UNCTAD, UN Policy Notes
Transport and Infrastructure	Rural roads; social infrastructure; affordable public transport; non-motorized transport for households (bicycles, buffalos, horses)	Large (and costly) infrastructure investments that the poor/excluded do not use or do not benefit by taxation	World Bank's PRSP Sourcebook, DFID
Urban Development	Slum upgrading; accessible universal design	Large urban infrastructure projects in wealthy areas	World Bank's PRSP Source Book, UN HABITAT, UNICEF
Water and Sanitation	Rural water supply and sanitation	Poorly negotiated privatizations	UNICEF, UNDP, World Bank's PRSP Source Book

Source: Ortiz (2008)

6.C. Financing equitable policies: Transfers across three levels

Given the large extent of global income asymmetries, financing an equitable development agenda requires a degree of transfer from the wealthy to the poor across three levels:

- **North-South transfers**: The justification for more equitable international distribution cannot be stronger. For globalization to be accepted, it will have to be a globalization that benefits the majority, a globalization for all and not just for a privileged few. While the predominant channel for international redistributive flows is official development aid (ODA), international commitments continue to fall short. Of the 0.7% of gross national income (GNI) promised by high-income countries, actual ODA flows remain at only 0.3% (OECD DAC 2010). Given the failure of donors to meet aid commitments, new international sources of development finance have been proposed, mainly taxing luxury goods and services or those with negative social or environmental externalities. Recent proposals have included: taxing the arms trade, global environmental taxes (carbon-use tax), taxing speculative short-term currency flows (the so-called "Tobin tax") and taxes on international airplane tickets (Atkinson 2004). Proposals for an International Tax Organization have been suggested by both IMF staff and by the United Nations. Some point out that the overall amount of north-south transfers needed to vastly improve the well-being of millions of persons is trivial; Jeffrey Sachs, Director of the United Nations Millennium Project, estimates that extreme poverty could be eradicated with only one percent of the combined GDP of OECD countries (Sachs 2005).

- **South-South transfers**: South-South cooperation is becoming increasingly important. Though still minor in amount, South-South transfers are occurring in three main forms (Ortiz 2009): (i) bilateral aid (China, Saudi Arabia and Venezuela are noticeable examples), (ii) regional development banks (e.g. Islamic Development Bank, Arab Fund for Economic and Social Development, Andean Development Corporation or the Bank of ALBA) and (iii) regional integration (e.g. the South American Common Market, MERCOSUR; the Bolivarian Alternative for the Americas, ALBA; the League of Arab States;

the Southern African Development Community, SADC; and the Association of Southeast Asian Nations, ASEAN).

- *National transfers*: There is untapped capacity to fund more equitable policies even in the poorest countries. This may require moving away from orthodox approaches. Main options to increase fiscal space to ramp up equitable spending include: improved taxation, reprioritization of expenditures, external financing and debt relief, domestic borrowing, adopting a more accommodating macroeconomic framework (e.g. tolerating some inflation and/or fiscal deficit), fighting illicit financial flows or use of reserves for national development.

7. Impacts of the Global Economic Crisis and the Need for a Recovery for All

A global financial and economic crisis quickly swept across the world beginning in 2007. While comprehensive data are not yet available to evaluate the aggregate impacts on income inequality, many factors suggest that inequality may be increasing dramatically. Above all, historical analyses show that financial crises often deepen poverty and worsen income inequalities (Baldacci et al. 2002). In general terms, as a financial crisis causes a country's average income to decline, a more-than-proportional fall in the income share of the lowest income quintiles of the population leads to higher income inequality, which is worsened if coupled with an increase in the income share of the richest quintile. While this largely reflects the lopsided impact of changes in labour demand, inflation and public spending on the bottom quintiles over the short term (Lustig and Walton 1999), there are also longer-term effects on the capabilities of the poorest as a result of household coping mechanisms related to children and expenditures on essential food, health and education (Mendoza 2008). In aggregate poverty terms, Cline (2002) estimated a seven percent increase in the average poverty headcount of a developing country due to a financial crisis. The distributional impacts of financial crises are accordingly uneven, with inequality often worsening and adding further pressure to poverty levels (Ravallion 2008). Given the current trends in employment, food and fuel prices, as well as in government spending, it is predictable that income inequality will increase during 2011.

7.A. Employment

First, an employment crisis continues to affect much of the globe. The world experienced jobless growth prior to the crisis, and this intensified as labour demand weakened (ILO 2010a:7). ILO's (2011) latest analysis notes that, while there is evidence of employment recovery in some East Asian countries, the outlook worsened for many others during 2010. The ongoing economic recovery is not yet leading to a sufficient expansion in employment opportunities for most. At the global level, trends in the employment-to-population ratio, which indicates whether the employment-generating capacity of a country or region is rising or falling, show that economies are simply not generating sufficient employment opportunities to absorb growth in the working-age population. For example, in 64 countries for which quarterly data are available, the number of countries with falling employment-to-population ratios was still twice the number that had rising ratios as of the second quarter in 2010. More recently, in rich countries, estimates for the return to pre-crisis employment levels were revised an additional two years—to 2015. Near the end of 2010, ILO (2010a) also estimated that nearly 40% of jobseekers had been unemployed for more than one year in a sample of 35 countries, and more than four million had stopped searching altogether by the end of 2009 due to, for example, demoralization. The public response in many countries has included major protests against the government in its role as employer and failure to address dogged unemployment (ILO 2010a:40).

In terms of inequality, evidence shows that rising unemployment causes the bottom of the earnings distribution to fall off relative to the median (Heathcote et al. 2010). Further, total wage inequality—defined as the difference in the earnings of those at the 90th and 10th percentile of the overall wage distribution—had increased dramatically in many countries since the 1970s (Machin and van Reenen 2007, OECD 2008). More recently, evidence points that the trend has continued during the crisis. In advanced economies, for example, banks and corporations provided near-record bonuses to executives and financial sector workers in 2010 and 2011.[37] Given the severity and persistence of unemployment across much of the world, inequality in earnings is likely to be perpetuated through 2011 and beyond.

Young men and women have been disproportionately affected by unemployment since the onset of the crisis. Earlier experiences have shown that it takes, on average, over 11 years for youth unemployment to return to pre-recession levels (ILO 2010a:13). According to ILO estimates, youth unemployment has risen by nearly eight million globally since the onset of the crisis in 2007. Moreover, the percent increase in youth unemployment globally was over twice that for the overall working population. However, this dramatic increase masks an even more striking trend towards decreasing youth participation in labour markets and growing informality and precarity of youth employment (ILO 2010b). ILO further reports that young women have more difficulty than young men in finding work.

7.B.   High commodity prices

Second, households have been dealing with unabatedly high food prices since 2008. According to the FAO's Food Price Index, global food prices surpassed the peak levels of the 2007-08 food crisis in January 2011 and continued to set new record highs in February and March 2011. At the local level, UNICEF recent analysis finds that food prices closely trailed those in global food markets during the latter half of 2010; it also found that domestic food prices remained alarmingly high compared to pre-crisis levels as of November 2010 (Ortiz et al. 2011). As high food prices continue to erode disposable income, most poor families have already exhausted available coping strategies, such as eating fewer meals, cutting health expenditures, increasing debt and working longer hours in the informal sector. Given that poor families spend a much higher share of their income on food than wealthier groups, the link between higher local food prices and inequality is clear. For

---

[37]See Wall Street Journal, "On Street, Pay Vaults to Record Altitude," on 23 February 2011, and Wall Street Journal, "Executive Bonuses Bounce Back," on 18 March 2011.

example, studies of Asia and Latin America show that inequality rates rose as a result of the 2007-08 food price shocks (Save the Children 2009 and World Bank 2008), and the ADB (2008) estimates that a 20% nominal food price increase leads to a one percent increase in the Gini coefficient.

The food price outlook is bleak and further complicated by rising oil prices. The sharp rise of petroleum prices beginning in early 2011 is likely to persist as political uncertainty inundates much of the Middle East and North Africa, thus adding more pressure on employment-generating economic activities and scarce household resources. As the resilience of poor populations for further increases in food—or energy—costs is extremely limited, continued high prices can be expected to increase income inequality during 2011.

7.C.   Fiscal austerity

Third, while most governments launched fiscal stimulus plans during the first phase of the global economic crisis, fiscal stimuli were abandoned during the second phase, and governments are now scaling back public spending at a time when economic and social recovery remains fragile. UNICEF analysis of public expenditures in 126 developing countries (Ortiz et al. 2010) shows that many governments are planning to remove or phase out crisis response policies in 2010-11 as part of fiscal consolidation efforts. In particular, cuts/caps in public outlays on social programmes, transfers to households, and wages and salaries are being considered. The ILO (2010a:40) finds that such austerity measures have been met by severe social unrest and public protest in many countries, including 16 of 28 countries studied. In terms of inequality, reductions in government spending on basic education, health care and social security programmes—the main ways tighter fiscal policy affects the poor—are associated with falling incomes and investment for the poorest groups. A recent Economist analysis finds evidence of this effect in a set of developed countries.[38] Following examination of changes in income levels among regions within individual countries, The Economist concluded that income

---

[38]The Economist, "Internal Affairs: The Gap between Many Rich and Poor Regions Widened because of the Recession," 10 March 2011.

inequality had increased between richer and poorer regions since the start of the global recession and is likely to be exacerbated since lower government expenditures disproportionately impact poorer regions.[39] Current debates on reducing development assistance in donor countries should be considered in this context.

In sum, the ongoing patterns in employment, food and fuel prices, and public spending do not appear to bode well for equity outcomes. What is needed is a Recovery for All that ensures that the economic recovery benefits the most excluded households, and invests in the future of their members, rather than perpetuating or accentuating existing disparities (UNICEF 2010c).

8.   Concluding Remarks

Gross asymmetries in income distribution matter to people. To start with, they are a sign of social injustice. Irrespective of methodology, we inhabit a planet where, as an aggregate, the wealthiest quintile of the population enjoys more than 70% of total income compared to a meager two percent for the poorest quintile (83% versus one percent under market exchange rates). We also live in a world where more than eight million young children die each year (some 22,000 per day), and most of their deaths are preventable (UNICEF 2011:84). Hunger, malnutrition and lack of safe drinking water contribute to at least half of child mortality, and their incidence is highly concentrated among the poorer quintiles. The urgency to address these inequalities cannot be more stressed.

But inequality also matters to economic growth. Developing countries with higher income inequality tend to grow slower. Inequality is economically inefficient and dysfunctional: consumption is concentrated in the top income quintile in most developing countries, making their markets smaller. In contrast, most high-income economies developed by expanding domestic

---

[39]For example, USAID Administrator Rajiv Shah testified before the United States House Appropriations State and Foreign Ops Subcommittee on 30 March 2011 that the passed budget bill (to be approved by the Senate) would result in the deaths of at least 70,000 children who depend on American food and health assistance globally.

markets as a strategy to raise demand and promote economic growth. This happened through public policies that focused on generating employment and household income, ensuring access to land and assets, as well as infrastructure and services, and enhancing human capital and labour productivity. Likewise, developing country governments can focus on expansionary macroeconomic policies that support employment and broad-based economic activities, introduce new schemes to extend health services and social protection for all, and invest in education, water supply, sanitation, food security and nutrition.

Last but not least, inequality matters to political stability. Gross inequities tend to generate intense social tensions and even violent conflict. Equitable policies, on the other hand, are able to enlist the political support of citizens in democratic systems, and can build social stability.

A more equitable world can be achieved. This requires action at national and international levels.

Some questions for policy makers include:
- How can national development strategies and socio-economic recovery plans address inequality and better prioritize the needs and rights of lower income groups?
- How can inclusive development outcomes be accelerated?
- How can governments best guarantee the right to food, housing, education and medical care, along with the right to employment and social security, with special attention to families and children?
- How can employment-generating activities at the local level be fostered, including decent employment for young people?
- Are all possible fiscal space options being considered to ensure a Recovery for All and accelerate inclusive development?
- How can government spending be refocused on the bottom quintiles to push them up? Is the government doing all that it can?
- Are the long-term economic, social and political costs of leaving out low- and middle-income households and vulnerable children in the current economic crisis being considered?

- Are policies being selected and designed through inclusive processes—in other words, through open and public discourse?

At the global level, some of the initiatives that could support and complement the efforts of national governments include:

- Consider the social impacts of different global policies, such as international trade and finance, and promote those options that have larger positive impacts on inclusive national development and directly benefit the majority of households in a country.
- Promote a universal global social protection floor to support adequate income and services for all, which also supports investment in the human capital of poor people.
- Given gross income asymmetries at the global level, ensure donor commitments are upheld and pursue new international sources of development finance.
- Encourage South-South cooperation as a vehicle to promote regional solidarity.

Endnote: Estimating Income Inequality: Methodology and Assumptions

A.   Methodology

There are two common approaches for estimating global income distribution (see UNDP 1992 and 1995, Sutcliffe 2004 and Milanovic 2005). The first approach is known as the **inter-country** distribution accounting model, which looks at the average income differences between large groupings of countries. To do so, it treats all members of a country as if they have the same income (e.g. all Bolivians are assumed to earn the same amount of money in a given year). After ordering all countries in the world according to their levels of per capita income (smallest to largest), global income distribution estimates are derived by dividing the world population into five equal parts (or quintiles) and calculating the corresponding shares of total global income.

The data requirements for inter-country model are very basic and consist of GDP per capita and population for each country. As a result, this method allows for a very large sample size (about 98% of the global population for any given year) and covers very recent time periods. All calculations are based on data from World Bank (2011).

A second approach accounts for both inter- and intra-country distribution. Frequently referred to as the **global** distribution accounting model, this method decomposes national income by quintiles and compares those incomes across countries. Here, the average per capita income of those in India's bottom quintile is estimated on the basis of their share of total national income. While this method still assumes that large numbers of individuals have the same income (e.g. a quintile of India's population equals the entire population of Indonesia), it allows for the construction of a hypothetical world in which all persons can be lined up in a single distribution—within country population quintiles—regardless of where they live.

The global distribution model has much more stringent data requirements than the inter-country model. In particular, this method requires national income distribution estimates, which are commonly presented as the share of total income held by different population quintiles, from the poorest 20% (quintile 1 or Q1) to the richest 20% (quintile 5 or Q5). Annual quintile data were extracted from World Bank (2011) for all available countries and years and then supplemented by information from UNU-WIDER (2008) and Eurostat (2011). Since we are most interested in understanding trends over unique time periods (e.g. 1990, 2000 and most recent available), interpolation and nearest neighbor imputation were used as gap-filling procedures to maximize the number of observations using all three distribution data sources. We did not, however, estimate quintile values for all countries in the world, which means that all of our data points are derived from actual estimates.

B.   Assumptions behind income distribution estimates

Estimating income inequality based on national distribution estimates is no easy task. In an ideal world, there would be cross-nationally comparable household surveys for all countries over time with mean income estimates for different population deciles or quintiles derived from those surveys. In reality, however, household surveys are based on various methodologies, ranging from consumption (with and without transfers) and expenditure to earnings (gross and net) and income (monetary and taxable or disposable and gross). Moreover, household studies are not carried out on a regular basis in most countries, with methods often changing between studies. Since existing national income estimates must be converted from national currencies in order to be compared, there is also the issue of the most appropriate exchange rate (see Box 1 for discussion on using market versus PPP-adjusted exchange rates).

To date, the World Bank's PovcalNet offers the best attempt to create the ideal income distribution database (Note: distribution estimates published in the World Bank's World Development Indicators—referred as World Bank 2011 in this paper—are derived from PovcalNet). Using nearly 700 household surveys across 116 developing countries, it contains income/consumption distribution information along with mean per capita income/consumption estimates based on the latest PPP exchange rates (2005). Regrettably, however, PovcalNet does not include information for any developed countries and is further characterized by large data gaps over time.

Given our objective to understand global inequality trends since 1990, we sacrifice the quality assurance of income/consumption estimates offered by PovalNet in favor of an expanded sample of countries and across more time. We do so by complementing PovcalNet's estimates with income/consumption distribution data compiled by UNU-WIDER as well as by Eurostat. The UNU-WIDER and Eurostat data suffer from differing calculation methods and do not offer mean per capita income/consumption estimates based on household surveys. We further acknowledge the statistical inaccuracies in comparing distribution estimates from three unique data sources. Comparability shortcomings aside, combining these sources enables us to carry out rough approximations of income/consumption distribution estimates in a sample of 136 countries between 1990 and 2007.

The expanded sample requires us to use a less preferable income gauge: GDP. Using GDP as an income metric is inherently flawed given that investment and government spending are assumed to be distributed in the same way as household consumption (or disposable income). As a result, while GDP includes items which may have something to do with future welfare, it is not an accurate measure of current income (e.g. consumption expenditure in China is less than 40% of GDP as of 2009). Despite the measurement inadequacies, our intent is to show the general evolution of income distribution over time, and our calculations assume that the distribution of total household income/consumption and total GDP are equally proportionate. Adopting the GDP metric further allows us to carry out comparable distribution estimates using both the inter-country and global accounting models, which would otherwise not be possible.

Concerning populous countries, many global distribution estimates treat the world's most populous countries uniquely since the vast size of their populaces can have a significant impact on global projections. This usually involves dividing the populations of China and India into rural and urban groups and treating each group separately. We have not adopted this approach, and our estimates for all countries represent GDP per quintile of total population.

References

ADB (2008). "Food Prices and Inflation in Developing Asia: Is Poverty Reduction Coming to an End?" Economics and Research Department Special Report. Manila: Asian Development Bank.

Alesina, A. and D. Rodrik (1994). "Distributive Politics and Economic Growth." The Quarterly Journal of Economics, MIT Press, Vol. 109(2), pp. 465-90.

Atkinson, A. (ed.) (2004). New Sources of Development Finance. Oxford: Oxford University Press.

Baldacci, E., Inchauste, G. and L. de Mello (2002). "Financial Crises, Poverty and Income Distribution." IMF Working Paper 02/4. Washington, D.C.: IMF.

Birdsall, N. (2010). "The (Indispensable) Middle Class in Developing Countries, or the Rich and the Rest, not the Poor and the Rest." CGD Working paper No. 207. Washington, D.C.: Center for Global Development.

Birdsall, N. (2005). "Why Inequality Matters in a Globalizing World." UNU-WIDER Annual Lecture, Helsinki.

Bourguignon, F. (2004). "The Poverty-Growth-Inequality Triangle." Washington D.C.: World Bank.

Bourguignon, F. and C. Morrisson (2002). "The Size Distribution of Income among World Citizens, 1820-1990," American Economic Review, September, pp.727-744.

Callen, T. (2007). "PPP versus the Market: Which Weight Matters?" Finance and Development, Vol. 44, No. 1. Washington, D.C.: IMF.

Chang, H. J. (2003). Kicking Away the Ladder: Development Strategy in Historical Perspective. London: Anthem Press.

Chen, S. and M. Ravallion (2008). "The Developing World is Poorer than we Thought, but no Less Successful in the Fight against Poverty." Policy Research Working Paper 4703. Washington, D.C.: World Bank.

Cline, W. (2002). "Financial Crises and Poverty in Emerging Market Economics." Working Paper No. 8. Washington, D.C.: Center for Global Development.

Collier, P. (2007). The Bottom Billion: Why the Poorest Countries are Failing and What Can Be Done About It. Oxford: Oxford University Press.

Cornia, G. A. (2010). "Transition, Structural Divergence and Performance: Eastern Europe and the Former Soviet Union over 2000-2007." UNU-WIDER Working Paper No. 32. Helsinki: UNU-WIDER.

Cornia, G. A. (2005). "Policy Reform and Income Distribution." UN DESA Working Paper No. 3. New York: United Nations Department for Economic and Social Affairs.

Cornia, G. A. (2003). "The Impact of Liberalization and Globalization on Income Inequality in Developing and Transitional Economies." Working Paper No. 14. Geneva: International Labour Office.

Cornia, G. A. and B. Martorano (2010). "Policies for Reducing Income Inequality: Latin America during the Last Decade." UNICEF Policy and Practice Working Paper. New York: UNICEF.

Cornia, G. A. and J. Court (2001). "Inequality, Growth and Poverty in the Era of Liberalization and Globalization." Heksinki: UNU-WIDER.

Davies, J., Sandström, S., Shorrocks, A. and E. Wolff (2008). "The World Distribution of Household Wealth." Discussion Paper No. 2008/03. Helsinki: UNU-WIDER.

Davies, J., Sandström, S., Shorrocks, A. and E. Wolff (2006). "The World Distribution of Household Wealth." Helsinki: UNU-WIDER.

Deacon, B. (2010). "From the Global Politics of Poverty Alleviation to the Global Politics of Welfare State Rebuilding." Comparative Research Programme on Poverty Policy Brief.

Dowrick, S. and M. Akmal (2005). "Contradictory Trends in Global Income Inequality: A Tale of Two Biases." Review of Income and Wealth, Series 51, No. 2, June 2005.

Eurostat (2011). Income, Social Inclusion and Living Conditions Database. Luxembourg: European Commission. Accessed on 10 March 2011; available at: http://epp.eurostat.ec.europa.eu/portal/page/portal/income_social_in clusion_living_conditions/data/database.

Gilpin, R. (1987). The Political Economy of International Relations. Princeton: Princeton University Press.

Heathcoate, J., Perri, F. and G. Violante (2010). "Inequality in Times of Crisis: Lessons from the Past and a First Look at the Current Recession." VoxEU.org, 2 February 2010. Accessed 10 March 2011; available at: http://info.worldbank.org/governance/wgi/index.asp.

ILO (2011). Global Employment Trends: The Challenges of a Jobs Recovery. Geneva: International Labour Organization.

ILO (2010a). World of Work Report 2010: From one crisis to the next? Geneva: International Institute for Labour Studies.

ILO (2010b). Global Employment Trends for Youth. Special Issue on the Impacts of the Global Economic Crisis on Youth. Geneva: International Labour Organization.

ILO (2008). World of Work Report 2008: Income Inequalities in the Age of Financial Globalization. Geneva: International Institute for Labour Studies.

ILO (2004). A Fair Globalization: Creating Opportunities for All. Report of the World Commission on the Social Consequences of Globalization. Geneva: International Labour Organisation.

IMF (2007). World Economic Outlook: Globalization and Inequality. Washington, D.C.: International Monetary Fund.

Jomo, K. S. and J. Baudot (eds.) (2007). Flat World, Big Gaps: Economic Liberalization, Globalization, Poverty and Inequality. London: Zed Books.

Kanbur, R. and N. Lustig (1999). "Why is Inequality Back on the Agenda." Paper presented at Annual Bank Conference on Development Economics. Washington D.C.: World Bank.

Kaufmann, D., Kraay, A. and M. Mastruzzi (2010). Worldwide Governance Indicators (WGI) Project.

Lopez-Calva, L. and N. Lustig (eds.) (2010). Declining Poverty in Latin America. Baltimore: Brookings and UNDP.

Lustig, N. and M. Walton (1999). "Crises and the Poor: A Template for Action." Prepared for the Conference on Social Protection and Poverty in Washington, D.C.

Machin, S. and J. van Reenen (2007). "Changes in Wage Inequality." Special Paper No. 18, Centre for Economic Performance. London: London School of Economics.

Maddison, A. (2006). The World Economy: A Millennial Perspective. Paris: OECD. Historical tables available at: http://www.ggdc.net/maddison/Historical_Statistics/horizontal-file_03-2007.xls.

Mendoza, R. (2008). "Aggregate Shocks, Poor Households and Children: Transmission Channels and Policy Responses." Social and Economic Policy Working Paper. New York: UNICEF.

Mkandawire, T. (2006). Social Policy in a Development Context. Basingtoke: Palgrave Macmillan and UNRISD.

Milanovic, B. (2009). "Global Inequality and the Global Inequality Extraction Ratio: The Story of the Past Two Centuries." Policy Research Working Paper 5044. Washington D.C.: World Bank.

Milanovic, B. (2005). Worlds Apart: Measuring International and Global Inequality. Princeton: Princeton University Press.

OECD (2008). Growing Unequal? Income Distribution and Poverty in OECD Countries. Paris: OECD.

OECD DAC (2010). Aid Statistics. Paris: OECD. Available at: www.oecd.org/dac/stats.

Ortiz, I. (2009). "Financing for Development: International Redistribution." in Hujo, K. and S. McClanahan (eds.) Financing Social Policy. Basingtoke: Palgrave Macmillan and UNRISD.

Ortiz, I. (2008). "Social Policy" in United Nations National Development Strategies Policy Notes. New York: United Nations Department for Economic and Social Affairs.

Ortiz, I., Chai, J. and M. Cummins (2011). "Escalating Food Prices: The Threat to Poor Households and Policies to Safeguard a Recovery for All." Social and Economic Policy Working Paper. New York: UNICEF.

Ortiz, I., Chai, J., Cummins, M. and G. Vergara (2010). "Prioritizing Expenditures for a Recovery for All." UNICEF Social and Economic Policy Working Paper. New York: UNICEF.

Ravallion, M. (2009). "The Developing World's Bulging (but Vulnerable) Middle Class." Policy Research Working Paper 4816. Washington, D.C.: World Bank.

Ravallion, M. (2008). "Bailing out the World's Poorest." Policy Research Working Paper 4763. Washington D.C.: World Bank.

Reddy, S. and C. Minoiu (2006). "Real Income Stagnation of Countries, 1960-2001." UN DESA Working Paper No. 28. New York: United Nations Department for Economic and Social Affairs.

Reinert, E. (2007). How Rich Countries Got Rich ... and Why Poor Countries Stay Poor. London: Constable.

Sachs, J. (2005). Investing in Development: A Practical Plan to Achieve the MDGs. UN Millennium Project. New York: United Nations.

Save the Children (2009). "How the Global Food Crisis is Hurting Children: The Impact of the Food Price Hike on a Rural Community in Northern Bangladesh." London: Save the Children UK.

Simai, M. (2006). "Poverty and Inequality in Eastern Europe and the CIS Transition Economies." UN DESA Working Paper No. 17. New York: United Nations Department for Economic and Social Affairs.

Solt, F. (2009). "Standardizing the World Income Inequality Database." Social Science Quarterly 90(2):231-242. Accessed 10 March 2011; available at: http://dvn.iq.harvard.edu/dvn/dv/fsolt/faces/study/StudyPage.xhtml?studyId=36908&versionNumber=3.

Sutcliffe, B. (2005). "A Converging or a Diverging World?" UN DESA Working Paper No. 2. New York: UN DESA.

Sutcliffe, B. (2004). "World Inequality and Globalization." Oxford Review of Economic Policy, Vol. 20, No. 1.

Sutcliffe, B. (2003). "A More or Less Unequal World? World Income Distribution in the 20th Century." Political Economy Research Institute (PERI) Working Paper No. 54. Amherst: University of Massachusetts Amherst.

United Nations (2009). World Population Prospects: The 2008 Revision, CD-ROM Edition. New York: United Nations Department of Economic and Social Affairs.

United Nations (2008). National Development Strategies Policy Notes. New York: United Nations Department of Economic and Social Affairs.

United Nations (2007). "The United Nations Development Agenda: Development for All." New York: United Nations Department of Economic and Social Affairs.

United Nations (2005). The Inequality Predicament: Report on the World Social Situation 2005. New York: United Nations Department of Economic and Social Affairs.

UNDP (2005). Human Development Report 2005 – International cooperation at a crossroads: Aid, trade and security in an unequal world. New York: Oxford University Press.

UNDP (1999). Human Development Report 1999 – Globalization with a Human Face. New York: Oxford University Press.

UNDP (1992). Human Development Report 1992 – Global Dimensions of Human Development. New York: UNDP.

UNICEF (2011). State of the World's Children – Adolescence: An Age of Opportunity. New York: UNICEF.

UNICEF (2010a). "The Children Left Behind: A League Table of Inequality in Child Well-being in the World's Rich Countries." Innocenti Report Card 9. Florence: UNICEF Innocenti Research Centre.

UNICEF (2010b). Progress for Children: Achieving the MDGs with Equity. New York: UNICEF.

UNICEF (2010c). "Recovery for All: A Call for Collective Action." Social and Economic Policy Working Brief, July 2010. New York: UNICEF.

UNODC (2008). Homicide Statistics. Accessed on 10 March 2011; available at: http://data.un.org/Data.aspx?d=UNODC&f=tableCode%3A1.

UNRISD (2010). Combating Poverty and Inequality. Geneva: United Nations Research Institute for Social Development.

UNU-WIDER (2008). World Income Inequality Database (WIID). Accessed on 10 March 2011; available at www.wider.unu.edu/wiid.

Van der Hoeven, R. Dagdeviren, H. and J. Weeks (2001). "Redistribution Matters: Growth for Poverty Reduction." Geneva: International Labour Office.

Wilkinson, R. and K. Pickett (2010). The Spirit Level: Why Equality Is Better for Everyone. London: Penguin Group.

World Bank (2011). World Development Indicators (WDI). Accessed on 10 March 2011; available at: http://databank.worldbank.org/ddp/home.do?Step=12&id=4&CNO=2.

World Bank (2008). "Rising Food and Fuel Prices: Addressing the Risks to Future Generations." World Bank Human Development and Poverty Reduction and Economic Management Networks.

World Bank (2006). World Development Report 2006: Equity and Development. Washington, D.C.: World Bank.

The Spirit Level: Why Greater Equality Makes Societies Stronger

Bill Kerry, Kate E. Pickett and Richard Wilkinson[40]

More equal societies do better
We set out to find an explanation for problems with social gradients; that is, problems that are worst among the poorest in society, but also show a gradient across the whole society. Problems with social gradients include health, violent crime, and educational failure. We wanted to test a theory: that problems with social gradients are not caused by differences in material wealth, or by any kind of sorting or selection effects, but instead are due to social status differentiation itself - to the degree of hierarchy within a society.

We therefore looked at rich developed market democracies, specifically those where economic growth is no longer associated with life expectancy, happiness or wellbeing.

One may not be able to extend the analyses in *The Spirit Level* in its entirety to developing and emerging economies in a consistent way, due to lack of good quality data on income distributions and outcomes, but it is reasonable to assume (and there is indeed evidence from developing countries for life expectancy and infant mortality) that inequality is damaging in these contexts as well. The psycho-social mechanisms that link inequality to worse outcomes are common to all humans – inequality is socially divisive: status

---

[40]Bill Kerry is Co-founder and Director of The Equality Trust and works for the Trust as a part-time consultant
Kate Pickett is Professor of Epidemiology at the University of York. She is co-author of *The Spirit Level: Why More Equal Societies Almost Always Do Better*
Richard Wilkinson is Professor Emeritus of Social Epidemiology at the University of Nottingham. He is co-author of *The Spirit Level: Why More Equal Societies Almost Always Do Better*

competition and anxiety, feelings of inferiority and fear of being disrespected all increase. All of these are sources of chronic stress and this causes ill-health and makes the social environment more stressful, leading to other forms of social dysfunction – such as high levels of violence.

We found that amongst the 23 rich countries that we analysed (see figure), there was a very strong correlation between income inequality and an Index of Health and Social Problems endured in those countries. The Index of Health and Social Problems includes levels of trust, life expectancy and infant mortality rates, mental illness, obesity, educational scores, teenage birth rates, levels of homicides and rates of imprisonment, and social mobility.

Figure 1. Index of Health and Social Problems in relation to income inequality in rich countries.

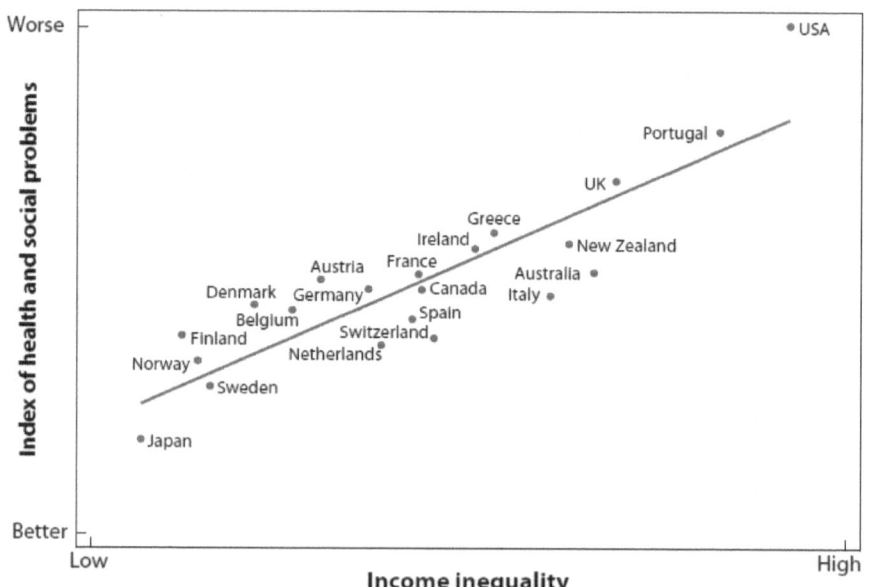

Source: Wilkinson & Pickett 2009.
Note: Income inequality is measured by the ratio of incomes among the richest compared with the poorest 20% in each country.

We were so struck by the correlations we were finding that we re-tested the relationships among the 50 US states, and found very consistent results. Correlation is, of course, not causation but each of these separate problems move together, which suggests there must be some underlying cause. And no one has yet suggested a better or more convincing explanation than inequality across these two settings.

We also found that the same Index of Health and Social Problems did not correlate with average national income (measured in equivalent US dollars) leading us to conclude that if developed countries really want to improve the quality of life for their populations they need to focus on how income is distributed within the economy, rather than just striving for more economic growth.

The effects of inequality on the poorest in society

Inequality has the greatest impact on the poor and those living in the most deprived areas of society. Children do particularly badly in unequal societies – from worse infant mortality rates, through to lower levels of participation in further education. In more unequal societies, children are more likely to be overweight, to be victims of bullying, and to become teenage mothers. Once they become adults in more unequal societies they are more likely to have mental health problems, to have problems with drugs and alcohol, to work longer hours and have more debt pressures on family life. And social mobility is lower in more unequal societies, so it is more difficult for children to escape from intergenerational cycles of poverty and deprivation.

There is a clear correlation between income inequality and the UNICEF Index of Child Well-Being in rich countries (UNICEF 2007, see Figure 2).

Figure 2. Child Well-being and Income Inequality

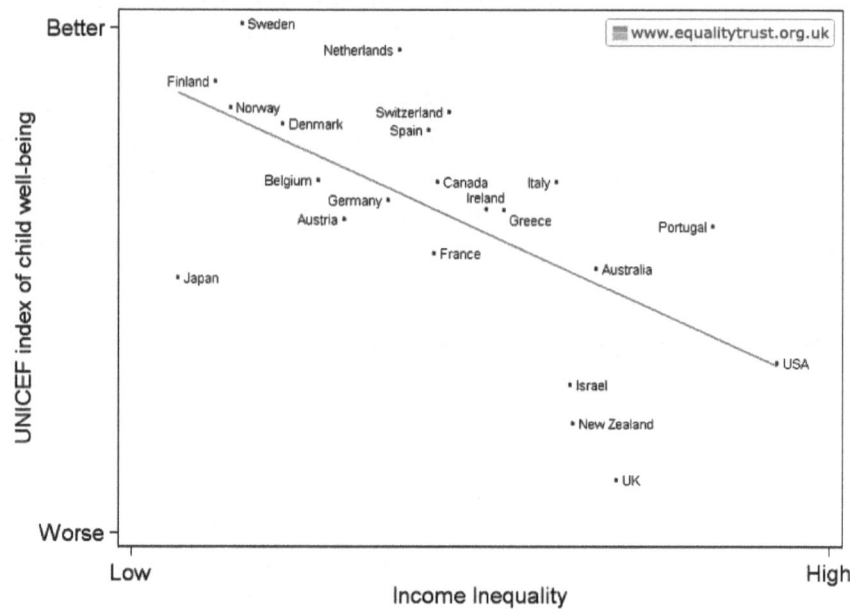

Source: The Equality Trust

Inequality as an indicator of deprivation

Both poverty and inequality are important for the well-being of populations. However, in the rich developed countries, absolute poverty no longer affects more than a very small percentage of the population, whereas relative poverty and relative social status affect the vast majority. The problem with focusing on poverty to the exclusion of inequality is that it is the distribution of incomes across society as a whole that matters; efforts to alleviate poverty do little to constrain income inequality driven by the rich getting richer.

Our evidence suggests that the developed world reaps diminishing returns in quality of life from economic growth, and at the same time the world is facing increasing environmental problems related to such growth. In this situation, dealing with inequality becomes important not only for improving health and social problems, but also for creating sustainable economies. This is grounds for optimism – if we need to rein in growth to rein in carbon emissions, we need not suffer from reduced quality of life but instead gain from improved social cohesion, improved health and fewer social problems.

Tackling inequality

We found that among the rich countries and the US States greater equality can be achieved in two quite different ways. For example, in Sweden and the other Scandinavian countries, higher levels of equality are achieved through progressive taxation, re-distribution, and strong welfare states. In contrast, in Japan, greater equality arises from narrower gaps between top and bottom incomes before tax. Amongst the US States, Vermont and New Hampshire are both examples of more equal states that do well in terms of health and social problems, yet Vermont achieves this through mechanisms similar to Sweden, and New Hampshire, like Japan, has smaller income differences before taxes and benefits, and low levels of public expenditure.

So it seems that it does not much matter how societies move towards greater equality, the point is that they should get there somehow. In terms of policies, this opens up a wide range of options. The idea of embedding greater equality within the institutional structures of the economy is perhaps particularly appealing. More economic democracy, more co-operatives, more mutuals, stronger trade unions and more employee-ownership will help to boost low pay and curb excessive levels of executive pay and bonuses.

The Equality Trust

The Trust is currently focused on education and campaigning in the UK but we are pleased that it is now being emulated around the world, in places like Latin America, South Africa and New Zealand. The aims of the Trust are to reduce income inequality through a programme of public and political education designed to achieve:

- A widespread understanding of the harm caused by high income inequality;
- Public support for policy measures to reduce income inequality; and
- The political commitment to implementing such policy measures.

Furthermore,

- We are non-partisan and call on all political parties to prioritise this issue.

- We would like to see the UK halve its current level of inequality to the levels found in Sweden or Japan. More generally, we hope to put inequality centre-stage on the national and international policy and development agendas.

- We use empirical evidence to bolster the traditional moral argument for equality that has been based on the grounds of human rights and social justice. One of the key findings in The Spirit Level is that the benefits of greater equality extend to the vast majority of the populations of rich, developed countries. This has profound implications. It opens up, perhaps as never before, the opportunity to present greater equality as being in the interests of the majority of the world's citizens, children as well as adults. We do not have to despair; the research evidence suggests that we can solve such seemingly intractable problems as persistent health inequalities and the challenge of sustainable living – greater equality is the key.

References

Conversation with Wilkinson and Pickett on the *Spirit Level* (video): http://www.youtube.com/watch?v=w4bPIMRmLGo&feature=related

Hills, J., Sefton, T. and K. Stewart (2009). *Towards a More Equal Society?: Poverty, Inequality and Policy Since 1997. CASE Studies on Poverty, Place & Policy*. Bristol: The Policy Press.

Tam, H. (2010). *Against Power Inequalities: Reflections on the struggle for inclusive communities*. Birbeck: London University

The Equality Trust: http://www.equalitytrust.org.uk/

UNICEF. (2007). "Child poverty in perspective: An overview of child well-being in rich countries." Innocenti Report Card 7. Florence: UNICEF Innocenti Research Centre.

Wilkinson, R. (2006). *The Impact of Inequality: How to Make Sick Societies Healthier*. London: Routledge.

Wilkinson, R. and K. Pickett (2009). *The Spirit Level: Why Greater Equality Makes Societies Stronger*. New York: Bloomsbury Press.

We're all in this together: Why fighting inequality is central to development

Alex Cobham[41]

The Post-2015 agenda

The report sets out our analysis of the Millennium Development Goals (MDGs), and draws some conclusions for the post-2015 successor framework. In particular, we highlight the gap between the ambition of the Millennium Declaration and the eventual form of the MDGs, in three main areas: sustainability, accountability and inequality.

Since its inception after the Second World War, Christian Aid has worked in countries around the world with partner organisations focused on people and groups of all faiths and none, who are systematically marginalised, economically and socially, and otherwise excluded from political processes. It was natural then that our critique of the Millennium Development Goals would focus on the extent to which inequality is not addressed.

We argue that in practice it is not possible for development processes to be inequality-neutral. By being largely inequality-blind, the MDGs may well have exacerbated inequality. The paucity of data, and in particular the lack of granularity that would allow major inequalities to be tracked and responded to, is a fundamental obstacle to both the MDGs and any eventual successor. That successor must include both data and targets that reflect the horizontal and vertical inequalities present in each aspect of development that is included.

Implications of inequality for child poverty

The child poverty implications of the inequality analysis in the report are absolutely stark. What we see time and again where data

---

[41]Alex Cobham is Chief Policy Advisor for Christian Aid

are available, is that systematic and predictable inequalities play an enormous role in determining life prospects before a child is even born. If policy fails to respond to those inequalities it is not neutral, but will instead reinforce and further embed the patterns.

Figure 3 from *We're All in This Together* shows the extent to which income inequality is related to differences in malnutrition rates. More than 40% of children in bottom quintile families across the developing world are malnourished, with all the immediate and long-term physical and mental impacts that follow, compared to around half that in top quintile families. These effects, however, differ markedly across countries and regions – making it very clear that the effects of inequality can be managed, or not. There are choices about the response to inequality, as well as about addressing it directly, that will have powerful effects for child poverty.

Figure 1. Inequality and Malnutrition

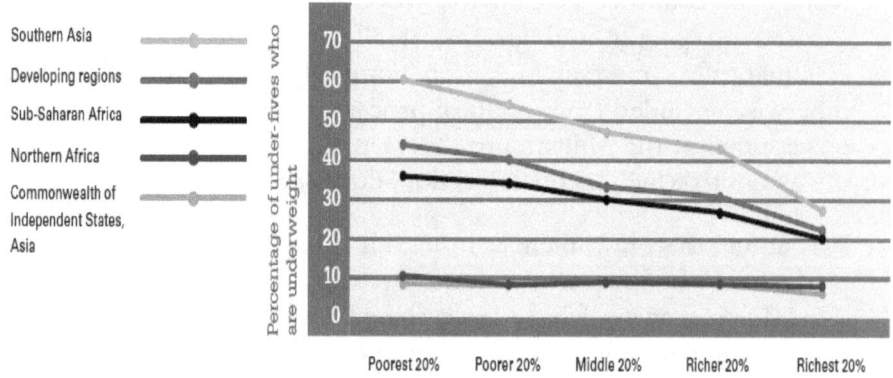

Source: Christian Aid (2010).
Note: Data is from the *Millennium Development Goals Report 2010*

The following figure shows data for an important horizontal inequality instead, the infant mortality premium suffered by indigenous groups across South and Central America. The numbers in the columns are the indigenous infant mortality rates per 1,000 births, while the height of the columns shows the ratio to non-indigenous mortality rates. While the scale of the effect varies greatly, its consistency across quite different political, social and economic contexts is striking.

Figure 2. Ratio of indigenous to non-indigenous infant mortality rate, 200-2002

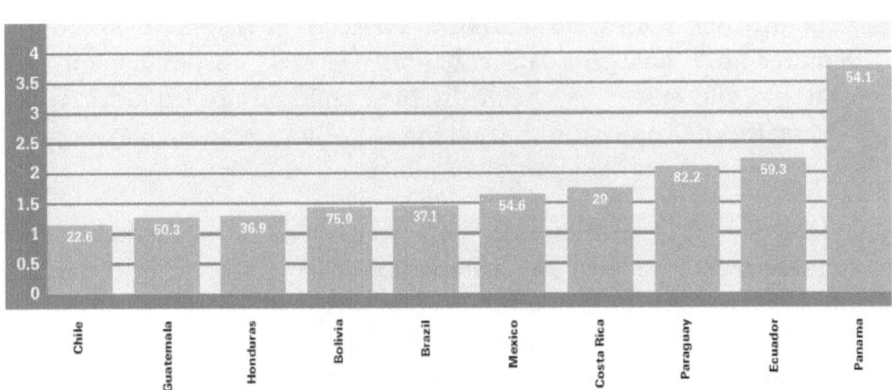

Source: Christian Aid (2010).

Opportunities and challenges for the post-2015 successor to the MDGs

There is a broad and growing consensus that inequality must be central to the post-2015 framework (and in development more generally). At the moment, however, there are open questions about how that happens, and whether there exist both the political will and the resources to do so.

On the first of these, there are two main schools of thought. One sees the 'solution' to this weakness in the MDG framework as being achieved by adding an inequality goal; the other stresses the importance of capturing the major inequalities within existing (and any additional) goals. Both of these raise further questions, of course.

A single income inequality indicator, especially if based on the Gini coefficient or similar, would be controversial. More powerful, and accurate as a reflection of in-country inequality, would be a ratio of income among quintiles – potentially the top: bottom ratio and/or the ratio of top quintile: bottom three quintiles. These would have the further advantage of being relatively straightforwardly replicable for regions and globally; and the idea of a development goal around global inequality is certainly appealing. There would, of course, be substantial resistance to more progressive proposals of this type.

The problems are as much practical as political with capturing inequalities, and in particular the major inequalities between groups, in a broader set of post-MDGs. A major investment would be required to enable the data collation necessary to understand, for example, the extent to which disabled children are excluded from access to education; or the extent to which gender, HIV status, caste, ethnicity and religion determine economic opportunities.

The necessary investment may be hard to envisage, with aid budgets tightening in the face of austerity measures, and with the ever-present pressure on governments to invest in people rather than numbers. Nevertheless, substantial progress could be made simply by joining up and sharing more effectively the existing data and the future data collation efforts of major players such as UNICEF. It is worth thinking about what kind of progress could be achieved by the September 2013 summit.

The overarching challenge for the next eighteen months is to turn the consensus on the importance of inequality into agreement on practical, specific elements in the post-2015 framework and the process to agreeing on it.

References

Christian Aid (2010). *We're All in This Together.* http://bit.ly/pOVERty

Kabeer, N. (2010). "Can the MDGs provide a pathway to social justice? The challenges of intersecting inequalities." Report for the Institute of Development Studies/Millennium Achievement Fund.

te Lintelo, D. (2011). "Summary: Inequality and Social Justice Roundtable Consultation." IDS/MAF: http://www.ids.ac.uk/files/dmfile/InequalityRoundtablereportFINAL.pdf

Sir Richard Jolly, Baroness Kinnock and others. (2011). Audio of inequality debate at UK parliamentary group: http://www.ids.ac.uk/news/inequality-is-top-development-challenge-parliamentary-meeting-told.

Policies for Reducing Income Inequality: Latin America during the Last Decade

Giovanni Andrea Cornia and Bruno Martorano[42]

From the mid-to-late 1990s, Latin America witnessed profound economic, political and distributive changes. During the 1990s, the region experienced slow growth followed by the 'lost half-decade' of 1998-2002. However, from 2003 to 2008 Latin America experienced an unprecedented expansion which generated an average GDP growth of 5.5% a year, second only to the growth registered from 1967 to 1974 (Ocampo 2008). Such steady expansion was, to some extent, a rebound from the stagnation recorded during the "lost half-decade" of 1998-2002, but featured also a sharp increase in investment rates which grew by 5 GDP points relative to 2002. However, from the third quarter of 2008, Latin America was affected by the global financial crisis which is expected to reduce GDP by 1.9% and produce a moderate growth of 3.4% in 2010 (CEPAL 2009). A second important change concerns income distribution. Contrary to the adverse distributive trends observed in the 1990s, between 2003 and 2007, income inequality declined in the vast majority of the countries of the region. Finally, since the mid-1990s, the region has also experienced a steady shift towards democratization and the election of Left-of-Centre (LOC) governments (Panizza 2005)[43]. As underscored by the election in mid-March 2009 of Mauricio Funes in El Salvador, during the last decade the region's political centre of gravity has shifted with surprising regularity towards regimes which

---

[42]G. A. Cornia is Professor of Development Economics, University of Florence. He is a former Chief Economist at UNICEF
Bruno Martorano is Staff Consultant at UNICEF's Innocenti Research Center.
[43]In the following analysis LOC group comprises countries which were ruled for at least four of the six years spanning 2002-2007 by left-of centre regimes. The countries responding to this criterion are: Argentina, Brazil, Chile, Costa Rica, Ecuador, Panama, Uruguay, and Venezuela.

attribute greater importance to social issues while avoiding the populist excesses of the 1980s. However, the recent coup in Honduras, the election of a centre-right president in Panama in July 2009, and the poor results of the *Justicialista* Party of President Fernandez during the July 2009 parliamentary elections in Argentina, may signal that such trend has reached its peak.

To what extent are these changes explained by shifts in external economic conditions, and to what extent are they instead the result of the adoption of new economic and social policies in the region, especially those adopted by LOC countries? To what extent are the distributive improvements recorded since 2003 likely to be overturned by the present crisis? These are the main issues explored in this paper. Part 2 reviews the recent decline in income inequality. Part 3 discusses the factors that could explain it, i.e. improved external conditions, a positive business cycle, a fall in educational inequality, and changes in macroeconomic, labor and social policies. Part 4 tests econometrically the relative importance of these factors, while Part 5 analyzes the impact of the financial crisis and uses the econometric model estimated in part 4 to predict the inequality changes that may be expected in 2008 and 2009.

1. The Latin American income distribution in historical perspective

With the exception of Uruguay and Argentina, in the early-to-mid 1950s, Gini coefficients in Latin America ranged between 0.45 and 0.60, among the highest in the world (Altimir 1996). This acute income polarization was rooted in an unequal distribution of land, industrial assets and educational opportunities that benefited a tiny agrarian, mining and commercial oligarchy. The rapid GDP growth which followed the adoption of the import substitution strategy in the 1950s and 1960s had, on average, a disequalizing impact. In the 1970s, however, inequality declined moderately in most of the region except for the Southern Cone (Altimir 1993, Gasparini et al 2009), where an extreme version of neo-liberal reforms had been implemented by the *juntas*. The combination of a rise in inequality over the 1950s-1960s, and a decline over the 1970s, meant that by 1980 all medium-to-large

Latin American countries had a higher income concentration than in the early-to-mid 1950s.

During the 'lost decade' of the 1980s, inequality in Latin America was affected by the 1982-84 world recession, the debt crisis, a large decline in commodity prices, and the recessionary adjustments introduced to respond to these shocks. Altogether, the 1980s were characterized by regressive distributive outcomes, as income inequality fell only in 3 countries (Colombia, Uruguay and Costa Rica) out of 11 with available data (Altimir, 1996). Despite the return to moderate growth and the extensive liberalization of the external sector, income polarization did not decline during the 1990s, and in half of the cases it worsened further if at a slower pace than in the 1980s (Gasparini et al.2009, and Figure 1). A review of inequality changes over the 1990s, based on 76 standardized surveys for 17 countries covering 90% of the regional population, shows that inequality rose in 10 countries and stagnated or declined in 7 (Székely 2003). The worsening was particularly acute during the "lost half-decade" of 1998-2002.

One of the key features of the rise in income inequality was a decline in the labor share in total income and a parallel rise in the capital share. For instance, between 1980 and the late 1980s, the labor share declined by 5-6 percentage points in Argentina, Chile and Venezuela and by ten in Mexico. These trends were not reversed during the mild recovery of 1991-98. In several countries, such as Chile during the military dictatorship, the fall in the labor share was due, *inter alia*, to the relaxation of norms on workers dismissals, a restriction of the power of trade unions, the suspension of wage indexation, a reduction of public employment and the coverage of the minimum wage, as well as to the reduction or elimination of wealth, capital gains and profit taxes. From an analytical perspective, the fall in the labor share can be decomposed into five components. First, sluggish growth resulting from a slowdown in jobs creation (Tokman 1986). Second, informal employment became more common. Third, formal sector wages evolved less favorably than GDP per capita. Fourth, the minimum wage fell in relation to the average wage. Fifth, wage differentials by skill widened, particularly during the 1990s, in parallel with widespread trade liberalization (Székely 2003).

In contrast to the trends observed in the 1980s and 1990s, during the 2000s income inequality fell in most of the region, particularly after 2002. Figure 1 shows that during this time, income inequality declined in 7 of the 8 LOC countries and in 7 of the 10 centre-right regimes. These results are confirmed by a study by Gasparini et al. (2009) that shows that inequality declined between the early 2000s and the mid-2000s in 14 of 17 countries analyzed, with the exception of Colombia, Nicaragua and Honduras. While the average regional decline in the Gini coefficient was 2-3 points, in countries ruled for most of the 2002-2007 period by LOC governments, the drop was more pronounced. Lustig (2009) arrives at a similar conclusion, noting that the decline among the LOC countries was faster than the decline among the NO-LOC centre-right regimes. She notes also that among LOC countries, the decline was more pronounced among the 'populist' than among 'social-democratic-left' regimes. The recent drop in inequality was also characterized by greater convergence at a lower level of inequality, a trend opposite to that experienced during the prior two decades, when the countries' Gini coefficients converged at a higher level of inequality[44]. Finally, Figure 1 suggests that the decline in inequality from 2003 to 2007 was greatest in those countries which experienced the largest increases from 1990 to 2002.

---

[44] Gasparini et al (2009) show that the coefficient of variation of national Gini coefficients fell from 0.10 to 0.07 over 1992-2006.

Figure 1. Changes in the Gini coefficients of the distribution of household income per capita, between 1990 and 2002 (light blue bars), and between 2003 and 2007 (dark bars) in LOC vs. NO-LOC countries

Source: authors' elaboration on the SEDLAC (2007) data and other data when SEDLAC data are missing. Note: Countries are assigned to the LOC group if a progressive government has ruled for at least 4 years between 2002 and 2007.

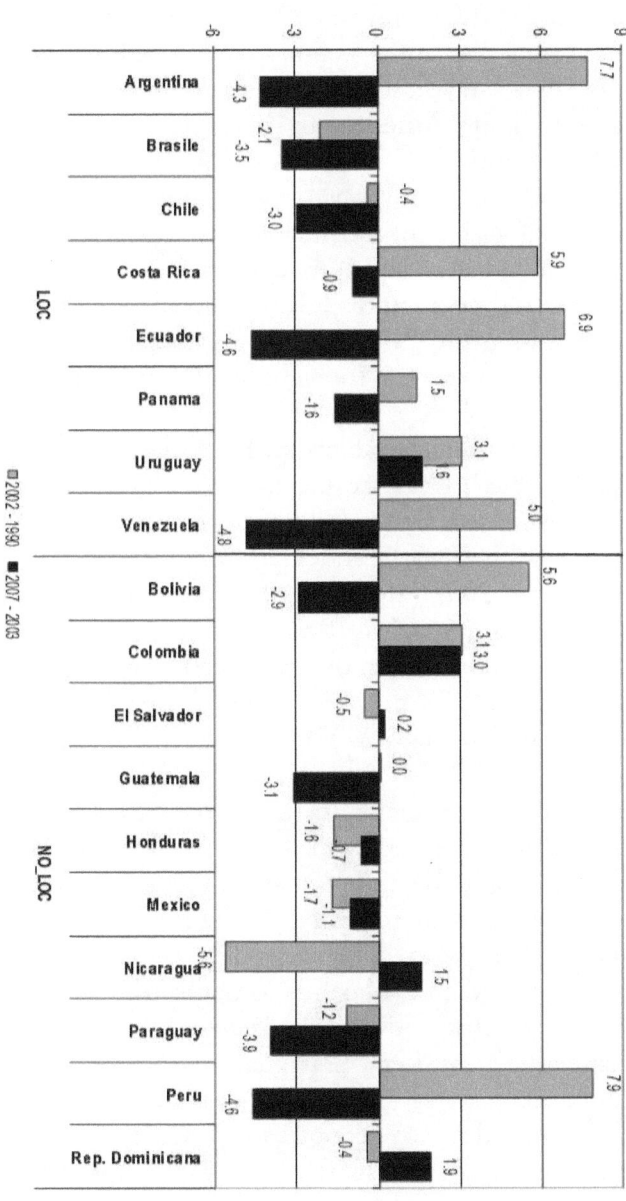

2. Factors explaining the changes in income inequality from 1990 to 2007

2.A. External shocks

(i) Terms of trade gains. During the 1990s, the international terms of trade of the region (2000=100) followed the business cycle, with declines during 1990-93, and the 1998-99 and 2000-02 crises. Since the beginning of the new century, the rapid growth of Asian countries exerted a favorable impact on the exports and economic performance of Latin America. In 2006, China alone accounted for a third of world coal, iron ore and aluminum consumption, a quarter of world copper consumption, and a large share of the world imports of agricultural commodities. The pull effect of Asian economies resulted in a rapid growth of Latin America's exports. As a result, the region's export/GDP ratio rose from 13% to 24% on average between the 1990s and 2007. The rapid increase in the value of exports was due to significant improvements in both export prices and volumes, with the highest increases recorded in energy and agricultural products such as vegetable oils, flour and seeds (CEPAL 2007). As a result, in 2007, the regional terms of trade index exceeded by 33% its average level of the 1990s, generating a positive yearly shock of 3.7% of the regional GDP between 2003 and 2007 (Ocampo 2008). In the five main oil-metal exporting Andean countries (Bolivia, Chile, Ecuador, Peru and Venezuela) the terms of trade gains from 2003 to 2007 were massive and generated a positive shock of between seven percent and 15% of GDP (Ocampo 2009).

However, these improvements in the terms of trade hide varying situations within the region. For instance, between the 1990s and 2007, the terms of trade index rose by 52% for South America (thanks to the huge gains recorded by the Andean countries), 21% for Mexico, and 13% for Mercosur, but fell by 13% in Central America, a region which depends on imported energy (CEPAL 2007). Of the countries adversely affected by the recent terms of trade changes, a subset (Paraguay, Uruguay, Panama and Nicaragua) remained specialized in the export of traditional agricultural commodities. A second group (Costa Rica, El Salvador, Guatemala, and Honduras) switched to the export of textiles and

growing emigration (Perez Caldentey and Vernengo 2007).

What was the inequality impact of the recent changes in terms of trade and export volumes? A partial equilibrium analysis would suggest that, given the high concentration of ownership of land and mines (where the presence of TNCs[45] is very important) in the region, the gains in terms of trade likely generated, *ceteris paribus*, a disequalizing effect on the functional and size distribution of income. Indeed, production in these sectors is very land, resource and capital-intensive, and has a limited employment generation capacity[46].

Changes in international terms of trade also affect income inequality via changes in tax and non-tax revenue. If mining and oil rents accrue to the state (as in Bolivia) either as an owner or in the form of royalties, an improvement in terms of trade raises government non-tax revenue in line with the increases in international prices. In addition, with a constant 'government tax effort', a rise in the international prices of exported goods generates an expansionary effect on income and consumption, which generate greater direct and indirect tax revenue. Due to this effect and to tax buoyancy, the tax/GDP ratio therefore rises. The tax/GDP ratio may also increase further if governments intensify their 'tax collection effort'.

What does the empirical evidence for Latin America show about the relation between terms of trade and tax and non-tax/GDP ratio? The top-left panel of Figure 2 suggests that there is a strong association (r= 0.97) between **average** regional terms of trade and **average** regional tax/GDP ratio. Yet, such aggregate relation hides more than it reveals. Indeed, when looking at country data for the 18 Latin American countries analyzed in this paper the relation appears much weaker (r=0.18) (top-right panel). The situation does

---

[45]An important part of the commodity price increase left the region in the form of profit remittances, as the exploitation of natural resources in Latin America is often in the hands of TNCs. Chile and Peru account for over half of the regional outflow of profit remittances, though they account for only 8 percent of the region's GDP.

[46]For instance, in Argentina, agriculture accounts for a modest 8 percent of the total labor force

not improve if the sample is restricted to the eight main commodity exporters (bottom-left panel), but improves (0.39 for 1990-2007, 0.63 for 2003-07) when considering the impact of terms of trade changes on **non-tax revenue** for these countries between 2003 and 2007. Overall, there is only limited evidence that gains in international terms of trade raised tax/GDP ratios. The impact on income inequality (which could derive from the distribution of a greater amount of rents via the budget) does not seem strong. In addition, the impact of such redistribution is not automatic, as it depends on the incidence of transfers carried out with the additional revenue. In contrast, it is likely (see Figure 4) that the main distributive effect of terms of trade takes place via the increase in GDP growth.

Figure 2 (A, B, C, D). Average international terms of trade and tax revenue/GDP ratio, Latin America, 1990-07

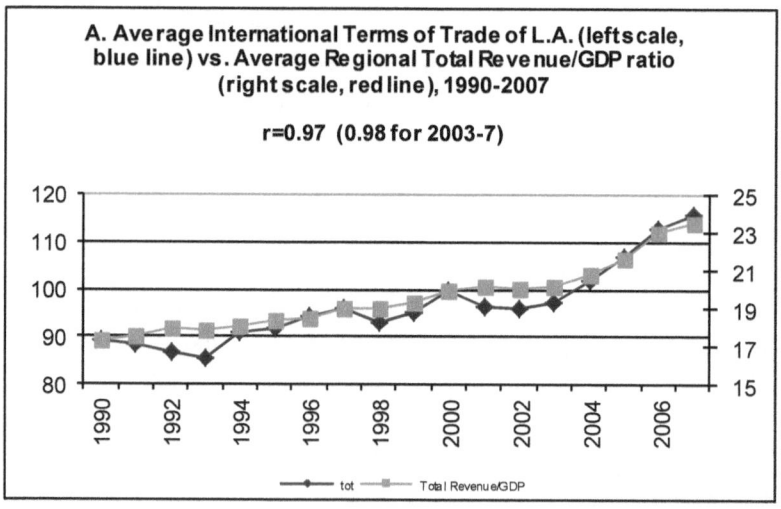

A. Average International Terms of Trade of L.A. (left scale, blue line) vs. Average Regional Total Revenue/GDP ratio (right scale, red line), 1990-2007

r=0.97 (0.98 for 2003-7)

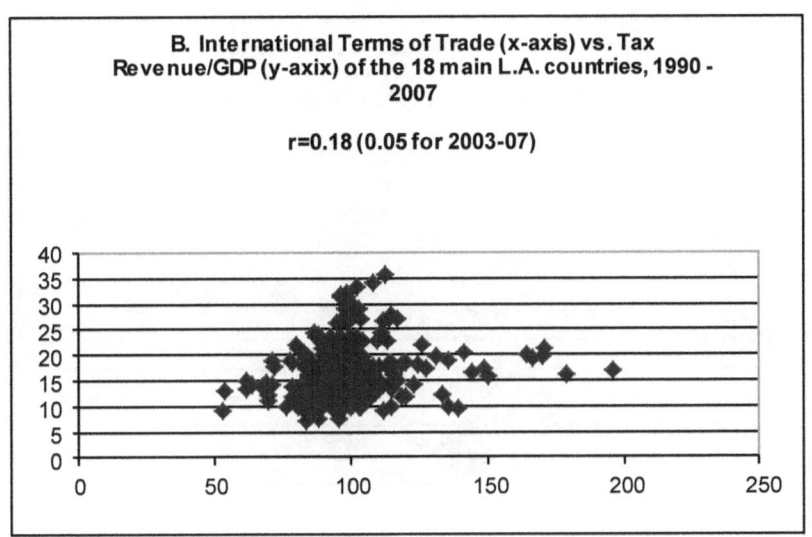

B. International Terms of Trade (x-axis) vs. Tax Revenue/GDP (y-axix) of the 18 main L.A. countries, 1990 - 2007

r=0.18 (0.05 for 2003-07)

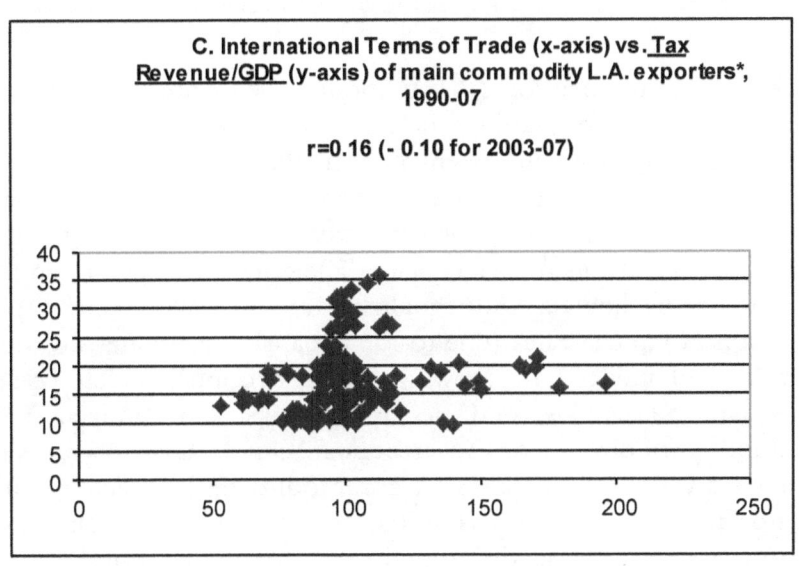

C. International Terms of Trade (x-axis) vs. Tax Revenue/GDP (y-axis) of main commodity L.A. exporters*, 1990-07

r=0.16 (- 0.10 for 2003-07)

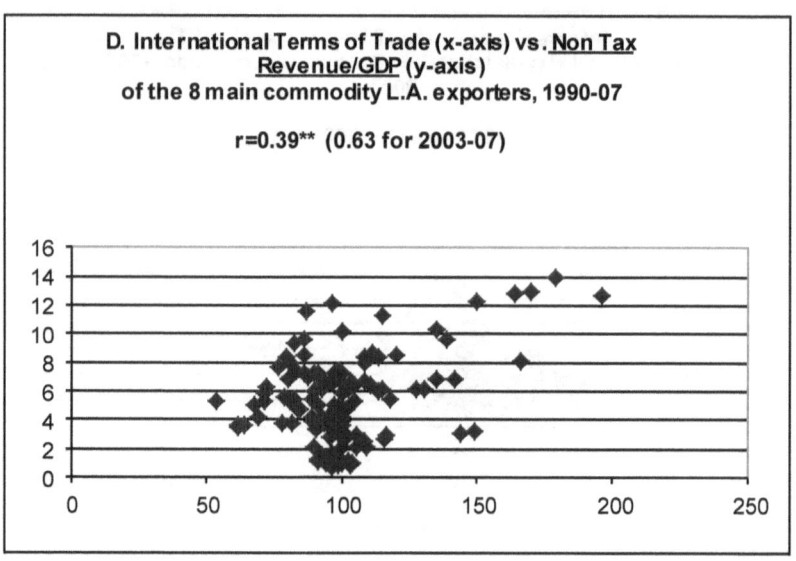

Source: authors' elaboration on the basis of the ECLAC's BADECON database. Notes: Tax revenue does not include non-tax revenue (such as royalties) which accrues to governments. *Argentina, Bolivia, Brazil, Chile, Ecuador, Mexico, Peru, and Venezuela; **r=0.56 without Argentina and Brazil.

Thus, in the absence of a CGE model, the general equilibrium effects of the commodity boom on income inequality are difficult to map out. Improvements in the balance of payments do relax the foreign-exchange constraint to growth and may stimulate production in labor-intensive industries with the effect of reducing income inequality. The effect via tax and non-tax revenue seems limited. An equalizing effect could occur via a reduction in interest rates (due to the expansion in money creation from abroad induced by growing export receipts), which favors firms and households, and penalizes banks and rentiers. Yet, commodity booms also can produce 'Dutch Disease' effects which slow growth in the non-commodity traded sector, with the possible effect of increasing income inequality, as many low-income people work in the traded sector of the economy. All in all, while it is plausible that the recent commodity bonanza had a favorable effect on growth, the impact on inequality is undetermined as it depends to a large extent on the use of the additional resources.

(ii) Migration and migrant remittances. Traditionally, emigration has not played a central role in promoting growth in developing countries. Yet, with the increasing integration of the world economy, the fertility decline and aging of the population of the OECD countries, and the lowering of migration costs, remittances have emerged as a possible growth driver in some developing nations. While the relation between migration and development remains controversial, remittances' weight in GDP and the current account balance has risen over time. In 1990, migration played a limited role in Latin America. However, they grew from 1.12% of the regional GDP in 1990, to 6.71% in 2007 (USAID 2008).

The sharp increase of remittances over the last decade benefitted in particular Central America, the Caribbean countries, Mexico and Ecuador. The surge in migration and remittances occurred mainly during the crisis years of 1998 and 2003, though it did not decline during the boom years of 2003-2008. Official remittances to the region increased from US$ 2 to 59 billion dollars, or from 0.23% to 2% of regional GDP between 1980 and 2006 (Table 2). In 2007, they accounted for 2.3% of the regional GDP (CEPAL 2007) but for over 11% in Central America, 2.8% in Mexico and about 20% in Grenada, Guyana and Jamaica. Interestingly, with the exception of Ecuador and Uruguay, remittances played a greater role in countries which did not experience terms of trade gains, meaning that Latin American countries support their current balance by exporting either primary commodities or migrant labor, and only a modest amount of manufactured goods.

Table 1. Remittances/GDP in countries affected by positive and negative terms of trade.

	1980-1990	1991-2001	2002-2006
Countries that recently experienced <u>favourable</u> terms-of-trade effects			
Argentina	0.1	0.2	0.4
Bolivia	2.0	2.2	2.5
Colombia	1.5	1.9	3.3
Ecuador	0.6	3.5	6.5
Peru	0.8	1.6	2.1
Venezuela	-0.4	-0.2	-0.1
Mexico	1.0	1.2	2.4
AVERAGE	0.7	1.3	2.1
Countries that recently experienced <u>unfavourable</u> terms-of-trade effects			
Dominican Republic	4.4	8.7	11.4
El Salvador	8.8	14.0	15.9
Guatemala	1.5	1.9	10.5
Honduras	3.6	8.1	20.5
Nicaragua	5.5	10.0	14.5
Paraguay	...	1.9	2.9
Uruguay	0.2	0.3	0.8
AVERAGE	3.6	4.9	8.8

Source: Adapted from Perez Caldentey and Vernengo (2008)

For the above group of countries, one may be tempted to establish a causal link between rising remittances and falling inequality. Yet, the literature on the inequality impact of remittances suggests that their short and medium term effect tends to be disequalizing. Indeed, in developing countries only middle-class persons are able to finance the high costs of illegal migration. As a consequence, the remittances will accrue not to the poor, but mainly to middle-income groups. In addition, in the countries of origin, the migration of skilled workers tends to raise their wage rate in relation to that of unskilled workers. The final distributive effect depends on how the families of migrants receiving remittances share them with low income families. In addition, remittances may reduce inequality over the long term, if the creation of migrant networks reduces migration costs, thus making migration accessible to low income/unskilled people as well. The long term inequality impact of migration depends also on whether it triggers a brain drain, brain gain, or brain waste. The cross country evidence (IMF 2004) shows that remittances raise current consumption, reduce volatility and improve the creditworthiness of the countries of origin, but do not have a significant impact on the investment rate and GDP growth. In light of all this, one would not expect that migrant remittances played a central role in reducing income inequality, either directly or indirectly.

(iii) Availability of external finance. Between 2004 and 2008, the region recorded a rebound in capital inflows after their decline in the early 2000s. The increase in capital inflows between 2002 and 2007 amounted to 2.4% of the region's GDP (Ocampo 2008). Portfolio flows to the private sector accounted for most of this increase. The cost of such funds dropped markedly with the decline of country spreads, i.e. from a regional average of 11.5% in May 2004, to less than seven percent in May 2007, and 7.3% in May 2008. This financial exuberance affected the region in several ways (Ocampo 2009): first, the decline in international interest rates exerted a downward pressure on domestic interest rates; second, capital inflows led to an appreciation of the nominal exchange rate; third, portfolio inflows mainly consisted of purchases of shares and securities, generated a boom in regional stock markets and, as a result, the stock market capitalization of the 7 largest regional economies quadrupled in value between mid-2004 and the end of 2007 (*ibid*); fourth, the inflows facilitated the accumulation of international reserves which reduced country spreads on international loans. In contrast, the FDI stock stagnated at 22% of the region's GDP, after having risen from 8% to 22.6% of GDP between 1995 and 2002 as a result of several foreign acquisitions of privatized state assets (Unctad 2008).

Also in this case, it is difficult to trace the general equilibrium effect of the 2004 to 2007 financial exuberance on inequality. As in the case of rising terms of trade gains and remittances, it is likely that these inflows affected growth (and therefore employment and inequality) indirectly, via the relaxation of the balance of payments constraint. Yet, financial exuberance also caused an appreciation of the nominal exchange rate in the majority of countries from May 2006 to September 2008 (Ocampo 2009). Such trends penalized the labor-intensive traded sector and, with it, the distribution of income (Taylor 2004). As for the direct effect, increased availability of finance benefitted mainly large capital- and skill-intensive companies and banks while it did not ease the problems of access to credit by labor-intensive small and medium enterprises, possibly inducing in this way adverse distributional effects.

2.B. Business cycle effects

From the end of 2002, the region recorded a strong recovery thanks to favorable external conditions, better policies (see later) and improved domestic conditions. G rowth of GDP/c doubled in the 1990s and from 2002 to 2007 in South America, and rose by half a point in Central America. Only a few countries (such as Chile, which enjoyed Tiger-like growth in the 1990s) did not improve their performance. While all countries recorded positive performance, growth was on average 2 percentage points higher in LOC countries t han in NO LOC ones (Figure 3).

Figure 3. Macroeconomic and growth performance of LOC versus NO-LOC governments, 2003-7

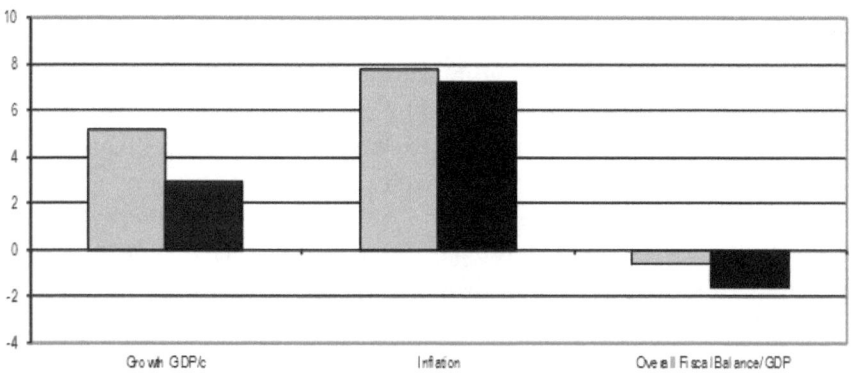

Source: Authors' elaboration based on ECLAC's Badecon for the growth of GDP/c and overall fiscal balance/GDP, and IMF's World Economic Outlook 2008 Database for inflation. Note: The inflation rate of LOC countries would be 6.6% (i.e. lower than the NO-LOC countries' average) if Venezuela (which recorded an average inflation of 21% during this period) is excluded.

Economic theory suggests that in developing countries an increase in GDP/c improves labor absorption and, under certain conditions, the wage rate, with positive distributive effects. In contrast, a GDP contraction raises inequality as wages drop and redundant workers are not covered by unemployment insurance. The evidence in Figure 4 on Latin America confirms this view and shows that, on average, a one percent yearly increase in GDP/c over the cycle (which has an average duration of 4-6 years) reduces the Gini coefficient by 0.12 percentage points, thus confirming the prediction of the above theory. Yet, a decline in inequality following a return to growth is of course, far from automatic, as growth patterns can be pro-poor, neutral or immiserizing.

Figure 4. Percentage changes in Gini coefficients (y- axis) versus percentage change in GDP/c (x-axis) over the business cycle in 18 countries, 1990-2007

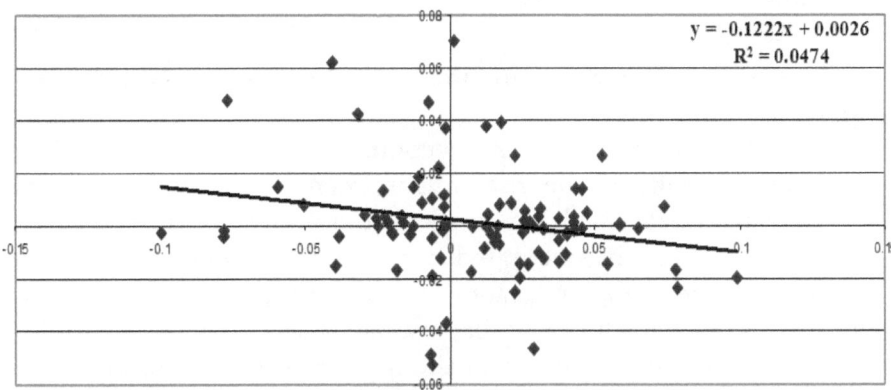

Source: authors' elaboration.

The evidence would thus suggest that the recovery recorded from 2003 to2007, as well as the labor policies discussed in section 3.4, generated a positive effect on employment and the distribution of wages. As shown in Table 2, from 2002 to 2007, the unemployment rate dropped by 5.3 points in LOC countries and 2 points in NO-LOC countries. Over 5.3 million new jobs were created each year in the region, i.e. at a much greater rate than during the previous decade. The new jobs were mainly taken by low–income groups, contributing significantly to the drop in inequality.

Table 2. Labour market trends for LOC and NO-LOC countries in Latin America, 1990-2007

Country groups	Variables	1990	2002	2007
LOC countries	Unemployment rate (%)	8.9	13.2	7.9
	Share of informal employment	40.5	38.9	38.1
	average wage index (2000=100)	92.2	98.6	103.4
	Minimum wage index	86.1	100.4	138.6
NO-LOC countries	Unemployed	8.5	10.0	8.0*
	Share of informal employment	48.5	53.7	49.2
	Average wage index** (2000=100)	79.5	102.2	102.0
	Minimum wage index (2000=100)	104.1	104.2	109.9

Source: authors' compilation on ECLAC's Badenso database and ECLAC's 2008 Panorama Social, ILO's Labour Overview (various years), and data from national statistical offices for the initial and last years.
Notes: *Guatemala is not included in the average for 2007; the Dominican Republic and Honduras are not included at all due to lack of data.

2.C. An improvement in the distribution of educational achievements

Another factor that might have contributed to the recent fall in income inequality is the rise in enrolment rates recorded at all educational levels since the early-to-mid 1990s (Gasparini et al. 2009), and the subsequent reduction in enrolment inequality in primary and secondary education. For instance, the probability that a child from the bottom decile completes secondary education in relation to that of a child from the top decile rose from 36.7% to 50% between 1990 and 2005 (CEPAL 2007a)[47]. The surge in enrolments raised also the average number of years of education of the working population.

---

[47]However, during the same period, the gap between rich and poor in accessing tertiary education widened.

Figure 5. Percentage changes in average years of education of the adult population and the Gini of educational achievements between the mid-1990s and the mid-2000s in 18 Latin American countries.

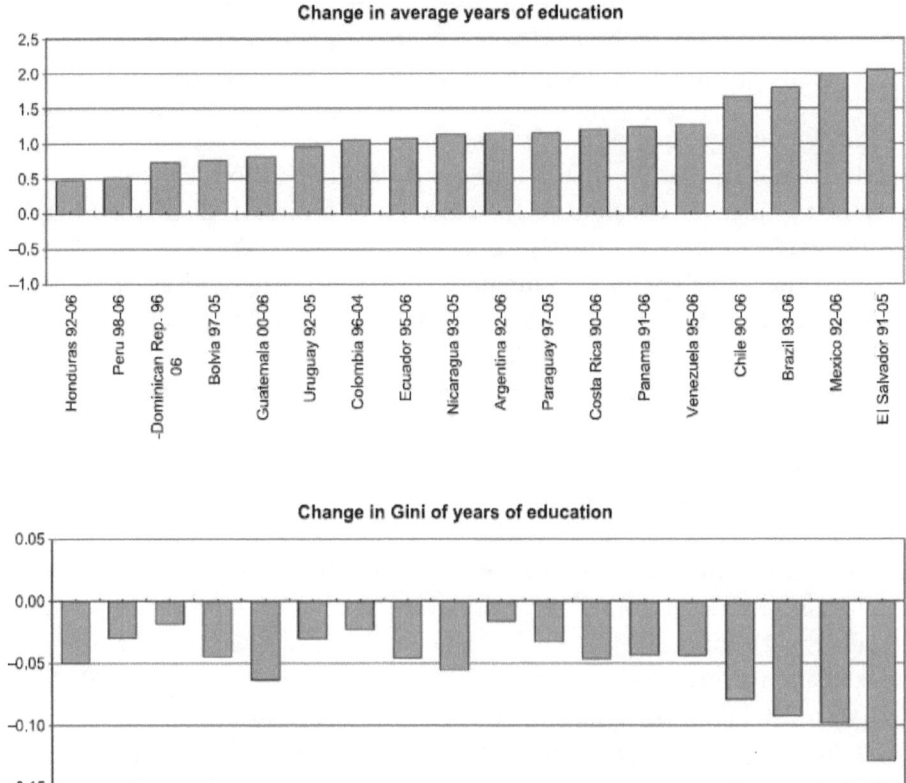

Source: Gasparini et al (2009)

Figure 5 provides evidence of the gains that were recorded under both LOC and NO-LOC regimes. All in all, the countries of Latin America made substantial inroads in the field of human capital formation and in reducing many dimensions of inequality in education. Yet, the effect of these trends on current and future inequality are not automatic, as an expansion of the stock of human capital leads to an increase in employment and drop in wage inequality only if additional jobs are created. In this regard, an IPEA study (cited in CEPAL 2006) decomposed the fall in inequality observed in Brazil between 2000 and 2006 and concluded that two thirds of the decline was due to a fall in labor incomes inequality caused by a drop in educational inequality among workers and in wage premium by education level.

2.D. Recent policy approaches

Latin America has been for long a symbol of authoritarian political systems, unequal distribution of assets, and limited redistribution by the state. However, during the last twenty years, the political landscape has been dominated by a steady drive towards democratization and, starting from the mid-late 1990s, a steady shift in political orientation towards LOC regimes. As documented by the results of different waves of the *Latinobarometro*[48], such shift was to a large extent, explained by growing frustration with the poor results of the Washington Consensus policies implemented in the 1980s and 1990s. Among other things, such policies caused a shrinkage of the industrial working class, a weakening of the unions, rising unemployment, and a substantial enlargement of informal sector and self-employment. The shift away from such approach began with the election in 1990 of the centrist Patricio Alwyn in Chile, but intensified in the 2000s (Table 3). Figure 5 shows that in mid-2009, of the 18 Latin American countries analyzed, only three countries (including Colombia and Mexico) were run by centre-right governments.

[48]Corporación Latinobarómetro is a non-profit NGO based in Santiago, Chile. Since 1995 it carries out public polls on economic and political topics by means of sample surveys of 19,000 households based in 18 countries of Latin America accounting for 400 million people (http://www.latinobarometro.org).

Table 3. Changes in political orientation in 18 Latin American countries, 1999 - 2009

Country	President	Party	Assumed office
Chile	Ricardo Lagos	*Partido Socialista de Chile*	11-03-00
	Michelle Bachelet	*Partido Socialista de Chile*	11-03-06
Venezuela	Hugo Chávez	*Movimiento Quinta República*	02-02-99
		Partido Socialista Unido de Venezuela,	03-12-06
Brazil	Luiz Inácio 'Lula' da Silva	*Partido dos Trabalhadores*	01-01-03
			01-01-07
Ecuador	Lucio Edwin Gutiérrez Borbúa	*PSP (Patriotic Society Party)*	15-01-03
			20-04-05
	Rafael Correa	*Alianza PAIS (Patria Altiva I Soberana)*	15-01-07
Argentina	Nestor Kirchner	*Partido Justicialista*	25-05-03
	Cristina Fernández de Kirchner	*Partido Justicialista*	10-12-07
Panama*	Martin Torrijos	*Partido Revolucionario Democratico*	02-05-04
Uruguay	Tabaré Vásquez	*Frente Amplio*	01-03-05
Bolivia	Evo Morales	*Movimiento al Socialismo*	22-01-06
Costa Rica	Oscar Arias	*Partido Liberacion Nacional*	08-05-06
Nicaragua	Daniel Ortega	*Frente Sandinista de Liberación Nacional*	10-01-07
Guatemala	Álvaro Colom Caballeros	*Social-democratic National Union of Hope*	14-01-08
Paraguay	Fernando Lugo	*Alianza Patriótica por el Cambio, APC*	15-08-08
El Salvador	Carlos Mauricio Funes Cartagena	*Farabundo Martí National Liberation Front)*	01-06-09

Source: authors compilation on the basis of national sources as reported by Wikipedia.
Notes: * on 2 July 2009 Ricardo Martinelli, of the right-of-centre Democratic Change party was elected and replaced Martin Torrijos.

Figure 6. Changes in political orientation in 18 Latin American countries, 1990 - 2009

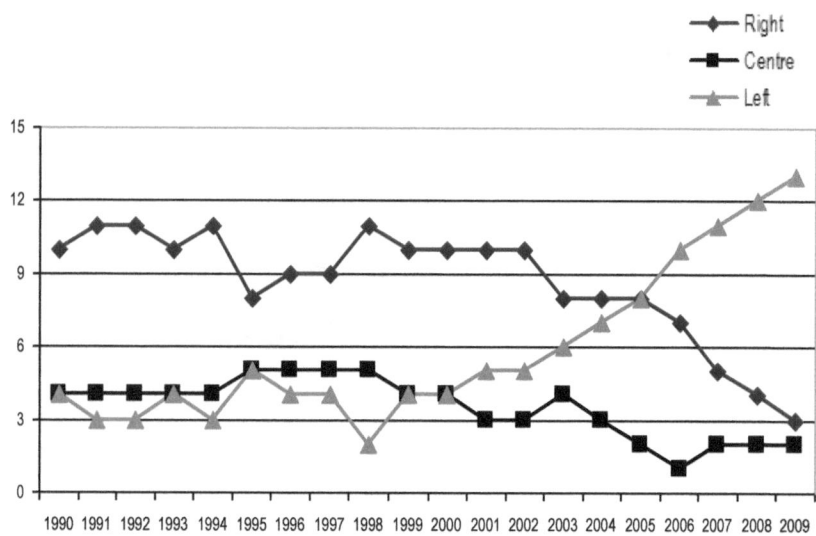

Source: authors' compilation on the basis of Keefer (2006) and national data reported by Wikipedia for the years 2006-09. Notes: a few corrections were made to the Keefer database, as in the case of: Chile 1990-99 that we treat as a centre (and not a right) regime and a left (not a right) regime since 2000; Colombia 2003-07, that we treat as a right (not an independent) regime; Costa Rica 1990-94, that we treated as a left (instead of right) regime, and between 1998 and 2007 when we treat as a centre -left (instead of right) regime; Mexico between 1990 and 2000 which we treat as a centre (instead of a left) regime; and Uruguay 1995-2004, that we consider a centre (instead of a right) regime; Venezuela 1990-93 that we treat as a left (not a right) regime, 1994-8 that we treat as a right (not left) regime, and from 1999 onwards that we consider a left (not an independent) regime.

As noted by Panizza (2005) and Lustig (2009), such regimes vary substantially among each other. Some of the LOC regimes now dominating the region can be defined as social-democratic, as in is the case of Chile's *Partido Socialista*, Uruguay's *Frente Amplio* and Brazil's *Partido dos Trabalhadores* (*ibid*, see also Lustig 2009). These parties have their roots in organizations of the working class, but have evolved into broad coalitions comprising sectors of business and the middle classes, the urban and rural poor, the unemployed and those working in the informal sector. They have abandoned any notion of revolutionary break in favor of electoral politics and respect for the institutions of liberal democracy. In contrast, a second group of countries (such as Argentina and Ecuador) developed left-nationalist platforms, while Venezuela, Bolivia and Nicaragua are characterized by a radical left-populist approach entailing a redistribution of assets both nationally and internationally.

Matters of social justice and economic development are at the core of the new LOC parties' identity. However, in the pursuit of such objectives, the LOC parties avoided the ill-conceived approach to budget deficits and inflation typical of the heterodox-populist policies of the 1980s (Dornbusch and Edwards, 1991). In fact, the LOC economic model incorporates into its paradigm some liberal policies such as a sound fiscal policy and low inflation, an awareness of the inefficiencies associated with some forms of state intervention and protectionism, the primacy of the market in setting prices, regional trade integration and openness to foreign investment. At the same time, its concern for poverty and inequality, recognition of market failures and the increasing importance assigned to strengthening state institutions are in sharp contrast with the neo-liberal emphasis on shrinking the state and the self-sustained role of the markets (Panizza 2005).

LOC governments have thus developed a new economic paradigm and social contract that binds together their traditional and emergent constituencies through a combination of macroeconomic stability, neo-corporatist and participatory institutions, redistribution via taxation and targeted social programs (Panizza 2005a). There are, however, built-in tensions within the new social contract. For instance, tension exists between the fiscal and monetary constraints required to maintain macroeconomic stability, and the demands for higher public investment and social spending. In addition, in some cases (such as Brazil), macroeconomic stability was achieved by means of high interest rates and primary surpluses, which dampened economic growth and favored financial rents over public investment. The main components of the new LOC model are reviewed hereafter.

(i) Macroeconomic policies. With some country variation, the measures introduced are broadly aligned with the 'pro-poor macroeconomics' paradigm (Cornia 2006). Its key elements are:

A fiscal policy aiming at balancing the budget in the context of an expansionary expenditure policy

Traditionally, Latin America adopted pro-cyclical macroeconomic policies that boost growth during periods of external buoyancy, but build up vulnerabilities which explode when the favorable conditions disappear. This stance has partially changed over the recent decade. A decline in the budget deficit was targeted in all countries, despite an increase in public expenditure, with LOC countries achieving better results than NO-LOC countries (Figure 3). Overall, fiscal deficits have typically been reduced below one percent of GDP (much lower than the EU and US) and in several cases were turned into surpluses. As a result, in 2006 and 2007 the average central government budget for the region as a whole was in equilibrium. This suggests a shift towards countercyclical fiscal management (Ocampo 2007). A **'strong version'** of such policy, which requires the extra revenue collected during upturns to be saved and used to support public expenditure during bad years, was followed in Chile, Peru and Argentina. A **'weak version,'** consisting in balancing the budget during the upturn, was followed in most other countries. As noted by Ocampo (2008), the latter approach was followed because of difficulties faced by democratic regimes in convincing the population of the need for continuing a policy of austerity in periods of relatively abundant revenue.

Rising tax/GDP ratios

Tax policy underwent gradual but deep changes, both during the 1990s and even more so since 2002, particularly in LOC countries. As a result, for the region as a whole, the tax and non-tax revenue of the central government, including social security contributions, rose from 15% of GDP in 1990 to 17% in 2000, and 20.2% in 2007 (CEPAL, 2007). Large revenue increases were recorded over 2002-2007 in Argentina and Brazil (9 points of GDP), Colombia (8.5 points), Bolivia (10 points), and Venezuela (6 points), and only Mexico experienced a small decline. By mid 2000s, Brazil, Argentina, Uruguay and Costa Rica had reached levels of taxation similar to those of the US and Japan. In contrast, with tax/GDP ratios at around 10-12%, Group 3 countries (see Table 4) remained mired in a 'low revenue development trap' which made them unable to fund pro-poor and pro-growth public goods, merit goods and goods generating large positive externalities. The revenue increase recorded in most of the region constitutes an important achievement, as the traditional inability or unwillingness to raise revenue was an important factor in the large accumulation of public debt during the 1970s, the subsequent debt crisis of the 1980s, and the macro instability of the 1990s.

The revenue increase resulted from a widespread reduction in excise taxes (due to administrative simplification) and tariffs (following trade liberalization), a rise in indirect taxes (VAT *in primis*), an increase in personal and corporate income tax, and stagnation of wealth taxes and social security contributions following the informalization of employment (Table 4).

Table 4. Tax Revenue and Non Tax Revenue GDP ratio of the central government in 1990, 2002, and 2007, and changes in tax structure in LOC and NO-LOC countries

Tax revenue/GDP			Non-tax revenue/GDP				Changes over 2002-07 (% points of GDP)				
1990	2002	2007	1990	2002	2007	Country Group	Trade taxes	Excises +other ind tax	VAT	Direct Taxes	Social Security
17.5	19.2	23.7	5.4	5.3	5.9	LOC	+0.38	-0.23	+ 1.35	+ 2.56	+ 0.45
9.9	14.2	16.1	2.8	2.5	3.4	NO-LOC	- 0.20	- 0.72	+ 1.19	+ 1.49	+ 0.13

Source: Authors' elaborations on ECLAC's BADECOM.

Between 2002 and 2007 there was also an increase in non-tax revenue linked to terms of trade gains. From 2002 to 2007, LOC countries appear to have performed somewhat better, both in terms of additional tax and non-tax revenue raised, and in terms of the progressivity of the tax instruments used[49] (Table 4).

---

[49]A regression analysis (1990-2007, 18 Latin American countries) of tax revenue/GDP was carried out to test for differences in tax behavior between LOC and NO-LOC countries. OLS estimates confirm that LOC countries taxed 2.5 GDP points more than NO-LOC countries. However, the LOC dummy is non-significant when using the fixed effects estimator. The countries were then split between LOC and NO-LOC and tests were carried out separately on the two subsamples by means of the fixed effects estimator. The results show that tax/GDP ratio rose on average by 0.20-0.22 GDP points a year in both types of countries due to greater effort at tax collection and, in some cases, a

Countries benefiting from large increases in the price of hydrocarbons, metals and agricultural exports recorded important growth in public revenue, as they taxed part of the land and mining rent by imposing special taxes on the operating revenues of mining companies. In turn, Argentina appropriated part of the benefits accrued from the real exchange rate depreciation of 2002 by means of a selective *ad valorem* export tax, the incidence of which is progressive[50]. While the improvements in terms of trade contributed to the increase in total revenue/GDP ratio, such increase preceded the commodity boom and also resulted from efforts at broadening the direct and indirect tax base and at reducing evasion. In addition, several countries introduced a "surrogate" tax on financial transactions which, while potentially distortive (Cetrangolo and Sabaini 2006), is a 'second best' tax on highly concentrated financial assets which would otherwise remain untaxed.

It is still an open question whether the recent revenue increase was enough to achieve the equity objectives of LOC governments, or whether it exacerbated the regressive features of tax systems in

---

formalization of the economy. Such parameters are higher (0.75 and 0.54 respectively) for the boom years 2003-07. The test shows, in addition, that while an increase in GDP/c lead to higher tax/GDP in LOC countries, no effects were observed in NO-LOC countries. Overall, the hypothesis that LOC countries have a more active tax policy seems broadly verified.

	OLS (all sample)	FE(all sample)	FE (LOC)	FE (NO-LOC)
GDP/c	0.0001***	0.0005	0.002***	0.0001
Year	0.1835***	0.2454***	0.200*	0.220***
Dummy LOC countries	2.5315***	-0.1019	--	--

Source: authors' elaboration on ECLAC's BADECON and national data. Note:*, **, *** significant at 10%, 5% & 1%

[50]Governments developed a variety of fiscal mechanisms for appropriating part of the increase in commodity prices (CEPAL 2007, p.31). Argentina introduced an export tax on selected agricultural goods. In turn, Venezuela, Bolivia and Chile introduced new taxes to raise the revenue generated from their non- renewable resources. As a result, the share of fiscal resources represented by such revenue in Bolivia, Chile, Colombia and Mexico rose from of 27.8%, 7.6%, 9.9% and 29.4% in the 1990s to 34.8%, 20%, 14.2% and 37.5% in 2006-2007.

the region. Table 5 suggests that while tax reform still has a long way to go, the 2002-2007 increase in tax/GDP ratio was achieved in part by raising progressive direct taxes, while reducing regressive excises and general sales tax. In addition, the selective export tax used in Brazil and Argentina is likely progressive, as it captures part of the 'windfall profits' due to rising world prices, accruing to a sector characterized by high asset and income concentration.

Monetary policy and inflation targeting
As suggested by the 'impossible trinity theorem,' in economies with an open capital account, such as those of Latin America, the monetary authorities can count only few tools (accumulation of reserves and sterilization of the increase in money supply induced by capital inflows) to control the fall in interest rates and credit expansion occurring during periods of export bonanzas and financial exuberance. The only other instrument utilized was the introduction of capital controls, as done in part from 2002 to 2008 by Argentina, and in 2007 by Colombia (Ocampo 2008). In most other countries, both LOC and NO-LOC, monetary policy was therefore either accommodating or neutral, tolerating (with the major exception of Brazil) lower or even negative real interest rates and higher inflation rates. Monetary policy also aimed at reducing the extensive dollarization of the financial system. Argentina conducted a radical de-dollarization during the crisis of 2002, while Peru, Bolivia and Uruguay adopted a policy of gradual de-dollarization. In particular, there was a decline in the floating of dollar-denominated public-sector bonds in domestic markets. Finally, there was a general strengthening of Central Bank independence.

Exchange rate regime
With the exception of Brazil and Venezuela, most LOC and several other countries abandoned the free floating and fixed pegged regimes adopted during the prior decade, and opted instead for a competitive exchange rate regime, as in the case of Argentina (Frenkel and Rapetti, 2008), or employed managed floats aimed at preventing an appreciation of the real exchange rate. As noted by Ocampo (2007), consistent with this approach, Central Banks

reduced the supply of foreign exchange through interventions in the currency market, particularly during the massive capital inflows of 2006 and 2007, adopted a coherent fiscal policy, and in a few cases, introduced capital controls. The clearest example of this policy can be seen in Argentina, where a competitive exchange rate was a cornerstone of macroeconomic policy. There is evidence that such policy shifted labor towards the labor-intensive traded sector (mainly manufacturing) with a strong equalizing effect (Damill 2004, cited in World Bank 2005).

In 2006 and 2007, this policy approach came under pressure owing to large increases in export prices, capital inflows and remittances, and several countries – both commodity exporters, and particularly non-commodity exporters - experienced a mild-to-moderate real appreciation (Figure 6). Indeed, the large current and capital account surpluses realized in most of South America in 2006 and 2007 led to an appreciation of 4.8% of the extra-regional real exchange rate for the region as a whole. Stronger effects were felt in Colombia, Brazil and Venezuela (Figure 6, and CEPAL 2007). Only Argentina, Bolivia (till 2006) and Panama experienced a modest real depreciation, while in other countries there were no changes (Figure 6). It must be noted however, that without a huge accumulation of reserves and parallel sterilization efforts, several countries would have shown stronger symptoms of Dutch Disease and accelerating inflation in the non-tradable sector which would have generated adverse distributive impacts (Taylor 2000).

Figure 7. Trends in the index of the real effective exchange rate (REER), 2002=100 in commodity and non-commodity exporters, 2002-8 (a decline denotes an appreciation)

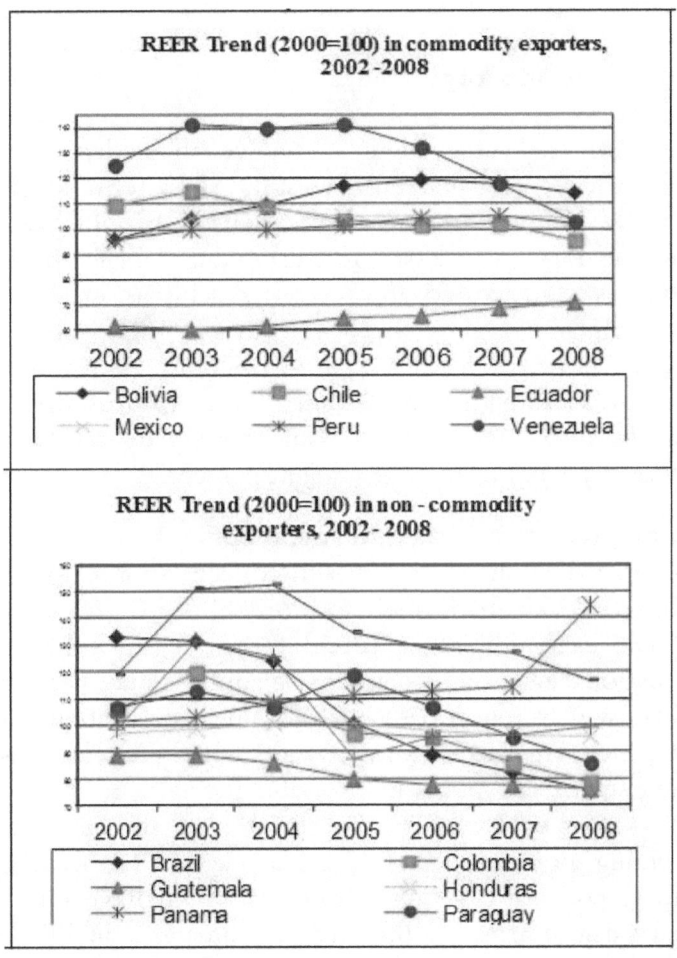

Source: authors' elaboration on the basis of ECLAC data. Notes: Argentina (which recorded a huge real depreciation in this period), as well as El Salvador, Costa Rica and Nicaragua (which maintained a broadly constant REER) were omitted to render Figure 6 more legible.

Trade and external indebtedness

The free trade policies adopted in the past have not been overturned. In contrast, the trend towards international trade integration points to some reorientation. The Free Trade Area of the Americas seems to have stalled while regional trade integration seems to have developed rapidly, especially in the field of manufacturing exports. Free trade agreements with industrialized countries have, in contrast, strengthened the exports of primary commodities. A possible exception is Mexico, which increased its exports of manufactured goods with high import contents and limited backward and forward linkages.

LOC governments attempted to reduce their dependence on foreign borrowing and generally, existing short-term stabilization agreements with the IMF were not renewed. Brazil (in 2005) and Argentina (in 2006) prepaid their outstanding debt to the IMF. A few countries restructured their foreign debt, as in the case of Argentina which – against the advice of the IMF – successfully renegotiated its private debt at a 70% discount. As a result, Latin America's gross foreign debt declined from 42% of the regional GDP in 2002, to 20% in 2007, while foreign debt/GDP net of currency reserves fell from 33% to eight percent.

(ii) Income, redistributive, and social policies

Measures to reduce the glaring wealth concentration existing in the region have seldom made their way on the LOC governments' agenda. The exception are 'radical LOC' regimes like Bolivia (which nationalized mines and is planning land reform) and Venezuela (which renegotiated oil royalties and nationalized key industries, including steel, electricity and telecommunications). The moderate stance adopted by social-democratic/reformist LOC countries is likely explained by the fact that – in the absence of overwhelming political support, and in view of the heterogeneity of the LOC coalitions – radical reforms would have unavoidably generated tensions affecting the business climate, capital flights, and electoral support. In addition, the power of progressive regimes did not reduce the influence of dominant interest groups which – though small in number – are still powerful and can sway the public opinion on controversial issues. As a result, and with the two exceptions mentioned above, the LOC policy model resembles the 'Redistribution With Growth' (Chenery et al 1978) model more than its more radical alternative of 'Redistribution Before Growth' which sees the redistribution of assets and opportunities as a way to overcome the under-consumption trap and lack of human capital afflicting developing countries. In contrast, the measures introduced in the field of labor market social expenditure, and conditional transfers, discussed hereafter, were more far reaching.

Income and labor market policies
The LOC policy model differs from the liberal one regarding the extent to which labor policies explicitly addressed the problems inherited from the 1990s, i.e. rising unemployment, job informalization and instability, falling unskilled wages, diminishing coverage of social security, and the weakening of institutions for wage negotiations and dispute settlements.

Argentina enacted income policies to strengthen the purchasing power of poor and middle-income earners, including a rise in minimum wages, a large-scale public works program, a deliberate attempt to extend the coverage of formal employment, and the re-birth of trade-unions. In Uruguay the *Frente Amplio* administration reinstated the 'wage councils', i.e. tripartite collective bargaining bodies composed of representatives from the business sector, unions and government that negotiate wage settlements for major industries. In Brazil the government set up an Economic and Social Development Council composed of representatives of business, labor and a wide variety of civil society organizations as an advisory body on economic and social issues. Most LOC governments decreed hikes of the minimum wage, which were far from excessive when considering their very low initial levels. This led to important increases in the minimum wage index in LOC countries and to a moderate increase in NO-LOC countries (Table 2 above).

A recent empirical assessment of 19 Latin American countries for the years 1997-2001 (Kristensen and Cunningham, 2006) suggests that the increases of minimum wage introduced during the 2000s in the region likely produced an equalizing effect. Indeed, the study shows that the minimum wage[51] raised the pay at the bottom of the distribution and was generally associated

[51]Minimum wage varied between 20% and 143% of low-skilled wages, with the number of beneficiaries varying between 1% and 20% of the labor force.

with lower dispersion of earnings. The minimum wage coverage was found to be more far reaching than the neoclassical theory would predict, as the minimum wage was found to lift wages in both the formal and informal sectors. Indeed, though the minimum wage is not binding in the informal sector, the study found that, in 14 of the 19 countries analyzed, the wage distribution in this sector was also enhanced.

Average wages rose even more slowly (*ibid*) and, despite their recent hike, remained generally below their 2000 level, with the exception of Chile. Such wage restraint policy may reflect the greater concern of policy makers for creating jobs over improving earnings. It also reflects the recognition that, unless backed by increases in productivity, nominal wage raises may fuel inflation with little effect on real wages. The emphasis placed on this approach is confirmed by the rapid decline in unemployment in both LOC and NO-LOC countries and a faster rise in wage employment than in self-employment (Table 2), suggesting that the policy of 'formalizing employment' produced some results. Finally, in several countries, there is evidence that the wage premium declined due to a growing supply of educated workers (section 3.3) and a shift in production towards the unskilled labor-intensive tradable sector. Overall, the labor market outcomes support the view that LOC regimes paid greater attention to equity issues.

Rising public social expenditure and redistribution
Public social expenditure started rising in the early-to-mid 1990s and continued growing in the 2000s in most of the region (Table 6). Most of the rise concerned social security, social assistance and education (*ibid*). The rise was nearly universal and, of the 21 countries in the region, only Ecuador had in 2005 a social expenditure/GDP ratio lower than in 1990 (CEPAL 2005). While there still is a huge intra-regional variation in social expenditure[52], it appears that political orientation influenced the extent of the

---

[52]In 2006, Cuba, Uruguay, Brazil, Argentina, Bolivia, Costa Rica, and Panama had social expenditure/GDP ratios in the 15-20% bracket, while in most Central American and Andean countries they were below 10 %.

2003-06 increase. Indeed, this rise was greater (by about one percent of GDP) in the LOC than in the NO-LOC ones (Table 6). A factor in the public expenditure rise was the increase in tax/GDP ratios (see above). Changes in the structure of public expenditure also played a role. For instance, the debt cancellation enjoyed by HIPC countries permitted reallocating to social activities monies used to service the foreign debt[53], while ODA-recipients increased rapidly their social expenditure, possibly due to growing conditionality for achieving the MDGs.

Table 5. Average public expenditure/GDP in LOC versus NO-LOC countries (18 countries)

Year	Social public expenditure as percentage of the Gross Domestic Product (GDP)				
	Total	Education	Health	social security	Housing
1990	9.0	2.8	2.1	3.3	0.7
1996	10.9	3.4	2.4	4.0	1.0
2003	12.8	4.3	2.8	4.6	1.1
Around 2006	13.3	4.3	2.9	4.6	1.4
LOC Δ (2006 – 2003)	1.33	0.20	0.38	0.46	0.29
NO LOC Δ (2006 – 2003)	0.48	-0.12	0.06	0.11	0.43

Source. Authors' elaboration on the basis of the ECLAC database Badenso. Notes: the data refer to the 18 countries analyzed in this study, including Bolivia (using national data) omitted in similar studies by CEPAL (2005 and 2007a).

The rise in public social expenditure likely generated positive redistributive effects. Analysis of studies on the incidence of public social expenditure by income quintile for 18 countries over 1997-2003 (CEPAL 2007, Gasparini et al 2007) suggests that: all components of public social expenditure (including social security) are less concentrated than private incomes (Table 7); expenditures on primary education and social assistance are strongly progressive, those on secondary education and healthcare are mildly progressive or proportional (depending, in the case of health, on the approach to its financing), and those on tertiary education are as concentrated as the income distribution. In turn, social security outlays (pensions and unemployment benefit) are a bit less concentrated than those of private income, as they focus

---

[53]Since 1996-7, Bolivia, Honduras and Nicaragua benefitted from debt cancellations of 5, 6 and 2 percent of their GDP.

on formal sector workers and only seldom they provide non-contributory pensions to informal sector workers and their families. Furthermore, CEPAL (2005) suggests that the incidence of such expenditure is becoming more progressive, though at different speeds across the region, as shown by the increase in enrolments in secondary education, greater access to health services, social assistance and anti-poverty programs (see below).

Table 6. Incidence of government expenditure by quintile (18 countries over selected years, 1997-2004) and concentration coefficients of public expenditure by country subgroups

Shares of total public expenditure By sector and income quintile					Expenditure Sector	Concentration coefficients of public expenditure		
I quintile	II quintile	III quintile	IVquintile	V quintile		Group 1	Group 2	Group 3
7.4	6.5	6.3	5.9	5.6	Education	-0.067	0.116	-0.138
5.1	4.7	4.2	4.0	3.7	Health	0.074	-0.073	-0.192
2.0	2.8	4.3	6.3	16.5	Soc Security	0.504	0.568	0.349
3.3	2.1	1.6	1.3	1.1	Soc Assist.	-0.089	-0.154	-0.484
0.8	0.9	1.1	1.4	0.9	Housing	0.206	0.067	-0.026
19.6	17.0	17.5	18.9	27.8	Total	0.143	0.042	0.044

Source: Elaboration on CEPAL (2007a); Note: Group 1 includes Bolivia, El Salvador, Guatemala, Honduras, Ecuador, Nicaragua, Paraguay, Peru; Group 2: Colombia, Dominican Republic, Mexico, Panama, Venezuela; Group 3: Argentina, Brazil, Chile, Costa Rica, Uruguay.

As shown in Table 6, social security expenditure is not progressive, as it mainly covers formal sector workers with stable employment. This raises the question of how can governments best expand social security coverage, whether by actively extending the formal sector, or by setting up solidarity-based, non-contributory, universal or targeted funds to provide basic benefits to informal sector workers and their families. Both approaches were followed in recent years, though the latter has been more common. For instance, several LOC countries introduced non-contributory social pensions to start addressing this problem (Table 7).

Table 7. Coverage of non-contributory pensions in Latin America and Southern Africa, 2008

	Age of eligibility	Universal (U) Means tested (M)	Amount paid/month US $	% population over 60	% pop >60 receiving a pension	Cost of pension as % of GDP
Argentina	70+	M	88	14	6	0.23
Bolivia	65+	U	18	7	69	1.30
Brazil 1	67+	M	140	9	5	0.20
Brazil 2	60/55+	M	140	9	27	0.70
Chile	65+	M	75	12	51	0.38
Costa Rica	65+	M	26	8	20	0.18
Uruguay	70+	M	100	17	10	0.62
memo item						
Lesotho	70+	U	21	8	53	1.43
Mauritius	60+	U	60	10	100	2.00
South Africa	65/58+	M	109	7	60	1.40

Source: HelpAgeInternational (2006b); Notes: Brazil 1 and 2 = Beneficio de Prestacao Continuada; Previdencia Rural.

There are not yet detailed studies on the net redistributive effects of the tax and social expenditures discussed above. Until the late 1990s, the net redistributive effect of tax-and- transfer operations in Latin America was much smaller than that of the OECD countries (Table 8), with the exception of Argentina and Costa Rica. In most countries, redistribution operated exclusively on the expenditure side. An analysis of tax incidence in 11 Latin American countries (Gomez-Sabaini 2006) concludes that the distribution of income after taxation (but before transfers) remained broadly unchanged, and even worsened in Mexico and Nicaragua where the tax system mainly relied on regressive or proportional taxes such as excises and VAT. Yet, as noted above, the increase in income and wealth taxes recorded between 2002 and 2007, especially in LOC countries, points to a gradual evolution of the tax system towards greater progressivity.

Table 8. Redistributive effect of budget operations in OECD (2005) and Latin America, around 2000s

	Tax/GDP ratio, (incl. social security)	Share of taxes on income and profits * on total taxes	Gini of the distribution of income before taxes and transfers	Gini of the distribution of income after taxes and transfers	% decline in Gini due to budget operations
Sweden '05	49.5	39.2	0.487	0.230	-52.8
Finland '05	43.9	38.3	0.392	0.231	-41.1
Japan '05	27.4	33.9	0.340	0.265	-22.1
Germany '05	34.8	28.2	0.436	0.282	-35.3
USA '05	27.3	46.5	0.455	0.344	-24.4
Italy '05	40.9	31.5	0.510	0.345	-32.4
Costa Rica '00	18.9	16.7	0.430	0.350	-18.6
Argentina '98	21.0	13.5	0.510	0.400	-21.6
Bolivia '02	17.3	11.2	0.440	0.412	-6.4
Mexico '02	12.0	41.3	0.490	0.450	-8.2
Brazil '97	26.9	16.8	0.561	0.490	-12.7
Colombia '03	16.6	29.6	0.530	0.500	-5.7

Source: compilation on Cetrangolo and Gomez Sabaini (2006) for OECD, and CEPAL (2005) for the Latin American countries. Note: The Gini in the table refer to the distribution of private and public income.

Social assistance

During the last 15 years, the region has experienced a profound change in its social protection systems, i.e. away from social insurance for the relatively few employed in the formal sector and little spending on social assistance, and towards a better financed social assistance (Barrientos and Santibanez 2009). The new emphasis on social assistance (which continues to be supported by social insurance in the slowly expanding formal sector) has entailed the development of large scale programs focusing on poverty reduction and including three main types of interventions: i.e. unconditional income transfers such as non-contributory pensions; conditional transfers (such as most of those listed in Table 9); and integrated anti-poverty programs (such as *Chile Solidario*).

Contrary to the small, donor dependent, poorly sequenced and targeted Social Emergency and Investment Funds introduced to soften the resistance to structural adjustment in the late 1980s (Cornia 2001), the new social assistance transfers are better funded by the state (with programs absorbing up to 0.5 to one percent of GDP), and cover a considerably greater share of the population at risk (Table 9). Such programs are directed to new political constituencies such as the urban and rural poor and focus on: programs aimed at simultaneously reducing poverty and ensuring that children remain in school, providing access to health services and proper nutrition (such as Brazil's celebrated *Bolsa Família*); temporary employment schemes for the construction of public infrastructure (as in Argentina's *Programma Jefas y Jefes de Hogares* and Uruguay's PANES); training of unemployed workers and youth with the aim of facilitating their access to formal sector jobs; subsidized formal sector employment for youth; and the promotion of SME (Table 9).

Several studies document the favorable impact of such transfers, even though, in many cases, comprehensive evaluations are not yet available. However, the existing evidence suggest that these programs had greater success in ensuring investments in human capital (e.g. having children to attend schools and clinics) than in lifting the poor out of poverty (Barrientos and Santibanez 2009). Yet, an IPEA microeconometric study (cited in CEPAL 2006) decomposed the inequality reduction observed in Brazil between 2000 and 2006, and found that government transfers (pensions and *Bolsa Família*) explained one third of such decline.

Table 9. Summary of some main social programs introduced in recent times in the region

Program (reference year)	Cost (GDP)	N. Beneficiaries	Monthly subsidy ($)
Plan Jefas y Jefes (Argentina, 2002)	0.80%	1.85 million workers	US$45 (2002) US$ 150 (2007)
Plan Nacional Emergencia (Bolivia, 2002)	0.86%	1.6% of Active pop.	63 $ Wage manual workers
PANES (Uruguay, 2005)	0.50%	7.2% of active pop.	55 $
Bolsa Familia (Brazil, 2005)	0.36%	11.1 million families	62 R$ for poor families 15 R$ for children 30 R$ for youth

Program (reference year)	Cost (GDP)	N. Beneficiaries	Monthly subsidy ($)
Chile Solidario (Chile 2005)	0.08%	256.000 families	8-21 $ depending on poverty intensity
Oportunidades (México, 2006)	0.40%	5 million families (18% of pop)	12-74 $ depends on educ. level 17$ family health
Bono desarrollo umano (Ecuador 2005)	0.60%	5 million people (40% of pop)	15 $
Familias en accion (Colombia 2007)	0.20%	1.7 million families	8-33 US$ (educ subsidy/child) 30 US$ (health subsidy/ family)

Source: Authors' compilation on Fiszbein and Schady (2009) and Bouillon and Tejerina (2007).

3. Regression Analysis

3.A. Dataset and matrix of correlation coefficients

To test the relative importance of the sources of inequality declines discussed in Part 3, and to verify the hypothesis that such declines were stronger in LOC countries (in addition to the effect of the specific policies introduced) it was necessary to compile a dataset on Income Distribution in Latin America (IDLA). IDLA includes annual observations for 18 Latin American countries[54], the years 1990-2007 and large number of variables, including those used in regression analysis (Table 11). The database includes 324 (18x18) cells for each variable, though missing data reduce the number of non-zero cells by almost a third. The dependent variable is the Gini

---

[54]The countries included in the dataset represent the near totality of the population and GDP of the region. They are: Argentina, Bolivia, Brazil, Chile, Colombia, Costa Rica, Dominican Republic, El Salvador, Ecuador, Guatemala, Honduras, Mexico, Nicaragua, Panama, Paraguay, Peru, Uruguay, and Venezuela.

coefficient of the distribution of income (standardized in terms of Gini of household disposable income per capita)[55].

Table 10. Definition, description and data sources of the variables used in regression analysis

Variable name	Variable label	Source	Unit of Measure
Gini income	Gini coefficient of the current distribution of disposable household income per capita	SEDLAC complemented by WIID	Percentage points
Gini income 1990	Gini coefficient of the distribution of disposable household income per capita in 1990	SEDLAC complemented by WIID	Percentage points
GDP/c gr	Per capita average annual growth rates GDP in constant prices	ECLAC	Percentage based on US dollar figures at constant 2000 prices
Gini education	Gini index of the distribution of years of education among the working population (25-64 years old)	SEDLAC	Percentage points
Tot- fob	International terms of trade, fob	ECLAC	Index, 2000=100
Remittances	Workers' remittances / GDP	UNCTAD	Percentage of GDP
FDI	Net Stock of Foreign Direct Investment/GDP	UNCTAD	Percentage of GDP

---

[55] Of the 324 cells on current income inequality, 175 are filled with SEDLAC data, 11 from WIDER's WIID2c (of these 1 is taken from Szekely (2003), 3 from Gasparini (2003), 3 from (SEDLAC 2006), 1 from Deininger and Squire (2004), 2 from Szekely and Hillgert (2002), 3 from Badeinso-Eclac (2008), 13 from WDI (2007), 1 (Argentina 2007) from national sources. 98 data-points were interpolated by filling gaps of 1-2 years part of stable time series. In 3 cases the interpolation filled gaps of years, and in 3 cases of 4 years, especially for the early 1990s. 23 cells (for Ecuador, Guatemala, Nicaragua, and Paraguay in the early 1990s) are blank. In most cases, data refer to disposable household income per capita. A successful check was carried out to ensure that the trend of the data filled in by interpolation replicated the trend of other income concepts. While in most cases it was possible to ascertain that the data referred to disposable income, lack of information in survey questionnaires did not allow identification of the income concept used. This might introduce a measurement error in the dependent variable. However, in view of the strong co-variance of the Gini's for all income concepts, it is likely that including data referring to an unknown income concept may bias the country intercepts in the fixed effect estimation, without affecting the parameters of the explanatory variables.

Variable name	Variable label	Source	Unit of Measure
Capital flows	Portfolio investment/GDP	ECLAC	Percentage of GDP
REER	Index of Real Effective Exchange Rate	Econ Survey of L. America and the Caribbean	Index, 2000=100
Min-wage* (1 - % inform sector)	Minimum wage index multiplied by 1 minus the share of informal sector workers on the total	ECLAC	Min wage Index, 2000=100 Informal sector
Direct tax	Taxes on income, profits, capital gains, property/ GDP	ECLAC	Percentage of GDP
Indirect tax	(General taxes on goods and services + taxes on specific goods and services) / GDP	ECLAC	Percentage of GDP
Public exp. on social security	Public expenditure on social security and social assistance / GDP	ECLAC	as a percentage of GDP
Q5/Q1 Pensions	Ratio of pensions coverage between the top and the bottom quintile	Rofman et al. (2008)	Ratio
LOC	Countries with left of centre regimes	Authors' compilation	1 (LOC), 0 (center-right)

Source: authors' compilation

The explanatory variables included in the regression analysis are described in Table 10. They belong to five sets of explanatory factors: (i) **initial conditions** (proxied by Gini 1990, and expected to have a positive sign in regression, as current inequality changes only gradually in relation to its past values); (ii) the impact of the **current business cycle** measured by the growth rate of GDP per capita expected *ex ante* to have a negative sign; (iii) the **distribution of human capital** (i.e. the Gini coefficient of the distribution of years of education among workers, expected *ex-ante* to reduce inequality); (iv) **external conditions** i.e. international terms of trade, migrant remittances, FDI, and portfolio flows (all of which have *ex-ante* an uncertain, and possibly non-significant, direct impact on inequality, other than the effects mediated through GDP growth and other variables); and (v) **public policies**. These include the Real Effective Exchange Rate (REER) which proxies **macro policy**, and which is expected to reduce inequality for the reasons given in Part 3, and the minimum wage (expected *ex-ante* to reduce income inequality) which proxies **labor market policies**. As for **redistributive policies**, the following variables were used in regression analysis: the ratio of direct to indirect taxes (expected *ex-ante* to reduce income inequality); the public expenditure on social security as a share of GDP (expected to reduce mildly inequality, especially where the share of social insurance is dominant); and the ratio of pension coverage in the top versus the bottom quintile (expected *ex-ante* to raise inequality). Finally, (vi) a LOC **political dummy variable** equal to 1 when a country is ruled by a centre-right or centrist regime, expected *ex-ante* to reduce inequality (beyond the impact manifested via the adoption of progressive social policies). Table 11 presents the matrix of correlation coefficients between the variables to be included in regression analysis.

Table 11. Matrix of bilateral correlation coefficients among variables used in regression analysis

	Current Gini	Gini_90	Gdp/c g.r.	Reer	Min Wage index	DirTax / InTax on Tax/GDP	Public exp. On social sec./GDP	Remit./GDP	Internat terms of trade	Gini distr of years of educ. (-1)	FDI stock/GDP	ln_Q5/Q1 Pensions	LOC regime	Portal. investment/GDP
Current Gini	1.00													
Gini_90	0.81	1.00												
Gdp/c g.r.	-0.09	0.00	1.00											
Reer	-0.36	-0.41	0.06	1.00										
Min wage index	-0.24	-0.12	0.11	0.38	1.00									
DirTax : IndTax/ Tax/GDP ratio	0.06	0.18	-0.09	0.14	0.18	1.00								
Public exp. on social sec./DP	-0.26	-0.18	0.05	0.17	0.22	-0.55	1.00							
Remittances/ GDP	-0.08	-0.05	0.03	-0.26	-0.15	-0.22	-0.31	1.00						
Intel. terms of trade,	0.05	0.09	0.26	-0.13	-0.02	-0.20	0.14	0.00	1.00					
Gini years of education (-1)	0.46	0.50	-0.18	-0.35	-0.39	0.04	-0.39	0.22	-0.03	1.00				
FDI stock/GDP	0.05	-0.05	-0.06	-0.01	-0.23	-0.54	0.11	0.24	0.06	0.07	1.00			
Ln_Q5/Q1 Pensions	0.38	0.20	-0.11	-0.21	-0.36	0.23	-0.64	0.20	0.10	0.50	0.05	1.00		
LOC regime	-0.06	0.10	0.07	0.18	0.38	-0.04	0.16	-0.04	0.14	-0.09	0.06	-0.38	1.00	
Portfolio flows/GDP	-0.01	0.08	0.17	-0.08	0.05	0.06	0.07	-0.18	0.06	-0.13	0.19	-0.08	0.01	1.00

Source: authors' elaboration

In the vast majority of cases, the explanatory variables are strongly independent among each other. This is not true in five cases where medium bilateral correlation coefficients are 0.5-0.6 involving the correlation between pension and social security expenditure, pensions and the distribution of human capital, taxes and social expenditure, and FDI and Gini education. This may cause some problems of multicollinearity and render the related parameters of some of these variables non-significant. In more general terms, however, the small bilateral collinearity among variables suggests that there is no need to develop a structural multi-equation model – as it might be suggested by economic theory because of the possible (but not empirically verified) relations among regressors. Indeed, one might surmise that the growth rate of GDP/c depends on the international terms of trade, migrant remittances, or FDI, but the related region-wide correlation coefficients between these pairs of variables are only 0.26, 0.03 and -0.06.

3.B. Estimation procedure and regression results

The IDLA database is organized as a tri-dimensional matrix, with 18 countries on one axis, 18 years on the second, and the 12 dependent variables used in the analysis on the third. One may wonder if the use of a panel of different countries may cause heterogeneity in the data. Yet, the Breusch-Pagan test for data poolability refuses, at the zero percent probability level, the null hypothesis of heterogeneity of country data. As for the choice of the best estimator, this kind of dataset demands that the procedure chosen for the estimation of the determinants of income inequality takes into account that each country is observed over several periods. Such model takes therefore the following form:

$$y_{it} = \alpha + x_{it} \cdot \beta + u_i + \varepsilon_{it}$$

where y is the dependent variable (the Gini coefficient of the distribution of gross income per capita), x is a vector of explanatory variables (see above), the subscripts i and t represent respectively the countries and the years of the panel, u_i is the error term for each country, it is a joint error term for countries and time periods, and represent the parameters to be estimated. Given the nature of this dataset, the OLS procedure tends to yield inefficient and distorted estimates of the values of and Baltagi. The estimation procedure best suited to situations in which u_i varies from country to country is the fixed effects (FE) model in which u_i is not treated as a random variable. This means that the estimation with the fixed effects model includes, for each of the 18 countries considered, an intercept which captures specific country effects due to geography, institutions and unobservables. Besides fixed-country effects, the estimation procedure has included also year fixed-effects so as to capture the impact of yearly shocks. The F test of joint significance confirm at zero probability level that both country and year fixed-effects are different from zero. This indicates that their exclusion from the regression would bias the estimates of the other parameters.

The results of the regression analysis are presented in Table 13 in a basic model (column 1) and in two subsequent models where portfolio inflows/GDP (column 2) and the latter plus the ratio of the coverage of pensions in the top to the bottom quintile (column 3) were added. In the basic model, practically all variables have the sign expected *ex-ante* on the basis of the received theory reviewed in section 3. The addition of portfolio flows and pension has a minimal effect on the value of the parameters of model 1.

We turn now to the impact of the five sets of variables discussed before the regression. (i) **Initial conditions**: in the fixed effects approach, the time-invariant Gini income 1990 is absorbed in the country-specific constant term (but its effect is strong, in contrast, when using the OLS or random effect estimators, not shown here for reasons of space). (ii) The growth rate of GDP/c (which measures the impact of the **business cycle**) has a strong effect on inequality, falling by a quarter of a Gini point for every one percent in GDP/c growth. The recovery of 2003-07 appears therefore to have had an important equalizing effect. (iii) The Gini of the distribution of the years of education among members of the **labor force** (delayed one year) is, as expected, strongly significant, suggesting that improved access to secondary education had an important, if slow-moving, effect on the decline of income inequality.

(iv) As for the impact of the **external conditions**, the results suggest that their direct effect is significant but not large though, as noted in section 3, their impact might operate via the growth of GDP. The international terms of trade reduce inequality in a significant but moderate way (an increase of 100 points in the related index would reduce inequality by 1.5 Gini points); remittances appear to raise inequality (as suggested in section 3) but at a borderline levels of significance; portfolio flows are not statistically significant, possibly also because of errors of measurement of this variable. In turn, the FDI stock/GDP appears to increase inequality in a statistically significant but limited way.

For instance, a doubling of the FDI/GDP ratio from the current regional average of 20% to 40% for the region as a whole would increase Gini by 1.2 points, though the effect would be higher, for instance, in FDI dependent Andean countries. (v) As for the impact of **macroeconomic policy**, the results suggest that, as argued in section 3, a competitive exchange rate affects inequality in a convex way. Inequality at first falls, then rises beyond a given threshold requiring excessive nominal devaluations. As for the income and redistributive policies, the results suggest that the minimum wage (interacted with the share of formal sector workers) reduces inequality, but at a borderline level of significance. More significantly, the ratio of direct to indirect taxes indicates that the changes in the structure of revenue collection during 2003-07 (Table 5) generated a favorable distributive effect. In turn, social security expenditure/GDP has a clear and statistically significant impact on inequality (doubling such expenditure from 10 to 20% of GDP would reduce inequality by 3.1 points), and the impact would likely be larger if social assistance could be factored out. In contrast to *ex-ante* expectations, the ratio of pension coverage of the top to the bottom quintile is not significant. This is possibly because it correlates closely with the share of social security/GDP (see Table 11), or because this variable exhibited little variation over time in many countries.

Table 12. Fixed-effects regression results (dependent variable: Gini coefficient of distribution of disposable income/c)

Variable (sign expected ex-ante on the basis of theory)		(1)	(2)	(3)
Gini income 1990[a]	(+)			
Growth rate of GDP/ per capita	(-)	-5.2952*	-5.3988*	-5.0624^
Gini distribution of years of education (-1)	(+)	0.6100***	0.6143***	0.5967***
International terms of trade, fob	(+,-)	-0.0156*	-0.0151*	-0.0132^
Migrant remittances/GDP	(+, -)	0.1088^	0.1111^	0.0051
FDI stock_net/GDP	(+)	0.0598***	0.0620***	0.0494***
portafolio investment/GDP	(+)	....	0.0182	0.0181
REER	(-)	-0.0720**	-0.0701**	-0.0687**
REER2	(+)	0.0003***	0.0003***	0.0003***
Minimum wage index * (100 – share of informal sector) (-)		-0.0002^	-0.0002^	-0.0003**
Share of Direct Tax / Indirect Tax on Tax/GDP ratio (-)		-8.9762***	-9.0673***	-10.544**
Public expenditure on social security/GDP	(=,-)	-0.3269**	-0.3182**	-0.2695^
ln_Q5/Q1 Pensions	(+)	....	....	0.123
LOC countries	(-)	-0.8205**	-0.8263**	-1.2404***
Constant		40.0748***	39.5769***	41.5874***
Year Dummies		Yes	Yes	Yes
Observations		222	222	181
R-squared		0.45	0.45	0.45

Source: author's calculations. Notes: ***, **, *, ^ significant at 1%, 5%; 10%; between 10 and 15%. [a]/ In the fixed effect estimation procedure, this time-invariant variable is omitted and is subsumed in each country's constant.

(vi) Finally, the **dummy variable 'LOC'** is significant and indicates that left of centre governments tend to have, on average, a Gini coefficients lower by around one point than NO-LOC countries, in addition to the effects mediated by the adoption of more progressive economic social policies. The statistical fit of the regression is broadly satisfactory. Yet, these results need to be probed further, and have to be considered as an initial step in disentangling the sources of the inequality decline observed from 2003 to2007. For instance, the validity of the conclusions drawn on the basis of these results needs to be probed in a few ways, starting with considering the possibility of reverse causation among dependent and independent variables[56].

With these caveats in mind, on the whole, it appears that the recovery of the business cycle (which is certainly related to improvements in external conditions), together with the introduction of pro-poor macroeconomic, labor and social policies (which is related to the election of LOC regimes) played a major role, as expected *ex ante*, in reducing income inequality. Though this variable moves very slowly, the impact of the distribution of years of education (which has slowly improved during the last 15 years) also had an important impact. These results broadly confirm the theoretical considerations presented in Part 3 regarding the possible sources of the inequality decline that has taken place in Latin America in the 2000s. In addition, these results contradict the conclusions reached by Perez Caldentey and Vernengo (2008) which state that the recent growth acceleration and fall in

---

[56]Reverse causation is tested by means of the Granger test. However, such test is not suitable for the ADLI dataset in which each variable has, at most, 18 or fewer observations due to missing data. It is therefore more appropriate to deal with this problem from a theoretical standpoint. In this regard, it must be noted that reverse causality makes no sense in the majority of the relations in Table 13. For instance, it is not plausible that changes in domestic inequality affect the real exchange rate, or can affect lagged, exogenous or policy variables (such as Gini income 1990, migrant remittances, terms of trade, ratio of direct/indirect taxes, ratio of pension coverage Q1/Q5, and minimum wage). Also, a fall/increase in Gini income may affect the Gini of years of education only after a considerable lag. It is also implausible that a decline in inequality will affect the expenditure on social insurance/GDP, which depends on the coverage of formal employment as far as pensions are concerned, and on tax revenue and public expenditure allocation for conditional cash transfers. The only area where reverse causation may be plausible is between the Gini inequality and the growth rate of GDP/c. In this case, however, this relation would be characterized by time lags, thus excluding the possibility of reverse causation on synchronous data. Furthermore, the literature on the impact of higher inequality on GDP/c growth is not unanimous. Neokeynesian and neoclassical models postulate a positive relation between these two variables, while 'political economy' and 'incentives' models assume a negative one. On the whole, reverse causality does not seem plausible. However, the parameters in Table 13 may be distorted by the possible endogeneity of some explanatory variables. Solving formally this problem by means of a simultaneous equations system is however a difficult task in a panel with 18 countries.

inequality have nothing to do with the policy changes introduced by LOC and some conservative governments in the economic and social sphere. For sure, favorable changes in the external environment played a major role in accelerating growth and reducing inequality. It is also true, as argued by these authors, that the recent developments have not reduced the long-term dependence of the region on the export of primary sector. But, as this paper has indicated, changes in public policies adopted during the 2000s seem to explain part of the inequality improvements.

4. The Distributive Impact of the Present Crisis

The rapid growth and inequality decline which began in 2002-2003 was abruptly interrupted by the onset of the global financial crisis in mid-2008. In the early stages of the crisis, it was commonly believed that the region would be bypassed due to the solidity of its financial sector, steady growth of the Asian economies and good macroeconomic conditions.

However, the view of 'decoupling' has been rapidly abandoned as the region was affected not by 'financial contagion', but by a series of 'real economy' shocks including (Ocampo 2009 and CEPAL 2009b): (i) a modest improvement of terms of trade (three percent for the region as a whole) in 2008, and an aggregate decline of -10.8% by mid-2009 (year on year). By mid-2009, the drop in terms of trade was particularly acute (between -20 and -28%) for six Andean countries exporting primary commodities, but moderate (-6.2%) for the Mercosur, minimal for Mexico (-4.5%) and positive (+4.8%) for Central America. The terms of trade deterioration was, on balance, of medium intensity, bringing the regional index broadly to the same level of that of 2004, i.e. a relatively good year. (ii) A drop in the growth of export volumes began immediately after the onset of the sub-prime crisis in July 2008, and become negative in October of the same year. By the first quarter of 2009, the volume of exports had dropped (year-on-year) by 3% in Central America and by 6-14% in the rest of the region. According to Ocampo (2009), the shocks to international trade are the main factors affecting Latin America's performance since mid-2008. (iii) A 20% decline in migrant remittances by mid-2009, affected in a major way the Central American economies (which benefitted from a drop in oil prices), Mexico, Ecuador and Columbia. Tourist receipts also declined, though to a lesser extent, and affected a limited number of countries. (iv) A sharp drop in the value of FDI from their historical peak in 2008 was due to the large decline in the prices of primary commodities. (v) A substantial drop in portfolio inflows, coincided with the spread of the banking crisis in the advanced economies, and an increase in capital outflows from the region. The issue of bonds on the international market diminished from 41 billion US$ in 2007 to 13 billion for the first half of 2009. As a result, the net capital inflow became negative by between 5 and 10 billion US$ per trimester since the second semester of 2008. The related outflows also caused a drop in the stock market indexes which collapsed from an average of 500 in May 2008 to below 200 by mid-November, to recover slightly in early 2009. As a result, it is estimated that the net reserves of the region, which had reached the exceptional level of 500 billion US$ in mid-2008, started to decline. (vi) An average increase in interest rate spreads by 500 basic points between the lowest level reached in 2007 and the first trimester of 2009 occurred, though the increase was considerably lower than that (1100 and 1400 basic points) observed during the Russian and Argentinean crisis of 1998-99 and 2001-02, during which the fundamentals of the region were more fragile. The spreads have started to decline, but are still well above the pre-crisis level.

These external shocks have weakened the balance of payments and revenue collection and, with it, the budget deficit. As a result, the regional budget and current account deficit will reach (a tolerable) - 2.5% of GDP in 2009. Much of the increase in the fiscal deficit is due to a drop in tax and non-tax revenue, rather than to greater public expenditure. As noted by the 2009 ECLAC (2009) study by Gomez-Sabatini and Jimenez, the decline in revenue collection varies with the economic and tax structure of the different countries[57]. Commodity exporting countries are expected to see their revenue/GDP ratio fall by 3.8% (for the reasons given in section 2 and in footnote 17) while in the others the revenue/GDP

---

[57]The countries most affected are those high dependent on natural resources, with already low tax/GDP ratios, mainly depending on import taxes and VAT, and low proportion of income tax in the total (CEPAL 2009a).

ratio should drop by only half a point. Finally, the growing deficit of the current account triggered a wave of currency devaluations. Indeed, with the exception of Venezuela and Peru, between January 2008 and March 2009, the nominal exchange rate of the largest economies depreciated by between 15% (Argentina) and 35% (Mexico) (CEPAL 2009b). These devaluations may however be a blessing in disguise in light of the overvaluation of most currencies in the region prior to the crisis (Ocampo 2009), and may provide important incentives to diversify the economic structures of many countries. As a result, it is expected that the growth rate of GDP of the region will drop from 4.2 in 2008 to -1.9 in 2009, to recover to an estimated 3.1 in 2010 (CEPAL 2009b). While the majority of growth rates range between +1% and -2%, in Mexico the drop (-7%) is extremely severe.

What is the distributive impact of the crisis? Will the crisis erode the inequality declines recorded since 2002-03? To answer these questions, it is important to note that the current crisis hits a region which exhibits much better conditions than those prevailing during the crises of 1982-1984 and 1998-2002. To start with, the crisis is mainly a real economy crisis, and less a financial crisis, as in the US and parts of Europe or as experienced in the region during the 1980s and 1990s. This means that fewer funds are needed than in the past to recapitalize ailing banks, and that fiscal policy can expand pro-poor and pro-growth public expenditures. Second, this is even more true when considering that many countries in the region are in a position to follow countercyclical fiscal policies entailing deficits for a couple of years (the expected duration of the global crisis). This is due to the decline of the public debt/GDP ratio, large accumulation of currency reserves, and decline in inflation achieved over 2002-2008 (see Part 3). In turn, with few exceptions, Central Banks can also carry out a more flexible monetary policy without endangering their inflation targets.

Also, the recent devaluations of the exchange rate are likely to correct recent real appreciations, as in the case of Brazil, with a possible favorable impact on export growth, diversification of the economy and inequality. Third, the impact of the recession via international trade will not affect all countries equally. For instance, the Southern Cone nations, which trade mainly with East Asia, are less likely to be affected due to the milder recession experienced in that region. Fourth, most countries have introduced in recent years important public works and cash transfer programs (Table 10). At the moment, 85 million Latin-Americans receive a subsidy through some kind of CCT schemes (UNDP 2009). This prior institutional development should facilitate the expansion of safety nets during the crisis and help preserve some of the recent inequality declines. However, not all countries may have the administrative capacity to act in a timely manner. Finally, the inequality trends over 2009 and 2010 will depend on the ability of governments to sustain the measures introduced during the recent past in the fields of direct taxation, social expenditures, labor market policies and a gradual drive towards an integrated, universal social protection system, and away from the traditional highly segmented and informal systems. As noted, a feasible countercyclical fiscal policy should sustain some of these efforts over the years ahead, and preserve part of the inequality gains achieved during the recent past. It seems unlikely, therefore, that an 18-24 month crisis will undo the full distributive gains of 2002-2007.

One way to grasp the impact of the current crisis is to use the parameters of the column 1 model in Table 13 to estimate the likely inequality impact of the global financial crisis in 2009 on a few prototypical countries. Prototypical countries include a few oil-metal exporters (Chile, Ecuador, and Mexico – which as noted above will suffer a decline in tax revenue of 3.8 points of GDP) and more broad-based economies (Argentina and Brazil). In this regard, the 2008 and 2009 values of the right-hand side variable (terms of trade, GDP/c, real exchange rate, tax/GDP ratio, migrant remittances and FDI) were derived from various ECLAC publications or were projected (as in the case of 'stock variables' such as FDI/GDP stock and the Gini education) assuming only minimum changes in their level. What needs to be noted is that several of the non-policy explanatory variables in the model presented in Table 13 varied little in 2008 and in 2009, a strong impact is evident only in a few countries (Mexico above all). As for the policy variables, two scenarios were simulated, one assuming moderate cuts, and the other assuming more severe cuts. The first assumes: a modest decline (five percent of its initial value) in tax incidence among non-commodity exporters and of 35% among commodity exporters, as suggested above; a 10% drop from the initial level of social security expenditure/GDP in all countries; and that the likely increase in job informality will be compensated by a social safety net reflected in a rise in minimum wages. In contrast, the second, more pessimistic, policy scenario assumes: a drop in direct tax revenue/GDP ratio in relation to its initial level of 40% for the commodity exporters and of 15% for the other countries; a 25% reduction of social security/GDP from its initial level ratio in commodity exporters and of 15% in the others; a cut of the minimum wage of 5% in LOC countries and of 25% for the NON-LOC countries; and a 5% increase in the share of informal employment in all countries.

The results of this highly hypothetical exercise are presented in Table 14. They suggest that in 2008 the rise in inequality in relation to the values predicted by the model for 2007 was very modest, varying between 0.1 (Colombia and Brazil) and 0.6 (Ecuador). This is not surprising as the external conditions continued to improve till midyear, and the rate of growth remained acceptable in all these countries. Under scenario 1, the 2007-2009 Gini rises were somewhat more pronounced but still modest, ranging between 0.4 and 1.4 Gini points, i.e. much less that the drop realized over 2003-7. The largest increase was recorded among commodity exporters such as Chile, Mexico and Ecuador. In non-commodity exporting countries, the increase was around 0.5 Gini points. Even under the more pessimistic scenario 2, the Gini increase remains moderate, ranging between 1 and 1.7 Gini points. While these results may depend on the model specification (which takes into account structural rather than cyclical factors), and on the fact that some adverse changes in variables were not included in model 1 Table 13 – such as a drop in capital inflows, rising interest spreads on international loans, and rises in capital flights – may also negatively affect income inequality. But the limited increase in inequality seems to depend mainly on the fact that – except for Mexico – the crisis has not been as acute as that of 1982-84, or that currently experienced in the European economies in transition where GDP/c is expected to decline between 10% and 20% a year over two years.

In Latvia, for instance, private consumption per capita is expected to fall by a staggering 40% over 2008-2010. In fact, (CEPAL 2009b) estimates for 2009 include a two percent GDP growth in Argentina, Ecuador and Colombia, and a decline of just one percent or less in Chile and Brazil.

Table 13. Simulated impact of the crisis on income inequality

Δ Gini points	Argentina	Brazil	Chile	Colombia	Ecuador	Mexico
2007-2008	+0.42	-0.09	+0.31	+0.04	-0.57	+0.18
2007-2009 *(Scenario 1)*	+0.50	+0.55	+0.92	+0.50	+1.38	+0.79
2007-2009 *(Scenario 2)*	+1.00	+1.04	+1.27	+1.35	+1.70	+1.44

Source: authors' simulation using the parameters of model 1, Table 13.

Conclusion

Has the LOC model of prudent distributive and redistributive policies reduced inequality? Is the current crisis reversing these gains? The spread of democracy and dissatisfaction with Washington Consensus policies have led to the elections of LOC governments which introduced – thanks also to favorable external conditions – economic reforms broadly inspired by a 'prudent redistribution with growth' which committed to reducing the 'social debt' inherited from the colonial past and exacerbated by the liberal policies of the 1980s and 1990s. With few exceptions, the new policy model did not introduce a radical redistribution. Rather, it has emphasized orthodox objectives such as macro-stability, fiscal prudence, and the preservation of free trade and capital movements. Yet, in a clear departure from the 1990s, LOC governments opted for managed exchange rates, a neutral or countercyclical fiscal policy, reduced dependence on foreign capital, rapid accumulation of currency reserves and a more active role of the state in the field of labor and social policies.

As with European social democracies, LOC and to a lesser extent moderate centre-right governments raised the tax/GDP ratio (a trend facilitated but not explained, neither in its timing nor in its extent, by the recent terms of trade gains) as well as public spending for education, cash transfers and other forms of social assistance. There is micro and macro evidence that higher public and private spending reduced inequality in education and improved the distribution of human capital among the workforce. Redistribution was also pursued via macroeconomic policies favoring the labor-intensive traded sector and changes in labor market policies and institutions. Also in this case, the changes introduced were far from radical, and yet helped improve labor participation, increase the proportion of workers covered by formal contracts, and reduce unemployment.

Of the changes that determined the decline in income inequality between 2002 and 2007, the most important was the reduction of educational inequality among workers, which explains one third of the overall average decline in inequality (equal on average to 4 Gini points). Other key factors were the choice of a competitive real exchange rate (though such policy was not followed in all countries) and the increase in minimum wages (each of them caused a drop in inequality equal to around a fifth of the overall decline). The rise in public social expenditure in LOC countries reduced inequality by about one tenth of the total while the changes in direct relative to indirect taxes has only a modest impact on inequality. As for the changes in international conditions, the improvements in international terms of trade reduced income inequality by about one tenth of the total, while remittances and capital inflows had no impact, and GDP growth affected inequality only modestly. Finally, the LOC countries recorded an additional decline equal to about fifth of the overall decline in inequality.

While interrupting a positive cycle of six years, the impact of the crisis is, on average, considerably less intense than in the OECD countries and the transitional economies of Eastern Europe. The arguments and simulation results presented above tentatively suggest that the inequality deterioration expected for 2008 and 2009 should be substantially lower than the gains recorded in most of the region over 2002/3 and 2007.

Beyond the problems posed by the current financial crisis, Latin

American governments still face formidable hurdles to deepen the reforms of their economies, promote inclusive growth and further reduce inequality. First, the trend towards increasing taxation and social expenditure needs to continue in much of the region, with the objective of building a lean state that avoids the high costs of the European welfare model while offering universal coverage. Second, while the funding of the reforms has come in part from gains in t h e terms of trade, the revenue needed to sustain social expenditure in the future will have to come from a diversification of the economy into new labor- and skilled-intensive sectors. Third, an intensification of the new policy model by LOC governments in the region faces considerable political opposition, as shown by the case of Bolivia and Argentina, where a few doubtful policy decisions and the opposition of interest groups nearly stalled even moderate attempts at redistribution. Perhaps, the main effect of the financial crisis is that it may dig a gap between the responses expected from LOC governments and what they can actually do. In this regard, it is important to note that the region will undergo 24 national elections between 2009 and 2010 (UNDP 2009). An unchecked deterioration of living conditions might lead to a collective perception that the crisis is due to inadequate policy responses. Failure to stay – with the needed corrections - the policy course adopted in recent years may cause a credibility gap, undermine support for LOC governments, and push the region towards its traditional path of unequal development or towards more radical solutions, possibly overturning in this way the inequality gains of the recent past.

References

Altimir, Oscar (1993), "Income Distribution and Poverty Through Crises and Adjustment", paper presented at the ECLAC/UNICEF Workshop on Public Policy Reforms and Social Expenditure, Santiago, Chile, 14-15 June 1993.

Altimir, Oscar (1996), "Economic Development and Social Equity," *Journal of Interamerican Studies and World Affairs*, Summer/Fall 1996.

Baltagi, Badi H. (2005) "Econometric Analysis of Panel Data", John Wiley and Sons, Chichester.

Barrientos, Armando and Claudio Santibanez (2009), "New Forms of Social assistance and the Evolution of Social Protection in Latin America," *Journal of Latin American Studies* 41, pp 1-26

Bouillon, Cesar Patricio and Luis Tajerina (2007), "Do We Know What Works?: A Systematic Review of Impact Evaluations of Social Programs in Latin America and the Caribbean", Inter-American Development Bank, Washington D.C.

CEPAL (2009), 'La reacción de los gobiernos de América Latina y el Caribe frente a la crisis internacional : una presentación sintética de las medidas de política anunciadas hasta el 30 de enero de 2009' CEPAL, Santiago de Chile.

CEPAL (2009a), ' Crisis, Volatilidad, Ciclo Y Politica Fiscal en America Latina', Montevideo, 19-20 May 2009

CEPAL (2009b), "Estudio Economico de America Latina y el Caribe, 2008-9", CEPAL, Santiago de Chile, 17 July 2009.

CEPAL (2007), 'Preliminary Overview of the Economies of Latin America and the Carribean, 2007', CEPAL, Santiago de Chile.

CEPAL (2007a), 'Panorama Social de America Latina', CEPAL, Santiago de Chile.

CEPAL (2006), 'Panorama Social de America Latina', CEPAL, Santiago de Chile.

CEPAL (2005), 'Panorama Social de America Latina', CEPAL, Santiago de Chile.

Cetrangolo, Oscar and Gomez Sabaini (2006), "Tributacion en America Latina: En busca de nuevas agenda de reformas", Libros de la CEPAL, n.93, CEPAL, Santiago de Chile, December.

Chenery Hollis, Montek Ahluwalia, Clive Bell, John Duloy and Richard Jolly (1974), "Redistribution with Growth", Oxford University Press.

Cornia, Giovanni Andrea (2006), "Pro-poor Macroeconomics: potential and limitations", Palgrave Mc Millan, London

Cornia, Giovanni Andrea (2004), "Inequality, growth and Poverty in an Era of Liberalization and Globalization", Oxford University Press, Oxford.

Dornubush Rudiger and Sebastian Edwards (1991), "The Macroeconomics of Populism in Latin America. Chicago and London: University of Chicago Press.

Easterly, William, and Stanley Fischer (2001), "Inflation and the Poor." Journal of Money, Credit and Banking, 33: 160-78.

Fiszbein, Ariel and Norbert Schady (2009), "Conditional Cash Transfers: Reducing Presnet and Future Poverty", World Bank, Washington D.C.

Freeman, R.(2008), "labor Market Institutions Around the World", CEP Discussion Paper No 844, Centre for Economic Performance, London School of Economics and Political Sciences, Jan. 2008.

Frenkel, Roberto and Martín Rapetti (2008), "Five years of competitive and stable real exchange rate in Argentina, 2002-2007". International Review of Applied Economics: 215-216.

Gasparini, Leonardo (2007),"Monitoring the Socio-Economic Conditions in Argentina 1992-2006" Mimeographed, CEDLAS, Universidad Nacional de La Plata, June 2007.

Gasparini Leonardo, Guillermo Cruces, Leopoldo Tornarolli y Mariana Marchionni (2009) "A Turning Point? Recent Developments on Inequality in Latin America and the Caribbean "Documento de Trabajo Nro. 81, CEDLAS Universidad Nacional de La Plata, February 2009.

Goni, Edwin, Humberto Lopez, and Luis Serven (2008), "Fiscal redistribution and Income Inequality in Latin America", Policy Research Working Paper No. 4487, Research Department Group, the World Bank, Washington D.C. January 2008.

Helpage International (2006), www.helpage.org/Home

Keefer, Philip (2007), "DPI2006, Database of Political Institutions: Changes and Variable Definitions", Development Research Group, The World Bank, December 2007.

Kristensen, Nicolai and Wendy Cunningham (2006), "Do Minimum Wages in Latin America and the Carribean Matter? Evidence from 19 Countries", World Bank Policy Research Working Paper No. 3870, World Bank, Washington D.C., March 2006

IMF (2004).

Lustig, Nora (2009), "La pobreza y la disegualdad en America Latina, y los gobiernos de la Izquirda" , Cuadernos del Consejo Mexicano de Asuntos Internacionales,7

Moreno-Brid, Juan Carlos and Igor Paunovic (2006) " The Future of Economic Policy Making by Left-of-Centre Governments in Latin America: Old Wine in New Bottles? Post-autistic Economic Review, no. 139, 1 October 2006, pp.2-7.

Novick, Marta, Carlos Tomada, Mario Damill, Roberto Frenkel and Roxana Maurizio (2007), "Tras la crisi: El nuevo rumbo de la politica economica y laboral en Argentina y su impacto", Instituto Internacional de Estudios Laborales, ILO, Geneva.

O'Connell, Lesley (1999), "Collective Bargaining Systems in Six Latin American Countries", Office of the Chief Economists, Working Paper No. 399, Inter-American Development Bank, Washington, D.C.

Ocampo, José Antonio (2007), "The Macroeconomics of the Latin American Economic Boom," CEPAL Review, No.93. pp.7-28.

Ocampo, José Antonio (2008), "The Latin American Economic Boom"Revista de Ciencia Política, Volume 28, n. 1, p. 7-33.

Ocampo, José Antonio (2009), "Impacto de la crisis financiera mundial sobre América Latina" Revista CEPAL 97, April 2009, p. 9-32.

Panizza, Francisco E. (2005) "Unarmed utopia revisited: the resurgence of left-of-centre politics in Latin America". *Political studies*, 53 (4). pp. 716-734.

Panizza, Francisco E. (2005a) , " The Social democratisation of the Latin American Left", Revista Europea de Estudios Latinoamericanos y del Caribe, 79, October 2005.

Perez Caldentey, Esteban and Matías Vernengo (2008), "Back to the Future: Latin America's Current Development Strategy", www.networkideas.org/featart/aug2008/fa02_Back2Future.htm

Székely, Miguel (2003), "The 1990s in Latin America: Another Decade of Persistent Inequality but with Somewhat Lower Poverty", Journal of Applied Economics Vol. VI, No.2, 317-339.

Taylor, Lance (2004), "External Liberalization, Economic Performance and Distribution in Latin America and Elsewhere", in Cornia G.A. (2004) op.cit.

Tokman, Victor (1986), "Ajuste y Empleo: Los Desafios del Presente", PREALC, Regional Employment Programme for Latin America and the Caribbean. Mimeo. Santiago, Chile.

UNDP (2009), "The Global Financial Crisis: Social Implications for Latin America and the Caribbean" Crisis Update No. 2, February 10, 2009, Regional Bureau for Latin America and the Carribean.

UNCTAD (2008),

USAID (2008), "Development Statistics for Latin America and the Caribbean" http://quesdb.cdie.org/lac/index.html

World Bank (2005), 'Argentina: Seeking Sustained Growth and Social Equity: Observations on Growth, Inequality and Poverty', 21 October 2005, Washington D.C.

Annex 1. Multidimensional Child Poverty
Children experiencing deprivation of basic needs*
Selected countries (2001 – 2006)[58]

	Shelter	Sanitation	Water	Information	Food	Education	Health	Children experiencing two or more of any deprivations
Bangladesh	85	63	3	46	no data	29	55	76
Bhutan	35	9	15	22	no data	27	no data	27
Bolivia	56	37	13	5	28	33	36	45
Burundi	92	68	55	47	no data	32	42	90
Cambodia	86	75	29	8	47	17	34	76
Cameroon	60	69	42	26	37	19	39	67
Congo, Republic of	58	10	42	13	32	11	29	45
Congo, Democratic Republic of	79	60	64	26	43	26	51	78
Egypt	19	2	2	1	21	8	12	6
Ghana	59	42	30	19	30	17	31	52

[58]Methodology note: All figures are UNICEF's calculations, using University of Bristol approach. Figures are derived from household surveys, using the most recent survey available for the period 2001 – 2006. Most of the figures are from UNICEF's Multiple Indicator Cluster Surveys round 3, while some are from Demographic and Health Surveys

	Shelter	Sanitation	Water	Information	Food	Education	Health	Children experiencing two or more of any deprivations
India	78	64	17	16	57	17	38	66
Jamaica	no data	3	8	no data	no data	6	22	1
Kyrgyzstan	28	4	14	2	18	7	41	15
Lao	54	60	59	27	49	28	65	73
Madagascar	18	50	73	25	57	28	39	64
Malawi	82	80	49	27	51	15	43	85
Mali	82	20	46	8	45	57	39	67
Mongolia	70	24	38	7	24	8	14	46
Morocco	30	20	28	4	27	22	18	30
Nepal	85	67	18	4	56	14	21	71
Nicaragua	64	18	11	7	22	22	29	34
Niger	92	81	66	18	57	65	61	88
Nigeria	60	57	57	19	45	34	68	73
Pakistan	58	42	10	27	no data	28	38	49
Palestine	10	0	30	1	12	5	33	9

	Shelter	Sanitation	Water	Information	Food	Education	Health	Children experiencing two or more of any deprivations
Philippines	14	16	18	4	no data	6	28	15
Senegal	50	24	37	2	25	47	36	46
Sierra Leone	78	68	56	46	49	29	52	79
Tanzania	81	15	61	15	42	23	35	69
Thailand	24	1	30	2	19	1	9	11
Ukraine	5	5	4	0	no data	3	no data	1
Uzbekistan	18	1	9	1	19	5	34	7
Viet Nam	33	27	13	11	no data	14	27	28
Yemen	59	28	50	21	no data	33	64	55
Zambia	61	27	52	23	51	31	28	60
Zimbabwe	59	42	38	25	33	10	43	56

*See description of indicators and thresholds on the following page.

Dimensions of basic needs: Indicators and thresholds (adopted from University of Bristol methodology)

	Deprivation	Severe Deprivation
Shelter	Child living in a dwelling of 4 or more people per room or lives in a house with no flooring or in a house with natural roofing	Child living in a dwelling of 5 or more people per room or lives in a house with no flooring
Sanitation	Child that only has access to unimproved sanitation (public latrine, open pit latrine, service or bucket latrine)	Child with no available toilet facility
Water	Child using unimproved sources of water (unprotected well, unprotected spring, rivers or pond, vendor-provided water, bottled water, tanker truck water) or if water source is more than 30mn away (round trip)	Child using surface water (excluding spring water) or if water source is more than 30mn away (round trip)
Information	Child with no access to broadcast media (radio or TV)	Children with no access to information sources: radio, TV, newspaper, phone
Nutrition	A child -2 standard deviation from the international reference population for stunting or wasting or underweight	A child -3 standard deviation from the international reference population for stunting or wasting or underweight
Education	Child aged 7-17 who is not currently in school and who has not completed primary education	Child aged 7-17 who is not currently in school and who has never been to school
Health	Child that is not fully immunised by the age of 2, or a child is under 2 years of age and has not received any immunisation, or child had a recent serious illness and was not treated (for diarrhoea or acute respiratory infection)	Child who has not received any immunisation or if a child had a recent serious illness and was not treated (for diarrhoea or acute respiratory infection)

Annex 2. Income Distribution and Gini Index Data by Country, 1990-2008 (or latest available)[59] [60]

Country Name	Year	Q1	Q2	Q3	Q4	Q5	Gini Index
Albania	1995	8.7	13	17.4	23.2	37.8	27.8
	2000	8.9	13.2	17.5	23.1	37.4	28.6
	2005	7.8	12.2	16.6	22.6	40.9	31.8
Algeria	1990	6.5	10.8	14.8	20.7	47.2	38.7
	1995	6.9	11.5	16.3	22.8	42.4	35.5
	2000						36.4
	2005						35.6
	2000	2	5.7	10.8	19.7	61.9	59.4
	2005						58.7
Argentina	1990	4.7	9.1	14.3	21.9	50.1	43.3
	1995	4.1	8.4	13.7	21.6	52.2	43.7
	2000	3.3	7.5	12.8	21.2	55.2	46.4
	2005	3.4	7.8	13.3	21.6	53.9	46.1
	2007/8	3.6	8.2	13.4	21.7	53	43
Armenia	1990						24.2
	1995	5.4	9.5	14	20.7	50.4	40.9
	2000	7.6	11.6	15.5	21.2	44.1	40
	2005	8.6	12.7	16.4	21.4	41	40.2
	2007/8	8.6	13	17.1	22.1	39.2	40.6
Australia	1990*	7.1	12.3	16.8	23.1	40.6	30.5
	1995*	3.6	9.3	15.2	24	47.9	30.8
	2000*	3.8	9	15	23.8	48.5	31.7
	2005*	8.2	13.1	17.9	23.3	37.4	31.6
	2007/8						33.5
Austria	1990*	9.2	14	17.9	23.3	35.6	25.1
	1995*	9	15	17	23	36	27.7
	2000	8.6	13.3	17.4	22.9	37.8	25.7
	2005						26.8
	2007/8**	9.5	14.4	17.9	22.3	35.9	26.7

[59] Methodology Note: Annual quintile data were extracted from the WDI (2011) and then supplemented by quintile information from UNU-WIDER (2008) and the European Commission (2011). If a data point was not available for a specific year of interest (e.g. 1990, 1995, 2000 or 2007), the stated value reflects (i) interpolation or, if interpolation was not possible, (ii) nearest neighbour imputation (e.g. the most recent data point within two years of the missing year); if neither of these options were possible, no quintile data were reported. All Gini index values were derived from Solt (2009), and some values also reflect interpolation. See Endnote in Ortiz and Cummins for further details on the methodology and underlying assumptions.

[60] The source key is provided at the end of the table.

Country Name	Year	Q1	Q2	Q3	Q4	Q5	Gini Index
	1990						31.3
Azerbaijan	1995	6.9	11.9	16.5	22.6	42	40.5
	2000	7.4	11.4	15.6	21.5	44.2	33.2
	2005	13.3	16.2	18.7	21.7	30.2	18.5
	1990						30.1
Bahamas	1995						34.3
	2000						46.4
	2005						30.1
	1990	10	13.9	17.5	22.1	36.6	27.5
Bangladesh	1995	9.3	12.9	16.4	21.3	40.2	32.5
	2000	9.3	12.7	16.3	21.4	40.4	35.2
	2005	9.4	12.6	16.1	21.1	40.8	39.1
	1990	10.6	14.8	18.5	23	33.1	20.9
	1995	8.5	13.5	17.7	23.1	37.2	25.1
Belarus	2000	8.5	12.9	17.1	22.6	38.9	25.6
	2005	8.8	13.6	17.8	23.1	36.7	24.9
	2007/8	8.8	13.4	17.5	22.6	37.7	26.8
	1990*	9.6	14.4	18.4	22.7	34.9	23.3
	1995*	8	13	17	23	37	26.6
Belgium	2000	8.5	13	16.3	20.8	41.4	27.9
	2005**	9.1	13.7	17.8	22.5	36.9	25.7
	2007/8**	9.1	14.2	18.3	23.1	35.3	25.7
	1990						53.8
	1995	2.1	5.4	10.4	19.2	62.9	47.6
Belize	2000						47.4
	2005	6.9	10.9	15.1	21.2	45.9	36.9
	2007/8						36.5
Bhutan	2000						47.8
	2005	5.4	8.8	12.9	20	53	47.5
	1990	5.5	9.7	14.8	22.2	47.9	42.2
	1995	3.2	7.2	12.4	20.3	56.8	52
Bolivia	2000	1.4	5.7	11.4	20.4	61	55.5
	2005	1.8	5.9	11.4	20.2	60.7	52.8
	2007/8	2.7	6.5	11	18.6	61.2	53.3
	1990						37.2
Bosnia and	1995						33.3
Herzegovina	2000	9.1	13.6	17.5	22.6	37.2	28.4
	2005	6.8	11.4	16.1	22.7	42.9	33.9
	2007/8	6.7	11.4	16	22.9	43.1	
	1990	3.4	6.3	10.5	17.8	61.9	54.4
Botswana	1995	3.1	5.8	9.6	16.4	65	52.9
	2000						52.8
	2005						51.2
Brazil	1990	2.4	5.3	9.7	18.2	64.5	52.8

Country Name	Year	Q1	Q2	Q3	Q4	Q5	Gini Index
	1995	2.4	5.7	10.6	18.9	62.5	51.6
	2000	2.4	5.8	10.9	19.2	61.7	52.3
	2005	2.9	6.5	11.4	19.3	60	49.1
	2007/8	3	6.9	11.8	19.6	58.7	47.7
	1990	9.7	14.1	17.9	22.6	35.6	22.4
	1995	6.9	13.5	18.1	23.5	38.1	28.9
Bulgaria	2000	7.4	12.7	17.2	22.7	40	24.5
	2005**	7.6	12.9	17.6	23.2	38.7	27.2
	2007/8**	5.9	12.3	17.2	23.3	41.3	33.6
	1990						46.9
Burkina Faso	1995	5.3	8.2	12.1	18.5	55.9	42.9
	2000	6.3	9.8	13.6	19.3	50.9	51
	2005	7	10.6	14.7	20.6	47.1	47
	1990	7.9	12.1	16.3	22.1	41.6	33.7
	1995	6.5	11.2	15.7	21.8	44.8	36.8
Burundi	2000	6.1	10.7	15.2	21.3	46.7	38.4
	2005	8.5	11.7	15.4	21.1	43.4	34.5
	2007/8	9	11.9	15.4	21	42.8	33.8
	1990						43.2
	1995	7.9	11.1	14.6	19.9	46.6	43.5
Cambodia	2000*	6.1	9.9	13	18.8	52.2	44.5
	2005	6.7	9.9	13.6	19.5	50.3	42.9
	2007/8	6.5	9.7	12.9	18.9	52	
	1990						51.6
Cameroon	1995	5.7	8.9	12.9	19.3	53.3	53.8
	2000	5.6	9.3	13.7	20.5	50.9	44.3
	2005						41.8
	1990*	7.7	13.7	19	24.8	34.8	27.5
	1995*	7.5	12.9	17.3	23	39.2	28.7
Canada	2000	7.2	12.7	17.2	23	39.9	31.5
	2005						31.7
	2007/8						31.5
	1990						41
Cape Verde	1995						46.4
	2000	4.5	8.1	12.2	19.1	56.1	51.9
	2005						51.1
Central African Republic	1990*	1.9	4.7	8.9	17.7	66.7	
	1995	2	4.9	9.6	18.5	65	
	2000	4	7.7	12.5	20.5	55.2	
	2005	5.2	9.4	14.3	21.7	49.4	
Chad	2000						40.4
	2005	6.3	10.4	15	21.8	46.6	40.1
Chile	1990	3.4	6.9	11.4	18.6	59.7	51.9
	1995	3.5	6.9	11.5	18.8	59.4	51.5

Country Name	Year	Q1	Q2	Q3	Q4	Q5	Gini Index
	2000	3.5	7	11.4	18.5	59.6	51.6
	2005	4	7.6	12	19	57.4	49.1
	2007/8	4.1	7.7	12.2	19.3	56.8	48.4
	1990*	6.5	11.2	15.9	26.4	40	31.8
China	1995*	6.5	10.5	14.7	21.3	47.1	36.1
	2000*	4.7	9	14.2	22.1	50	38.3
	2005	5.7	9.8	14.7	22	47.8	44
	1990	3.4	7.7	12.9	20.9	55.2	47.7
	1995	3.1	6.8	11	17.9	61.2	52.8
Colombia	2000	2.6	6.5	11.2	18.9	60.8	50.8
	2005						51.3
	2007/8	2.3	6	11	19.1	61.6	51.8
Congo, Democratic Rep.	2005						43
	2007/8	5.5	9.2	13.8	20.9	50.6	42.2
Congo, Republic of	2005	5	8.4	13	20.5	53.1	42.1
	2007/8						45.2
	1990	4	9	14.6	22.6	49.9	41.8
	1995	3.9	8.7	14.2	22.2	51	42.2
Costa Rica	2000	4.1	8.8	14.1	21.8	51.2	43.9
	2005	4.2	8.6	13.9	21.7	51.8	44.6
	2007/8	4.4	8.5	12.7	19.7	54.6	45.9
	1990	6.8	11.1	15.8	22.3	43.9	39.8
Cote d'Ivoire	1995	7.1	11.2	15.6	21.9	44.3	38.3
	2000	5.4	9.2	13.4	19.9	52.1	45.7
	2005						46.4
	1990	10.5	14.8	18.5	22.9	33.4	23.7
	1995						31.7
Croatia	2000	8.3	12.7	16.9	22.5	39.8	31.1
	2005	8.8	13.3	17.3	22.7	37.9	28.4
	2007/8						29
	1990						22.6
	1995						24.1
Cyprus	2000						27
	2005						28.8
	2007/8						28.8
	1990	11.3	14.8	18.1	22.2	33.6	20.6
Czech Republic	1995	10.3	14.2	17.4	21.6	36.6	24.5
	2000*	10.5	14.4	18	22.8	34.3	25.5
	2005**	9.8	14.4	17.5	22.3	36	25.4
	2007/8**	10.1	14.5	17.7	22.1	35.6	25.3
	1990*	9.4	14.7	18.1	22.6	35.1	25.9
Denmark	1995	8.3	14.7	18.2	22.9	35.8	21.8
	2000**	9.6	15	18.6	22.4	34.4	22.5

Country Name	Year	Q1	Q2	Q3	Q4	Q5	Gini Index
	2005**	9.5	15.2	19	23	33.3	23.5
	2007/8**	9.2	15.1	18.6	22.7	34.4	25
	1995	6.4	11.5	16.2	22.7	43.3	37.8
Djibouti	2000	6.1	10.9	15.5	22.1	45.4	40
	2005						39.4
	1990	4.2	7.9	12.5	19.6	55.7	47.1
	1995	4.2	8.3	13.1	20.4	54.1	46.4
Dominican Republic	2000	3.5	7.5	12.5	20.2	56.3	47.2
	2005	4	8	12.9	20.6	54.5	47.7
	2007/8	4.4	8.5	13.1	20.2	53.8	47
	1990	3.1	8	13.3	21	54.6	47.2
	1995	3.1	7.5	12.8	20.7	56	50.6
Ecuador	2000	2.9	6.8	11.3	18.4	60.6	52.4
	2005	3.3	7.3	12.1	19.8	57.6	51.3
	2007/8	3.4	7.2	11.8	19.2	58.5	51.2
	1990	8.6	12.4	16.3	21.8	40.8	32.9
	1995	9.3	12.9	16.4	21.3	40.1	36.7
Egypt	2000	9	12.5	15.8	20.7	42.1	36.4
	2005	9	12.6	16.1	20.9	41.5	33.5
	1990	2.4	8.5	14.5	22.8	51.8	46.6
	1995	3.7	8.2	13.3	20.8	54.1	46.8
El Salvador	2000	2.8	7.5	13.1	21.4	55.2	47.9
	2005	3.3	8.1	13.6	21.6	53.4	45.5
	2007/8	4.3	9.2	13.7	20.8	52	
	1990	8.6	13.2	17.4	22.7	38.1	22.5
	1995	8	12.9	17.6	23.6	38	36.7
Estonia	2000	6.6	11.3	16	22.4	43.8	36.1
	2005	6.8	11.6	16.2	22.5	43	33.6
	2007/8**	7.4	12.3	16.8	22.6	40.9	32
	1990						37.1
	1995	7.2	10.9	14.5	19.8	47.7	39.8
Ethiopia	2000	9.2	13.2	16.7	21.5	39.4	34.5
	2005	9.3	13.2	16.8	21.4	39.4	29.7
	1990						43.1
Fiji	1995						43.3
	2000						43.4
	1990*	11.1	15.2	18.5	22.6	32.6	21
	1995*	10.8	14.8	18	22.1	34.3	21.7
Finland	2000	9.6	14.1	17.5	22.1	36.7	24.6
	2005**	9.8	14.2	17.9	22.2	35.9	25.7
	2007/8**	9.7	14.1	18	22.4	35.8	26
	1990*	7.3	12.7	17.1	22.7	40.2	27.1
France	1995*	8	13	17	23	38	28.2
	2000*	9	13	17	23	37	27.8

Country Name	Year	Q1	Q2	Q3	Q4	Q5	Gini Index
	2005**	9.2	13.8	17.6	22.3	37.1	27.8
	2007/8**	9.3	14.2	17.9	22.4	36.2	28
Gabon	1990						51.7
	1995						50.4
	2000						45.3
	2005	6.1	10.1	14.6	21.2	47.9	42.1
Gambia	1990*	1.1	3.4	6.8	14.9	73.7	55.4
	1995*	1.2	3	6.4	13.4	76	55.5
	2000	4.3	8	12.8	20.7	54.3	47.6
	2005	4.8	8.6	13.2	20.6	52.8	48.1
Georgia	1990						27.2
	1995	6.1	11.4	16.3	22.8	43.5	40.5
	2000	5.9	10.8	15.8	22.6	45	37.7
	2005	5.4	10.5	15.3	22.2	46.7	39.6
Germany	1990*	8.5	13.2	17.2	22.7	38.3	26.6
	1995*	8.2	14	17.8	22.9	37.1	27.1
	2000	8.5	13.7	17.8	23.1	36.9	27.5
	2005**	9.5	14.5	18.1	22	35.9	28.1
	2007/8**	7.8	13.7	17.5	22.5	38.5	30
Ghana	1990	6.9	11.3	15.8	22	44	37.6
	1995	6.1	10.5	15.2	22.1	46	35.7
	2000	5.6	10	15.1	22.6	46.8	38.5
	2005						41.5
	2007/8	5.2	9.8	14.8	21.9	48.3	40.8
Greece	1990*	6.6	12.2	16.6	25.8	38.8	31.5
	1995*	6	12	17	24	41	34.9
	2000	6.7	11.9	16.8	23	41.5	33.3
	2005**	7	12.6	16.9	23.2	40.3	33.4
	2007/8**	6.9	12.2	16.7	22.8	41.4	33.5
Guatemala	1990	2.2	5.7	10.5	18.8	62.9	55
	1995	2.8	6.5	11.1	18.7	60.9	53.5
	2000	3.4	7.2	11.6	18.6	59.2	52.3
	2005	3.3	7.1	11.9	19.5	58.1	51.6
	2007/8	3.4	7.2	12	19.5	57.8	50.7
Guinea	1990	3.1	8.2	14.7	23.9	50.1	47.3
	1995	6.4	10.4	14.8	21.3	47.1	41.9
	2000	6	9.9	14.4	21	48.7	41.2
	2005	5.8	9.6	14.1	20.8	49.7	39.3
	2007/8						38.6
Guinea-Bissau	1990	2.1	6.5	12	20.6	58.9	51.6
	1995	5.2	8.9	13.1	19.4	53.5	44.6
	2000	7.2	11.6	16	22.1	43	38
	2005						38.1
Guyana	1990						42.1

Country Name	Year	Q1	Q2	Q3	Q4	Q5	Gini Index
	1995	4.3	9	13.2	19.5	53.9	44.1
	2000	4.3	9.8	14.5	21.3	50.1	42.7
Haiti	1990						50.2
	1995						50.6
	2000	2.5	5.9	10.5	18.1	63	51.1
	2005						53
Honduras	1990	2.8	6.3	10.9	18.8	61.2	51.5
	1995	3.2	7	11.8	19.5	58.5	50.9
	2000	3.3	7.5	12.6	20.5	56	50.5
	2005	2.3	6.4	11.7	20	59.7	52.1
	2007/8	2.5	6.7	12.1	20.4	58.4	52.5
Hong Kong	1990*	4.9	10.2	14.4	21.2	49.4	34
	1995	5.3	9.4	13.9	20.7	50.7	38.1
	2000						40.5
	2005						43.5
	2007/8						43.9
Hungary	1990	10.2	14.1	17.6	22.1	36	26.7
	1995	9.8	14	17.5	22	36.7	28.9
	2000	9.6	13.8	17.5	22.2	37	27.7
	2005	8.6	13.1	17.1	22.5	38.7	28.9
	2007/8**	9.6	14.6	18	22.5	35.3	27.7
India	1990*	9.1	13.1	16.9	21.8	39.1	30.8
	1995*	8.3	12	15.8	21.4	42.5	33.2
	2000*	7.7	11.4	15.2	21.5	44.3	31.8
	2005	8.1	11.3	14.9	20.4	45.3	34.6
Indonesia	1990*	7.9	11.7	15.5	21.1	43.8	34.3
	1995*	7.3	11	14.9	20.9	45.9	35.6
	2000*	8	11.6	15.2	21	44.2	33
	2005	7.1	10.7	14.4	20.5	47.3	35.5
	2007/8	7.4	11	14.9	21.3	45.5	35.9
Iran	1990	5.2	9.6	14.5	21.6	49.2	44.2
	1995	5.4	9.6	14.4	21.5	49.1	43.7
	2000	5.1	9.3	14.3	21.6	49.7	43.9
	2005	6.4	10.9	15.6	22.2	45	41.5
Ireland	1990*	5.7	11.2	16.4	23.6	43.1	33
	1995*	7.4	11.3	15.7	21.9	42.8	33.6
	2000	7.4	12.3	16.3	21.9	42	31.3
	2005**	7.9	12.5	17.2	22.7	39.7	31.5
	2007/8**	8.2	12.6	16.8	23.1	39.3	30.7
Israel	1990*	4.8	9.9	15.9	23.7	45.7	30.6
	1995*	2.6	7.3	13	21.5	55.4	32.9
	2000	5.7	10.5	15.9	23	44.9	34.4
	2005						37
Italy	1990*	7.7	12.6	17.2	23.4	39.1	30.7

Country Name	Year	Q1	Q2	Q3	Q4	Q5	Gini Index
	1995*	6.4	11.9	16.7	23.3	41.8	33.8
	2000*	6.6	11.9	16.8	23.2	41.6	33.3
	2005**	7.2	12.8	17.2	22.7	40.1	34
	2007/8**	7.2	12.7	17.5	23.1	39.5	33.3
	1990	5.8	9.7	14.5	21.7	48.3	45.1
Jamaica	1995	6.5	10.9	15.3	21.6	45.7	38.6
	2000	5.1	9.2	13.8	20.8	51.1	49.4
	2005	5.2	9	13.8	20.9	51.2	48.1
	1990						28
Japan	1995	10.6	14.2	17.6	22	35.7	29.1
	2000						32.8
	2005						35.9
	1990	6.4	10.3	14.7	21.2	47.3	40.6
	1995	6.7	10.6	14.8	20.9	47	37.9
Jordan	2000	7	11.1	15.4	21.6	45	37.9
	2005	7	11	15.2	21.3	45.5	39.2
	2007/8	7.2	11.1	15.2	21.1	45.4	38.8
	1990	8.7	13.3	17.6	23.2	37.2	24.8
	1995	7	11.7	16.7	23.2	41.5	32.8
Kazakhstan	2000	8.1	12.5	17	23.1	39.3	33.2
	2005	8	12.3	16.6	22.5	40.6	34.3
	2007/8	8.7	12.8	16.6	22	39.9	36.3
	1990	3.4	6.7	10.7	17.3	61.8	54.3
	1995	5.7	10	14.6	21.3	48.4	48.2
Kenya	2000	5.5	9.4	13.9	20.7	50.5	47.1
	2005	4.7	8.8	13.3	20.3	53	48.2
	1990*	7.3	12.4	16.8	22.9	40.6	32
Korea, Republic of	1995*	5.8	13.3	18	23.5	39.4	29.1
	2000*	4.8	11.2	17.8	24.5	41.6	32
	2005						31.8
	2007/8						29.2
	1990	7.4	10.7	15.4	22.1	44.4	24.2
Kyrgyz Republic	1995	4.4	8.8	13.8	21.4	51.6	44.1
	2000	7.8	12	16.4	22.3	41.6	31.2
	2005	8.3	12	15.9	22.1	41.8	35.8
	2007/8	8.8	11.9	15.1	21.6	42.6	38.1
	1990	9.3	12.8	16.4	21.4	40.1	30.7
Lao PDR	1995	8.5	12.3	16	21.2	42	34.5
	2000	8.3	12.1	16	21.4	42.1	35.5
	2005						34.5
	1990	10.1	14.3	18.3	23.1	34.2	22.8
Latvia	1995	8	13.3	17.3	22.3	39.2	28.9
	2000	7.1	12	16.4	22.4	42.1	33.2
	2005	6.8	11.6	16.1	22.6	42.9	36.7

Country Name	Year	Q1	Q2	Q3	Q4	Q5	Gini Index
	2007/8	6.7	11.5	15.9	22.6	43.3	37.8
Lebanon	1995						43.7
	2000						43.5
	2005						43.1
	1990	2.7	6	10.7	19.5	61.1	59.1
Lesotho	1995	1.5	4.3	9	18.6	66.6	61.4
	2000	2.4	6.1	11.2	20.1	60.2	56.6
	2005	3	7.2	12.5	21	56.4	48.7
Liberia	2005						41.1
	2007/8	6.4	11.4	15.7	21.6	45	47.2
	1990	9.5	14	17.7	22.3	36.5	22.7
	1995	7.9	12.6	16.6	22	40.9	33.4
Lithuania	2000	7.9	12.5	17	22.8	39.9	32.8
	2005**	6.2	11.8	16.2	22.7	43.1	34.6
	2007/8**	7	12.3	16.8	22.7	41.2	34.9
	1990*	9.7	14.2	17.1	22.4	36.6	23.7
	1995*	9	13	17	22	38	25.4
Luxembourg	2000*	8.9	13.3	17.1	22.9	37.8	26
	2005**	9.3	14.2	17.9	22.6	36	27.4
	2007/8**	9.1	13.9	17.6	22.6	36.8	28.4
	1990						24.5
	1995*	5	11.1	18.4	25.8	39.8	33.4
Macedonia	2000	6.7	12	16.9	23.2	41.2	32.3
	2005	5.5	10.2	14.8	21.8	47.6	35.9
	2007/8	5.2	10	14.5	21.5	48.8	36.8
	1990						44.7
Madagascar	1995	5.7	9.9	14.5	21.1	48.8	42.2
	2000	5.4	9.1	13.7	21.1	50.8	43
	2005	6.2	9.6	13.1	17.7	53.5	44.3
	1990						59.2
Malawi	1995*	4.9	8.5	12.3	18.3	56.1	56.6
	2000	5.6	9.2	13.2	19.3	52.8	45.7
	2005	7	10.8	14.9	20.9	46.4	39.3
	1990	4.9	8.8	13.5	20.7	52.2	41.1
Malaysia	1995	4.4	8.3	13.1	20.6	53.6	43.5
	2000	5.2	9.3	14.2	21.5	49.9	40.1
	2005	6.4	10.8	15.8	22.8	44.4	37.1
Maldives	2005	6.5	10.9	15.6	22.6	44.3	
	1990	6.6	10.6	15	21.4	46.4	42.7
	1995	4.6	7.8	12.1	19.3	56.1	63.6
Mali	2000	6.1	10.2	15	22.1	46.7	43.4
	2005						38.9
	2007/8	6.5	10.7	15.2	21.6	46	38.8
Mauritania	1990	4.7	9	13.6	20.3	52.4	44.8

Country Name	Year	Q1	Q2	Q3	Q4	Q5	Gini Index
	1995	5.9	10.3	14.8	21.2	47.9	38.7
	2000	6.2	10.5	15.4	22.3	45.7	36.6
Mauritius	1990						35.8
	1995						40.3
	2000						40.2
	2005						39.9
	2007/8						39.4
Mexico	1990	3.7	7.6	12.2	19.6	56.9	47.2
	1995	4.1	8	12.8	20.2	54.9	48.4
	2000	3.9	7.8	12.4	19.6	56.4	49.1
	2005	4.6	8.9	13.6	20.8	52.2	46
	2007/8	4.2	8.3	12.8	19.8	54.9	46.9
Micronesia	2000	1.6	5.1	10.2	19	64	
Moldova	1990	8.4	13.2	17.6	23	37.8	24.5
	1995	6.6	11.6	16.4	22.8	42.7	37
	2000	6.9	11.4	15.9	22	43.8	42.2
	2005	7.1	11.5	15.8	22	43.6	38.3
	2007/8	6.7	11.1	15.6	22	44.6	37.3
Mongolia	1995	7.3	12	16.9	23.4	40.4	34.1
	2000	7.6	12.6	17.3	23.3	39.2	35.8
	2005	7.2	12.2	17.1	23.4	40.2	33.8
	2007/8	7.1	11.5	16.1	22.6	42.7	
Montenegro	1995*	9	13.8	17.9	22.9	36.5	
	2000*	8.4	12.6	16.4	21.5	41.2	
	2007/8	6.5	11.4	16.1	22.2	43.7	
Morocco	1990	6.6	10.5	15	21.5	46.4	37.3
	1995	6.5	10.5	15.1	21.6	46.3	39.9
	2000	6.4	10.4	14.9	21.6	46.8	40.3
	2005						41
	2007/8	6.5	10.5	14.5	20.6	47.9	41.3
Mozambique	1995	5.7	9.6	13.8	20.1	50.8	39.4
	2000	5.6	9.4	13.5	19.6	52	42.2
	2005	5.4	9.2	13.1	19	53.3	40.7
Namibia	1990						70.8
	1995	1.5	2.8	5.5	12	78.3	67
	2000						65.4
	2005						67.7
Nepal	1990						34.1
	1995	7.6	11.1	15	20.6	45.7	39.2
	2000	6.8	10	13.7	19.5	50	45.5
	2005	6.1	8.9	12.5	18.4	54.2	48.5
Netherlands	1990*	7.9	13.6	18.1	23.6	36.8	26.2

Country Name	Year	Q1	Q2	Q3	Q4	Q5	Gini Index
	1995*	8.5	13.6	17.8	23.1	36.8	25.6
	2000*	9.4	14.6	17.3	23.1	36.2	25.2
	2005**	9	14.5	18	22.5	36	27.4
	2007/8**	9.3	14.1	17.6	22	37	27.8
	1990*	4.6	10.5	16.3	23.9	44.7	31.6
	1995	6.4	11.4	15.8	22.6	43.8	33.4
New Zealand	2000						35.9
	2005						33.1
	2007/8						32.6
	1990						53.1
Nicaragua	1995	2.9	6.8	11.7	19.5	59.1	52.7
	2000	3.7	7.9	12.6	20	55.9	51
	2005	3.8	7.7	12.3	19.4	56.9	49.1
	1990	7.5	11.7	15.7	21.3	43.9	40.1
Niger	1995	6	10.1	14.6	21.2	48.1	49.8
	2000	5.9	9.9	14.3	20.7	49.2	45.9
	2005	5.9	9.8	13.9	20.1	50.3	43.6
	1990	4.9	9.5	15	23.2	47.5	49.1
Nigeria	1995	4.7	9	13.9	21.2	51.2	49.4
	2000	5	9.4	14.1	21.1	50.4	47.2
	2005	5.1	9.7	14.7	21.9	48.6	43.8
	1990*	6.2	12.2	18	24.7	38.7	23.2
	1995*	9.8	14.4	17.8	22.3	35.7	23.8
Norway	2000*	8.1	13	17.3	22.7	39	25
	2005**	9.3	14.4	17.6	21	37.7	25.3
	2007/8**	9	15.7	19	22.8	33.5	24.1
	1990	8.1	12.3	16.2	21.6	41.7	32.6
Pakistan	1995	9.7	13.2	16.5	21.2	39.5	32.2
	2000	9	12.6	16.1	21	41.4	29.5
	2005	9.1	12.8	16.3	21.3	40.5	30.8
	1990	1.9	6	11.8	21	59.3	51.3
	1995	2.1	6.2	11.6	20.2	59.9	51.7
Panama	2000	2.4	6.3	11.6	19.9	59.8	51
	2005						49.8
	2007/8	2.5	6.6	12.1	20.8	58	48.9
Papua New Guinea	1995	4.5	7.7	12.1	19.3	56.4	40
	2000						48.7
	2005						51.6
	1990	5.8	10.3	15.4	22.7	45.8	36.2
	1995	2.3	5.9	10.7	18.7	62.4	54
Paraguay	2000	2.2	6.3	11.5	19.7	60.2	52.2
	2005	3	7.2	12.2	20	57.6	51.1
	2007/8	3.4	7.6	12.2	19.4	57.4	49.3
Peru	1990	5.6	9.8	14.1	20.5	50	42.3

Country Name	Year	Q1	Q2	Q3	Q4	Q5	Gini Index
	1995	4.6	9.1	14.1	21.4	50.7	50.5
	2000	3.5	7.6	12.7	20.4	55.8	53.2
	2005	3.7	7.5	12.4	20	56.4	50.7
	2007/8	3.6	7.8	13	20.8	54.8	49.8
	1990	6.1	9.6	13.9	20.9	49.6	39.3
	1995	5.8	9.3	13.7	20.8	50.5	46.1
Philippines	2000	5.4	8.8	13.2	20.4	52.3	45.2
	2005	5.5	9.1	13.7	21.2	50.5	42.7
	2007/8	5.6	9.1	13.7	21.2	50.4	42.6
	1990	9.2	13.8	18	23.2	35.9	24.9
	1995	7.7	12.6	16.9	22.5	40.4	31.8
Poland	2000	7.9	12.3	16.6	22.4	41	28.8
	2005	7.3	11.7	16.2	22.4	42.4	31.3
	2007/8**	7.6	12.8	17	22.5	40.1	29.7
	1990*	7.1	11.8	16.4	22.6	42	31
	1995*	6	11	17	22	44	35.6
Portugal	2000*	7	12	17	22	42	35.3
	2005**	6.6	11.3	15.4	21	45.7	37
	2007/8**	6.9	11.5	15.4	21.8	44.4	35.9
	1990	9.7	14.7	18.6	23.2	33.7	20.8
	1995	8.8	13.5	17.6	22.7	37.4	27.7
Romania	2000	8.2	13	17.4	23	38.4	27.2
	2005	8.2	12.8	16.8	22.3	39.9	29.8
	2007/8	7.9	12.7	16.8	22.3	40.3	33
	1990	7.8	12.3	16.5	22	41.5	24
	1995	4.4	9.1	13.9	20.9	51.8	44.7
Russian Federation	2000	6.1	10.7	15.7	22.7	44.8	43.4
	2005	6.4	11	15.9	22.7	44.1	45
	2007/8	5.6	9.6	13.9	20.7	50.2	46.2
	2000	5.4	9	13.2	19.6	52.8	47.7
Rwanda	2005						42.3
	2007/8						44.1
São Tomé	2000	5.2	8.7	12.1	17.6	56.5	
	1990	3.5	7	11.6	19.3	58.6	62.5
Senegal	1995	6.5	10.4	14.4	20.4	48.4	41
	2000	6.5	10.3	14.4	20.5	48.3	39.2
	2005	6.2	10.6	15.3	22	45.9	36.7
	1990						32.9
	1995*	9	13.8	17.9	22.9	36.5	29.4
Serbia	2000*	8.4	12.6	16.4	21.5	41.2	35.7
	2005						36.1
	2007/8	9.1	13.6	17.4	22.5	37.5	35.1
Seychelles	2007/8	3.7	5.7	8.4	12.4	69.8	
Sierra Leone	1990	1.1	2.2	9.8	23.1	63.8	62.7

Country Name	Year	Q1	Q2	Q3	Q4	Q5	Gini Index
	1995	3.6	5.9	11.9	22	56.5	55.8
	2000	5.2	8.3	13.2	21.3	52	48.9
	2005	6.1	9.7	14	20.9	49.3	44.7
	1990						34.4
	1995						33.8
Singapore	2000	5	9.4	14.6	22	49	37.4
	2005						37.9
	2007/8						39.7
	1990	11.7	15.8	18.8	22.3	31.4	17
Slovak Republic	1995	9.5	15.2	18.7	22.7	33.9	22.4
	2000*	10.4	14.6	17.8	22.3	35	24.6
	2005**	9.1	14.6	18.3	22.5	35.5	24.9
	2007/8**	10	14.9	18.2	22.3	34.6	23
	1990	9.9	13.9	17.6	22.3	36.3	18.6
	1995	9.2	13.3	17.2	22.3	38.1	24.4
Slovenia	2000	8.8	13.3	17.5	22.9	37.5	24.8
	2005**	9.9	15	18.5	22.8	33.8	24.5
	2007/8**	10.1	15.2	18.5	22.8	33.4	25.4
	1990						61.9
South Africa	1995	3.6	6.1	10.2	18.4	61.8	57.8
	2000	3.1	5.6	9.9	18.8	62.7	64.5
	2005						67.8
	1990*	7.6	12.7	17.1	22.9	39.7	30.3
	1995*	6.5	12.3	16.7	23.3	42.2	35.3
Spain	2000*	7.6	12.5	16.7	22.2	40.9	33.6
	2005**	7.2	12.8	17.4	23.6	39	31.6
	2007/8**	7.3	12.8	17.8	23.5	38.6	31.3
	1990	8.7	12.5	16.1	21.2	41.5	33.5
Sri Lanka	1995	8	11.8	15.7	21.4	43.1	37.1
	2000	7.1	10.8	14.8	20.8	46.5	44.5
	2005						43.8
	1995						49.1
Suriname	2000	3.1	7.5	12.2	19.9	57.4	48.9
	2005						48.4
	1990						54.9
Swaziland	1995	2.7	5.8	10	17.2	64.3	54
	2000	4.2	7.6	11.9	19	57.3	49.7
	2005						46.8
	1990*	7.4	12.7	16.7	25	38.2	20.7
	1995*	9.3	14.5	18.4	23.4	34.5	22.1
Sweden	2000*	9.4	13.8	17.2	21.9	37.8	25.2
	2005**	10.1	15.2	18.5	22.7	33.5	23.7
	2007/8**	10	15.2	18.7	22.7	33.4	23
Switzerland	1990*	6.2	12.1	16.6	22.9	42.2	30.9

Country Name	Year	Q1	Q2	Q3	Q4	Q5	Gini Index
	1995	6.7	12.1	16.5	22.8	41.9	29.2
	2000	7.6	12.2	16.3	22.6	41.3	28
	2005	8.2	12.9	17	22.5	39.5	31.1
	2007/8**	8.4	13.2	17.3	22.4	38.7	
Taiwan	1990						27.1
	1995						27.7
	2000						28.9
	2005						30.5
Tajikistan	1990						29.5
	1995						30.3
	2000	8	12.7	16.9	22.4	40	31.3
	2005	7.8	12	16.4	21.9	41.9	33
Tanzania	1990	7.4	12.2	16.6	22.2	41.6	42.2
	1995	7.4	12	16.4	22.2	41.9	39.4
	2000	7.3	11.8	16.3	22.3	42.3	35.5
	2005						36
Thailand	1990	5.8	9.1	13.4	20.3	51.5	50.2
	1995	5.8	9.3	13.7	20.6	50.5	51.5
	2000	5.9	9.4	14.1	21.3	49.4	45.1
	2005	6.1	9.8	14.2	21	49	41.1
Timor-Leste	2000	6.7	10.4	14.8	21.3	46.8	
	2005	8.2	11.8	15.6	21.3	43.1	
	2007/8	8.9	12.5	16	21.2	41.3	
Togo	2005						34.7
	2007/8	5.4	10.3	15.2	22	47.1	34.8
Trinidad and Tobago	1990	5.2	10	15.2	22.7	46.9	38.1
	1995						37.3
	2000						37.4
	2005						37.6
Tunisia	1990	5.9	10.4	15.3	22.1	46.3	38.4
	1995	5.6	10	14.9	22	47.6	41.5
	2000	5.9	10.2	14.9	21.8	47.2	40.8
	2005						40.8
Turkey	1990	5.9	10	14.3	20.8	49	43.7
	1995	5.8	10.1	14.8	21.5	47.8	43.7
	2000	5.7	9.9	14.6	21.3	48.5	42.2
	2005	5.2	9.8	14.6	21.6	48.8	43.9
	2007/8	5.4	10.3	15.2	22	47.1	
Turkmenistan	1990	9.1	12.4	16.8	22.9	38.8	26.6
	1995	6.6	10.9	15.7	22.4	44.4	29.9
	2000	6	10.2	14.9	21.7	47.2	30.6
	2005						40.3
Uganda	1990	5.3	9.6	14.3	21.2	49.6	41.7

Country Name	Year	Q1	Q2	Q3	Q4	Q5	Gini Index
	1995	7	10.9	15.1	21	46	36.8
	2000	5.8	9.7	13.9	20.2	50.4	42.6
	2005	6.1	9.8	14.1	20.7	49.3	40.3
	2007/8						39.1
	1990	9.8	14.3	18.4	23.3	34.2	21.7
	1995	7.7	12.4	16.8	22.6	40.6	38.4
Ukraine	2000	8.8	13.4	17.5	22.8	37.6	30.5
	2005	9	13.4	17.6	22.9	37.2	33.4
	2007/8	9.3	13.5	17.5	22.7	37.1	32.5
	1990*	7.6	12.2	16.8	22.8	40.7	32.8
	1995*	7.4	12.3	16.6	22.7	41.3	34.4
United Kingdom	2000	7.7	12.5	16.6	22.4	41.2	34.5
	2005**	7.1	12.2	16.5	22.3	41.9	34.6
	2007/8**	7.5	12.6	16.9	22.6	40.4	35.8
	1990*	3.9	9.6	15.9	24	46.6	33.5
	1995*	3.7	9.1	15.2	23.3	48.7	36.3
United States	2000*	3.6	8.9	14.9	23	49.6	36.8
	2005*	3.4	8.7	14.7	23.2	50.1	37
	2007/8						36
	1990	5.3	10	14.9	21.8	48	40.6
	1995	4.9	9.6	14.8	22.2	48.5	40.5
Uruguay	2000	4.8	9.2	14.4	21.9	49.8	41.7
	2005	4.6	9	14.3	22.2	49.9	42.8
	2007/8	4.3	8.6	13.6	21.4	52.1	43
	1990	10.9	12.7	17.2	23.6	35.6	24
	1995	6.5	10.6	15.7	22.8	44.3	34
Uzbekistan	2000	5.9	10.7	15.4	21.9	46.1	33.5
	2005	7.1	11.5	15.7	21.5	44.2	36.4
	1990	4.9	9.6	14.7	22	48.8	40.6
	1995	4.2	8.8	13.9	21.6	51.5	43.5
Venezuela	2000	3	8.3	14.1	22.3	52.3	42.1
	2005	3.7	8.8	14.1	21.7	51.8	42.1
	2007/8	4.9	9.6	14.8	22.1	48.6	40.2
	1990						36
	1995	7.9	11.4	15.4	21.3	44	34.1
Vietnam	2000	7.7	11.2	15.2	21.1	44.8	36.2
	2005	7.1	10.7	14.9	21.3	46.1	38.1
	2007/8	7.1	10.8	15.2	21.6	45.4	38.3
	1990	6.1	10.8	15.4	21.8	45.9	39.2
	1995	6.8	11.5	16	22.3	43.4	35.4
Yemen	2000	7.4	11.9	16.3	22.3	42.2	33.6
	2005	7.2	11.3	15.3	21	45.3	38.6
	2007/8	7.2	11.3	15.3	21	45.3	
Zambia	1990	0.7	4.8	10.8	21.4	62.4	54.6

Country Name	Year	Q1	Q2	Q3	Q4	Q5	Gini Index
	1995	3.8	7.8	12.7	20.4	55.4	52.4
	2000	4.4	8.4	13.1	20.2	53.9	50
	2005	3.6	7.8	12.8	20.6	55.2	50.9
Zimbabwe	1990*	4	6.3	10	17.4	62.3	54.7
	1995*	1.1	3.2	6.5	12.5	76.7	57.5

Data Type	Asterisk	Source
		World Bank (2011)
Distribution	*	UNU-WIDER (2008)
	**	Eurostat (2011)
Gini		Solt (2009)

Note: For 2007/8, distribution estimates reflect 2007, and Gini estimates reflect 2008